摘 要

改革开放以来，我国经济增长速度较快，综合国力明显增强，人民生活显著改善，但区域经济差距也在不断扩大。在现实经济中，如果一个大国存在明显的区域经济差距，则不同地区对于宏观经济政策冲击的反应有可能不一致。统一货币政策的执行可能对不同的地区产生不同的影响，即货币政策区域效应。货币政策区域效应在一定程度上可能加剧我国的区域经济差距。本书实证检验了我国货币政策的区域效应，并提出了减轻货币政策区域效应的对策建议。

首先，在考虑货币政策溢出效应的影响后，本书采用结构向量自回归模型测度了1978—2011年期间我国货币政策的区域效应。结果显示，我国不同地区（不含港澳台地区）对货币政策的反应明显不同。溢出效应会显著影响货币政策的效果，考虑到溢出效应之后，各地区对货币政策冲击的反应明显增强。

其次，在货币政策传导机制理论的基础上，本书采用省际数据分析了货币政策区域效应的影响因素，特别关注不同地区大小银行结构的差异对于地区反应大小的影响。研究发现，小银行占比较大的地区对货币政策冲击的反应较小，而大银行占比较大的地区对货币政策的冲击反应较大。该结果与传统银行信贷渠道理论相悖，原因可能在于我国小银行的地方保护主义和大银行的国有性质影响了其对中央银行货币政策冲击的反应。

最后，本书以四川汶川地震灾区为案例，采用面板数据模型分析了定向降准对于四川汶川地震灾区灾后重建的影响，发现定向降准在一定程度上加快了地震灾区的灾后重建和经济增长。但定向降准、差别存款准备金率对于地区经济发展和经济结构调整的作用还需要进一步的证据支持。同时，央行还需要持续引入创新性的货币政策工具来减轻货币政策的区域效应，促进区域经济协调发展。

2018河北大学一流大学建设应用经济学项目资助出版

DIFFERENTIAL EFFECTS OF MONETARY POLICY IN CHINA

THE ROLE OF SPILLOVER EFFECT, LARGE AND SMALL BANKS, AND DIFFERENTIATED RESERVE REQUIREMENT RATIO

我国货币政策区域效应研究

——溢出效应、大小银行与差别存款准备金率的影响

GUO XIAOHUI

郭小卉　著

中国财经出版传媒集团

图书在版编目（CIP）数据

我国货币政策区域效应研究：溢出效应、大小银行与差别存款准备金率的影响/郭小卉著.—北京：经济科学出版社，2019.5
ISBN 978-7-5218-0460-7

Ⅰ.①我… Ⅱ.①郭… Ⅲ.①货币政策-研究-中国 Ⅳ.①F822.0

中国版本图书馆 CIP 数据核字（2019）第 071186 号

责任编辑：申先菊　路　巍
责任校对：蒋子明
责任印制：邱　天

我国货币政策区域效应研究
——溢出效应、大小银行与差别存款准备金率的影响
郭小卉　著
经济科学出版社出版、发行　新华书店经销
社址：北京市海淀区阜成路甲 28 号　邮编：100142
总编部电话：010-88191217　发行部电话：010-88191522
网址：www.esp.com.cn
电子邮件：esp@esp.com.cn
天猫网店：经济科学出版社旗舰店
网址：http://jjkxcbs.tmall.com
北京季蜂印刷有限公司印装
710×1000　16 开　13.5 印张　230000 字
2019 年 5 月第 1 版　2019 年 5 月第 1 次印刷
ISBN 978-7-5218-0460-7　定价：98.00 元
（图书出现印装问题，本社负责调换。电话：010-88191510）

ABSTRACTS

China is a huge country with great regional disparity. Common monetary policy would have different impacts across regions which may enlarge regional disparity. Therefore, the objective of this study is to examine and propose solutions to reduce the different regional effects of monetary policy.

Firstly, this study uses vector autoregressive model to gauge the effects of monetary policy after accounting for spillover in China from 1978 – 2011. The results confirm that monetary policy exert different impacts across regions. Spillover effect is very important since it can significantly amplify the magnitude of regions' responses to monetary policy shock.

Secondly, this study explores the factors, with a special attention on the role of small banks, which cause the differential effects of monetary policy using provincial data. The results show that bank lending channel works in China, implying that China's Central Bank should provide more assistance to small banks. Finally, this study examines the effect of specific tools introduced after the earthquake in Sichuan on growth of counties in this province. The results prove that the differentiated reserve requirement ratio can significantly help the disaster-stricken areas to gain more growth. From these findings, the inefficiency of monetary policy can be further improved by offering specific growth-enhancing instruments such as differentiated reserve requirement ratio. Thus, the other possible instruments can be time to time introduced to support the development of the Middle and/or Western regions in order to reduce the regional differential effects of monetary policy and promote a more balanced regional economic development.

ACKNOWLEDGEMENTS

First and foremost, I would like to take this opportunity to convey my highest appreciation to Associate Professor Dr. Tajul Ariffin Masron (Universiti Sains Malaysia) for his valuable suggestions and tremendous support throughout this book. His constant guidance and advice allowed me to successfully complete this study.

I would also like to thank the lecturers of School of Management (Universiti Sains Malaysia) for their suggestions, views and comments at various stages of the study. A special thank is accorded to Associate Professor Dr. Zamri Ahmad for his help during my study.

My deepest gratitude goes to my parents and my beloved wife whose constant encouragement and relentless support keep me going even during the most difficult period.

Special thanks also goes to all of my friends, who had always encouraged me to endure this difficult task, given me their warmest help along my path to success, and accompanied me during my most difficult as well as happiest moments on campus in Universiti Sains Malaysia.

List of Abbreviations

ABC	The Agricultural Bank of China
ADF	Augmented Dickey-Fuller test
AIC	Akaike Information Criteria
BOC	The Bank of China
CCB	China Construction Bank
CBRC	China Banking Regulatory Commission
CHIBOR	China Interbank Offered Rate
CNY	China Yuan
CPC	Communist Party of China
CPI	Consumer Price Index
DRRR	Differentiated Reserve Requirement Ratio
EU	European Union
FAVAR	Factor-Augmented Vector Autoregressions
FDI	Foreign Direct Investment
GDP	Gross Domestic Product
GLS	Generalized Least Squares
HQ	Hannan Quinn criterion
ICBC	The Industrial and Commercial Bank of China
IMF	International Monetary Fund
IRF	Impulse Response Function
KPSS	Kwiatkowski, Phillips, Schmidt and Shin
LR	Likelihood Ratio

LSDV	Least Squares Dummy Variable
ML	Maximum Likelihood estimator
NPL	Non-Performing Loan
OCA	Optimum Currency Area
OECD	Organization for Economic Co-operation and Development
OLS	Ordinary Least Squares
OMO	Open Market Operations
PBC	The People's Bank of China
POLS	Pooled Ordinary Least Squares
PP	Phillips-Perron
PPP	Purchasing Power Parity
RCC	Rural Credit Cooperative
RRR	Reserve Requirement Ratio
S&M	Small and Medium
S. D.	Standard Deviation
SC	Schwarz Criterion
SE	Small Enterprises
SOCB	State-Owned Commercial Bank
SOE	State-Owned Enterprise
SOHE	State-Owned and State-Holding Enterprises
SUR	Seemingly Unrelated Regression
SVAR	Structural Vector Auto-Regressions
UK	the United Kingdom
US	the United States
USD	the United States Dollar
VAR	Vector Autoregressive
VEC	Vector Error Correction
VS	Versus
WTO	World Trade Organization

Contents

Chapter 1

Introduction

1. 1 Background of Study

1. 1. 1 China's Economy

China's economy is huge and expanding rapidly. The growth of China's economy in the past forty years since the initiation of economic reform and opening up in 1978 has been another East Asian "miracle" of modern economic development. According to Figure 1. 1, China has undergone spectacular economic growth in the past three decades, with the nominal GDP rising on average by almost 9. 9% per annum from 1978 to 2010, reaching an historical high of 15. 18% in 1984 and a record low of 3. 84% in 1990. From 1980 to 2008, China's economy grew 14-fold in real terms, real GDP per capita (a common measurement of living standards) grew over 11-fold (Morrison, 2009). During this period, China's economic and comprehensive national strengths have been continuously enhanced, the living standards and welfare of the people have been further improved and hundreds of millions of people were raised out of extreme poverty. Previously suffering shortages of many necessities, China today instead has excess production capacity on the whole. At the same time, living standards have been greatly improved and the people in general lead a comfortably well-off life. Indeed, China currently had overtaken Japan and got the world's second largest GDP (PPP, 10.08 trillion USD) in 2010 (World Bank Database).

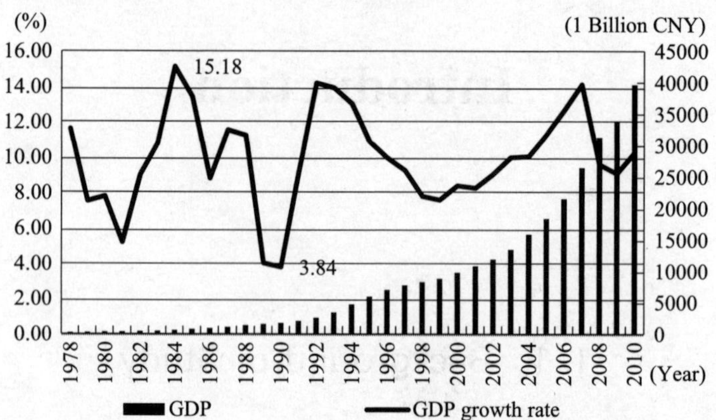

Figure 1.1 **China's Nominal GDP and GDP Growth Rate Per Annum**

Sources: China Statistical Book (2010).

Closely following the globalization process, China has been quickly integrating into the world economy since economic reform and opening up especially after WTO accession in 2001. Globalization makes the annual exports and Foreign Direct Investment (FDI) in China unceasingly increase, and this greatly promotes the economic growth in China (Wei, Yao & Liu, 2009; Chen & Groenewold, 2012). Now exports are supposed as an important engine of China's economy. China is the largest exporter and second largest importer in the world. A great amount of China's trade is conducted by enterprises with foreign investment. In 2010, China's total exports and imports were USD 2972.76 billion, exports totaled USD 1577.93 billion and total imports were USD 1394.83 billion. In recent years, China has been one of the leading FDI recipients in the world. For 2010, China's inbound FDI firstly exceeded USD 100 billion (almost USD 105.74 billion), and overseas direct investment of Chinese firms in non-financial sectors reached USD 59 billion altogether. Long time huge trade surpluses, together with large amount of the FDI inflows, have made China hold the largest foreign exchange reserves in the world at USD 3.18 trillion in 2011.

1.1.2 Overview of Monetary Policy in China

Since economic reform and opening up, monetary policy has played an increasingly important role on the economic growth in China (Dickinson & Liu, 2007; Sun, Ford & Dickinson, 2010; Fan, Yu & Zhang, 2011). The People's Bank of China (PBC, the central bank of China) functioned as a central bank in 1984① and began to play a crucial role in macro-economic regulation. Since 1978, China's economy has experienced four obvious high inflations: one in 1984 – 1985, one in 1988 – 1989, one in 1993 – 1994, and one in 2007 – 2008, while deflation occurred during 1998 - 2002. The first three inflations were caused by easy credit provided to state-owned enterprises (SOE) by four state-owned banks and excessive investments in hot industries and regions at the time (Fan, Yu & Zhang, 2010). In the process of each inflation, the PBC implemented tight monetary policy with the purpose to cool off the overheated economy.

In 1988, the inflation rate reached a record high of about 19%. The PBC raised interest rates, ordered cutbacks on construction projects and reduced loans to bring inflation down to a level of less than 10 percent in 1989. However, in 1994, the inflation rate saw its highest level again of around 24%. In 1995, the PBC adopted a moderately tight monetary policy in order to curb this high inflation. Meanwhile, many kinds of measures were used to cool off the economy and these measures are finally found to be effective (Fan, Yu & Zhang, 2011). The economic growth rate and inflation rate returned to the normal level. The

① Actually, before 1984, the PBC had already monopoly control over the supply and production of its currency and functions as a central bank.

moderately tight monetary policy played a key role in these processes (Dai, 2001).

The 1997 Asian Financial Crisis happened and made an apparent decline in demand. In 1998, the inflation rate firstly became negative and China underwent deflation. The PBC implemented the "prudent" monetary policy by using various kinds of monetary policy instruments and finally pulled the economy out of deflation. At the same time, the PBC decided to make several changes to monetary policy mechanism and monetary policy instruments. They cancelled the control of loan scale and began to extensively use open market operations. The regulatory way of monetary policy has been shifted gradually from direct control to indirect control within three years.

In 2007, China suffered from excessive liquidity and inflation, the economy was on the edge of overheating with bubbles in the real estate and stock markets. The consumer price index (CPI) reached a dangerous high level. Facing this situation, the PBC adopted tight monetary policy, raised the interest rate and reserve requirement ratio to reduce money supply. From July 2008, the inflation rate began to reduce from 7% in June to 4.6% in September. In September 2008, Lehman Brothers went broke and the subprime mortgage crisis in the United States started to spill over. The global financial crisis happened and China's economic growth slowed down. Then monetary policy shifted from tight to relative loose in order to stimulate the economic growth.

In recent years, China's economy has fast integrated into the world economy and became more and more market-oriented. Monetary policy has undertaken an increasingly heavy responsibility in ensuring sustainable economic growth and harmonious development in China. Despite deeper structural economic reforms may be the key factors of long-term economic growth, monetary policy really plays a key role in stabilizing macro-economic environment which is crucial for those reforms to take root (Goodfriend & Prasad, 2007).

1.2 Motivation of the Study

1.2.1 Monetary Policy and Regional Economy in China

In reality, monetary policy has played an increasingly important role on promoting economic growth in China since 1978 (Hsing & Haieh, 2004; Dickinson & Liu, 2007). However, the conduct of monetary policy by the PBC to a great extent depends on real economic condition of the whole country without accounting for the regional differences of economic conditions. China is a big country with great regional disparity. Common monetary policy may exert various impacts across regions.

Several studies addressed the issue of how monetary policy variables responded to macro-economic variables such as the output and the inflation rate (how the central bank formulated monetary policy). Taylor (1993) proposes a rule for central banks to set a nominal target interest rate based on the expected inflation rate gap and the output gap. The McCallum (1988) rule describes how money supply growth changes with the expected inflation rate gap and the output gap. The two rules describe how central banks raise (reduce) the target interest rate (money supply) when the expected inflation is higher (lower) than the desired target inflation rate and when the actual output is greater (smaller) than the natural output. Several studies (Wang & Handa, 2007; Burdekin & Siklos, 2008; Fan, Yu & Zhang, 2011; Sun, 2013) apply these two rules into China's economy and point out that the formulation of China's monetary policy follows these two rules.

Therefore, the formulation of monetary policy which follows the Taylor rule and McCallum rule is mainly based on national output and inflation rate. It focuses on macro-economic conditions of the whole country and never considers the regional and provincial economic conditions. As one of macro-economic policies and one important instrument regulating economic operation, monetary policy always shows highly unification. It cannot be enacted according to the real economic condition of certain region, such as to stimulate one region while at the same time cooling off another region. Unification is an important characteristic of monetary policy. The implementation of unified and national monetary policy takes regional economic homogeneity as a precondition (He, 2010). So if the country has a balanced economy, all regions share the same economic structure and economic condition, monetary policy will affect all the regions in the same pattern.

However, China is a huge country with great regional and provincial disparity. The regional and provincial economic development is apparently unbalanced. Given its size and geography, China can be divided into three regions: the more developed eastern region, the less developed middle region and the western region. According to Figure 1. 2, the gap among three regions has been widening since 1992, and being supported by other studies such as Yao and Zhang (2001), Jones and Owen (2003), Pedroni and Yao (2006), Lau (2010), Fan, Kanbur and Zhang (2011), Zhang and Zou (2012) among others.

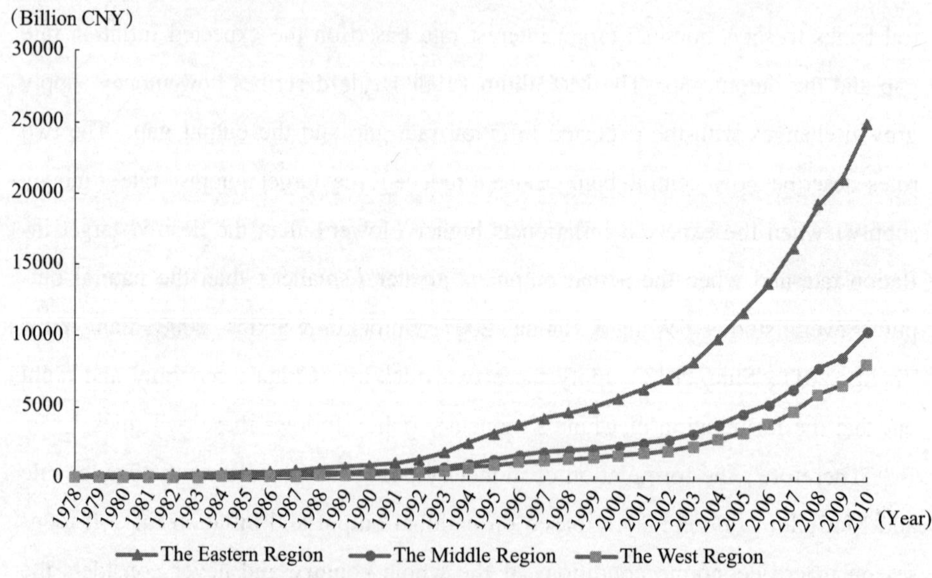

Figure 1. 2 The GDP of Different Regions from 1978 to 2010

Sources: The National Bureau of Statistics of China.

So what will be the results if the central bank implements common monetary policy in a country with great unbalanced regional economies? In reality, diverse regions within a big country which have different structures could respond differently to changing economic circumstances. Thus monetary policy may have varied influences on different regions (Carlino & DeFina, 1998). Walter Isard who is the founder of the Regional Science Association explains that:

"*Since each of [the nation's] regions has different resource potentials and confronts different problems and obstacles to growth, it follows that monetary and fiscal policy based on national aggregates alone generates both retarding factors for some regions and problem intensifying factors for other regions.*" (*Walter Isard, 1957*)

It is well-known that the implementation of monetary policy focuses on macro-economic regulation and keeping a sustainable economic growth. Different regional effects of monetary policy imply that monetary policy may exert a bigger influence on certain region (region *A*), while at the same time a small impact on another region (region *B*), especially, if region *A* is more developed and region *B* is less developed, then to some extent, these different influences of monetary policy may enlarge regional disparity.

At present, in China, the national economic development is badly hurt by the unbalanced regional economies (Lau, 2010) and the consequences may be very serious in China. Fan, Kanbur and Zhang (2011) indicate that spectacular economic growth has been accompanied by sharp rises in inequality and increasingly manifestations of social tension. Chen and Groenewold (2010) also consider the gap between rich and poor regions as a major potential source of political instability. Clearly, the control and reduction of regional disparity is a big challenge for the Chinese government. Aware of this, the PBC has tried to implement differentiated reserve requirement ratio to support certain less developed region and rural area since 2004 in order to reduce regional disparities and achieve harmonious development.

In short, monetary policy has played an important role on promoting the national economic growth in China in the past forty years. However, regional effects of monetary policy have also brought apparent negative impacts on regional economies. Although regional effect of monetary policy is not the main factor causing regional disparities, it indeed widens the gap among regions. Under the background that the whole country tries to narrow the gap and reach a more balanced regional economy, definitely it should not be ignored the different regional effects of monetary policy in China.

1.2.2 The definition of Region and Province

China is a big country. Given its huge size, China can be divided into three regions: the East, the Middle and the West (see Table 1.1). The East contains 11 provinces, the Middle is consisted of 8 provinces and the West is made up of 12 provinces①. This study firstly examines the impacts of monetary policy on three regions. However, the division of three regions in China is too general. Measuring the effects of monetary policy on the East (the Middle or the West) is equivalent to testing the responses of the eastern 11 provinces (the middle 8 provinces or the western 12 provinces) as a whole to monetary policy shifts. Obviously, only three responses are too rough to provide useful information to the PBC as a reference. In fact, when the PBC formulates monetary policy, it always refers to the detail information of 31② provinces. Therefore, in order to provide useful and detailed information to the PBC, this study also examines 31 provinces' responses to monetary policy in detail when considering spillover effects among provinces. The latter examination may be more important and meaningful for the PBC to formulate monetary policy.

① Province mentioned in this book refers to provincial administrative region, including province, autonomous region and municipality.

② There are 31 provinces, autonomous regions and municipalities in mainland China.

Table 1.1 Three Regions in China

East	Middle	West
Beijing	Shanxi	Inner Mongolia
Tianjin	Jilin	Guangxi
Hebei	Heilongjiang	Chongqing
Liaoning	Anhui	Sichuan
Shanghai	Jiangxi	Guizhou
Jiangsu	Henan	Yunnan
Zhejiang	Hubei	Tibet
Fujian	Hunan	Shaanxi
Shandong		Gansu
Guangdong		Qinghai
Hainan		Ningxia
		Xinjiang
11 provinces	8 provinces	12 provinces

Notes: The coastal area means the eastern region. The inland area refers to the middle and the western regions.

Sources: West Develop Experiment (2000).

1.2.3 The Role of Banks in China

Monetary policy influences regional economy mainly through monetary transmission channels. As a transition economy, indirect financing is the main form for corporate financing in China (Baek, 2005). Thus bank lending channel is the main monetary transmission channel in China (Liu & Xie, 2006; Du, 2010; Gunji & Yuan, 2010). Bank lending channel is based on the view that banks play a crucial role in the financial system (Kashyap & Stein, 1997). Therefore, to explore how monetary policy affects regional economy, it is necessary to get a clear understanding of China's banking system.

Since 1978, China has taken a series of significant reforms in its banking system, and strengthened its opening to the outside world. As at end of 2011, China's banking sector is mainly consisted of five large commercial banks, 12 joint-stock commercial banks, 144 city commercial banks, 212 rural commercial banks, 190 rural cooperative banks, 2265 rural credit cooperatives. Total assets of China's banking institutions increased to CNY 113. 3 trillion. Large commercial banks, joint-stock commercial banks, rural financial institutions and city commercial banks account for 47 percent, 16 percent, 15 percent and 9 percent of the total assets respectively (see Figure 1. 3).

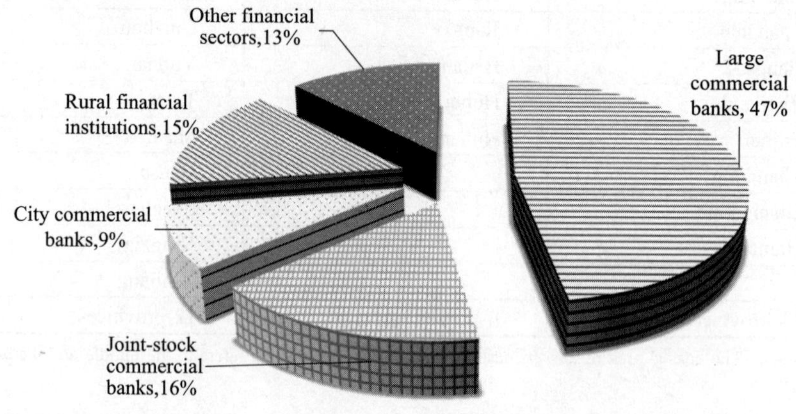

Figure 1. 3 Total Assets of Banking Institutions in 2011

Sources: China Banking Regulatory Commission Annual Report (2011).

On the basis of total assets, China Banking Regulatory Commission (CBRC) divides banking institutions into three categories: large banks, medium sized banks and small banks. According to this standard, there are five large commercial banks: the traditional big four: the Industrial and Commercial Bank of China (ICBC), the Bank of China (BOC), the Agricultural Bank of China (ABC) and China Construction Bank (CCB), and Bank of Communications also belongs to large banks. Medium sized banks contain 12 joint-stock commercial banks. Small banks are consisted of rural financial institutions and city commercial banks. Kashyap and Stein (1995) emphasize that they sort banks into size categories that reflect differences in the cost of raising external funds. This study mainly focuses on the role of small banks and large commercial banks on the regional effects of monetary policy.

Kashyap and Stein (1995) have suggested that the Federal Reserve System (Fed) policy actions could have varied effects on different banks' abilities to make loans. Regions with a disproportionately big share of loans made by small banks might respond more to monetary policy shocks than regions where a large proportion of loans are made by large banks. The size distributions of banks are different across provinces in China (see Table 1.2). This study selects three provinces: Guangdong (the East), Shanxi (the Middle) and Guizhou (the West) to make a contrast. According to Table 1.2, the scale of financial development in developed Guangdong province is much larger than that in the less developed Shanxi and Guizhou provinces considering the number of outlets, staff and total financial assets. The proportions of outlets of small banks are 40.07%, 50.70% and 52.86% in Guangdong province, Shanxi province and Guizhou province. The proportions of assets of small banks are 18.10%, 27.65% and 32.71% in Guangdong province, Shanxi province and Guizhou province. The differences are obvious and the distributions of small banks are unbalanced across provinces.

Table 1.2 The Distribution of Banks in Guangdong Province, Shanxi Province and Guizhou Province in 2011

Item	province	Large Commercial Banks	Joint-stock Commercial Banks	City Commercial Banks	Rural Co-operative Institutions	total
Number of outlets	Guangdong	5958	1022	392	5776	15393
	Shanxi	1656	102	180	2967	6207
	Guizhou	1034	6	185	2082	4289
Number of staff	Guangdong	139416	34961	14028	66108	280549
	Shanxi	46854	4012	5000	34778	105239
	Guizhou	18311	361	4133	20830	47685
Assets (Billion CNY)	Guangdong	5825.7	2629.2	859.2	1331.8	12103.7
	Shanxi	1076.23	342.73	150.6	542.14	2505.58
	Guizhou	482.7	53	141.6	213.7	1086.2
Corporate financial institutions	Guangdong	0	3	6	112	186
	Shanxi	0	0	6	114	147
	Guizhou	0	0	4	85	103

Notes: Large banks contain large commercial banks. City commercial banks and rural financial institutions belong to small banks. Rural financial institutions are consisted of rural credit cooperatives, rural cooperative banks and rural commercial banks.

Sources: Regional Financial Operation Report in China (2011).

1.2.4 Differentiated Reserve Requirement Ratio in China

In recent years, along with the deepening of economic reform and opening up, to cope with the complicated domestic and international economic situation, the PBC (the People's Bank of China, central bank of China) has begun to make some new attempts to affect the structure of monetary policy. The PBC has introduced the differentiated reserve requirement ratio (DRRR) policy since April 25th, 2004. The initial content of the DRRR policy is that the reserve requirement ratio (RRR) applicable to a financial institution will be linked with certain indicators such as its capital adequacy ratio and asset quality. The lower the capital adequacy ratio of a financial institution and the higher its non-performing loan (NPL) ratio, a higher RRR will be charged. The initial purpose of this policy is to limit loan expansion of those financial institutions with inadequate capital and poor asset quality, reduce financial risk and maintain financial stability.

The DRRR policy said that financial institutions whose capital adequacy ratios were below 4% would apply the DRRR 0.5% higher than normal level①. Since this policy applied, the Agricultural Bank of China and 38 joint-stock banks and city commercial banks such as Guangdong Development Bank, China Everbright Bank and Shenzhen Development Bank have been applied DRRR 0.5% higher than normal level as their loan growth is too fast and the risk is too high.

In practice, the PBC has also tried to implement the DRRR policy based on regions and the structure of credit to continuously extend the application of the DRRR policy. Since September 21st, 2003, all financial institutions that took deposits from the public have had to meet a uniform RRR of 7 percent, with the exception of the Urban and Rural Credit Cooperatives that still abide by the 6 percent standard. To support the development of rural area, the PBC did not

① The People's Bank of China: http://www.pbc.gov.cn/.

raise the RRR of Rural Credit Cooperative until 2006. On May 12th, 2008, a big earthquake hit Sichuan province and made lots of damage. To support the reconstruction of the disaster area, the PBC decided to apply the DRRR a little lower than normal level to corporate financial institutions in 39 counties in Sichuan province that suffered most in the earthquake on June 8th, 2008 (see Figure 1.4). The PBC also declared that this preferential DRRR would not be raised in the disaster area until June, 2011.

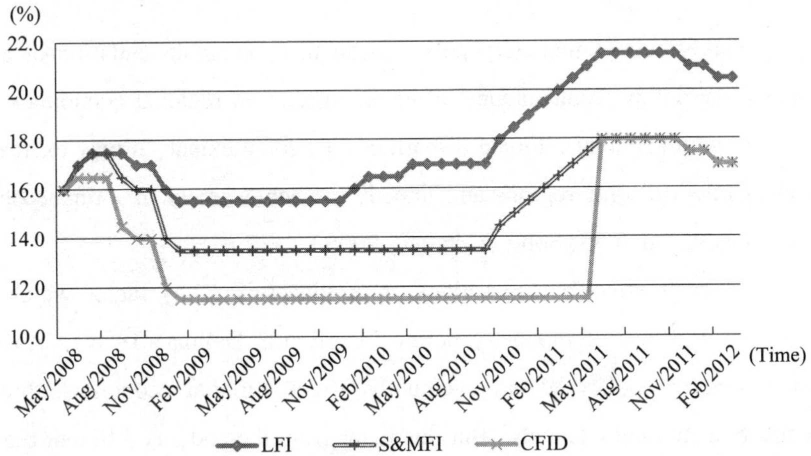

Figure 1.4 Differentiated Reserve Requirement Ratio in China from 2008 to 2012

Notes: LFI: reserve requirement ratio of large financial institutions. S&MFI: reserve requirement ratio of small and medium sized financial institutions. CFID: reserve requirement ratio of corporate financial institutions in disaster area (39 counties).

Sources: The People's Bank of China.

Global financial crisis happened in 2008 made the domestic and overseas economic condition become much more complicated. Facing this situation, the PBC decided to apply the DRRR to different sizes of financial institutions. On September 25th, 2008, the PBC applied DRRR to large banks and small & medium sized banks (S&M sized banks). Large banks applied the DRRR 1% higher than S&M sized banks. Large banks occupy a bigger market shares, applying a higher DRRR is helpful for the PBC to control money and credit supply. Considering most of loans made by S&M sized banks flow to S&M sized enterprises

(China Banking Regulatory Commission Annual Report 2011①), the PBC applies a little lower DRRR to S&M sized banks so as to solve the difficulty of financing in S&M sized enterprises. Currently large and S&M sized banks apply Differentiated Deposit Reserve Ratio separately (see Figure 1.4).

1.3 Problem Statement

Regional effects of monetary policy mean that the implementation of common monetary policy would induce different impacts on regional economies in a big country with apparent regional disparities. To some extent, it may exert negative influences on some regions and impede the achievement of ultimate objectives of monetary policy (Song & Zhong, 2006).

The spillover effect across regions or provinces is a key factor which can affect regional effects of monetary policy (Carlino & DeFina, 1998). As well known, monetary policy would eventually affect regional economies through monetary transmission channels. But this is far from the end, as different regions will interact with each other through interregional links. For example, 2008 Beijing Olympic Games promotes economic growth of Beijing to some extent through infrastructure construction such as the building of Bird's Nest Stadium and the Water Cude. In fact, most of construction workers come from the nearby province Hebei. Therefore, the infrastructure construction to some extent enhances the incomes and employment in Hebei province, indirectly promoting the economic growth of Hebei province and thus generating a positive spillover effect. Applying it into the regional effects of monetary policy, the spillover effect means that monetary policy is not only directly influenced the economy of province by monetary transmission channels, but also can further affect the nearby provinces through the interregional links such as trades, funds transfer, and so

① Available on: http://www.cbrc.gov.cn.

on. Thus a monetary policy shock to one region or province would affect other regions or provinces through spillover effects. Especially, the more developed eastern coastal provinces may get much spillover generated by positive monetary policy shock, while the poor western provinces may get less spillover, then the gap among provinces would be further widened. In opposite, if the poor provinces get more spillover and the rich provinces get less, the gap could be narrowed. Therefore, the spillover effect across regions or provinces is a key factor which can affect the regional effects of monetary policy (Carlino & DeFina, 1998).

In addition, bank lending channel suggests regional differences of small versus large banks might cause the regional effects of monetary policy (Carlino & DeFina, 1998). Samolyk (1991, 1994) suggest that regional financial disparity causes the regional impacts of monetary policy and the banking system plays a central role in some regions through transmission of monetary policy and provision of credit. Kashyap and Stein (1995) indicate that monetary policy could have different impacts on different banks' ability to make loans. Large banks not only have abundant capital but also have much access in securing non-deposit financing. So when facing tight monetary policy, large banks are less affected than small banks. They can make decisions of loan more depending on their own profits and the real conditions of regional economy. However, small banks do not have this way and have to shrink their credit when facing tight money policy.

The size distributions of small banks are different across provinces in China (see Table 1. 2). For example, the proportion of small banks in Jilin and Ningxia (less developed provinces) are 34. 61% and 36. 83%, but that in Beijing and Shanghai (more developed provinces) are only 13. 52% and 12. 33%. Generally speaking, the more developed eastern provinces have smaller proportion of small banks than the less developed western provinces. Thus, different provinces may respond differently to monetary policy shifts. Provinces with a large proportion of small banks would respond more to monetary policy shifts than provinces with a small percent of small banks. Therefore, to some extent, the different size distribution of small banks across provinces may explain the regional effects of monetary policy.

In June, 2008, the PBC applied DRRR policy in 39 earthquake-stricken counties in Sichuan province. In these 39 earthquake badly hurt counties, a preferential DRRR is implemented. While in the other counties in Sichuan province, the nomal RRR is still applied. One shortcoming of the normal RRR is that "one size fit all" practice doesn't consider the real condition of regional and provincial economies. The advantage of the DRRR policy is it gives some flexibility to monetary policy so that it can cope with regional economic disparity. The purpose of the DRRR policy implemented by the PBC is to help the earthquake-stricken counties to gain more growth and quicken the recovery process of the disaster counties. However, in reality, the role of the DRRR policy is quite uncertain. It may or may not help the earthquake-stricken counties recover quickly. Actually if it is proven that the DRRR policy really can quicken the reconstruction of earthquake-stricken areas, then the DRRR policy and other similar differentiated monetary policy instruments can be adopted as a national policy to promote the economic growth of poor provinces and narrow the gap among provinces.

1.4 Research Questions

The general research question that this study wants to address is to how to examine the regional effects of monetary policy in China. In order to address the above issue, we have the following sub-questions:

i. How much of the magnitude and timing of regions' and provinces' output responses to monetary policy when considering spillover effects in China?

ii. Can provincial different size distributions of small banks explain the regional effects of monetary policy in China?

iii. Does the DRRR policy have any effects on the outputs of the earthquake-stricken areas?

1.5 Research Objectives

The general objective of this study is to examine the differential regional effects of monetary policy in China. In order to address the above issue, we have the following sub-objectives:

i. To evaluate the magnitude and timing of regions' and provinces' output responses to monetary policy when considering spillover effects across regions or provinces;

ii. To examine whether or not provincial different size distributions of small banks can explain the regional effects of monetary policy;

iii. To examine whether or not the DRRR policy has some effects on the outputs of earthquake-stricken areas.

1.6 Significance of Study

1.6.1 Contributions

The study would extend the literature by making three main contributions.

Firstly, this study considers the influence of spillover effects on regional and provincial effects of monetary policy. To our knowledge, the previous literature does not account for it. For example, Cortes and Kong (2007) just use a single VAR system province by province to study regional effects of monetary policy without accounting for the spillover effects. In fact, when certain region (province) is affected by monetary policy, other regions (provinces) may also be affected through spillover effects. Therefore, it is not accurate to just consider the influence of monetary policy on one region or province. This study analyzes regional effects of monetary policy considering spillover effects across regions and provinces.

Secondly, this study introduces the size distribution of small banks across provinces as a factor to explain the regional effect of monetary policy. Samolyk (1991, 1994) develops a regional credit channel and indicates that it is regional differences in the distribution of bank sizes which really cause the regional effects of monetary policy (also the view of Kashyap & Stein, 1995). He emphasizes the role of banking system in the provision of credit and explains that monetary policy actions can affect different banks' abilities to make loans. By this way, monetary policy can affect the development of regional economies. In China, the size distributions of large and small banks are very different across provinces. The developed East has less proportion of small banks than the less developed Middle and the West. Thus this study uses the different size distribution of small banks (measured by the proportion of small banks in each province) to explain the regional effects of monetary policy. To our knowledge, no literature examines it before in China.

Finally, this study checks whether or not the differentiated monetary policy instrument (DRRR) can support the development of certain area and reduce the regional effects of monetary policy. To our knowledge, no literature does it previously. More importantly, if it can be proved the DRRR policy can reduce the regional effects of monetary policy, it can be extended to a great range. For example, the PBC can use it to support the development of the Middle and the West or less developed provinces to narrow the gap among regions. Moreover, the PBC has several monetary policy instruments whose functions are similar as reserve requirement ratio, such as interest rate and rediscount rate, the PBC can also try to use these preferential interest rates or differentiated rediscount rates to reduce regional effects of monetary policy and improve the effectiveness of monetary policy.

1. 6. 2 Significance

1. 6. 2. 1 The Implication for Central Bank to Enact and Implement Monetary Policy

In China, The PBC enacts and implements monetary policy with no consideration for regional disparities. They just collect regional or provincial economic information in order to measure aggregate economic conditions. Presumably, the PBC considers that monetary policy cannot and should not attempt to affect certain regions or provinces. However, this study demonstrates a good understanding of regional impacts of monetary policy is very helpful for policymakers.

Monetary policy may have differential effects in terms of timing and magnitude on regions with varied economic and financial structures. Monetary authorities must make an accurate assessment of regional impacts of monetary policy in order to successfully conduct monetary policy. This needs a good understanding of how monetary policy affects regional economy through transmission channels. Moreover, a better understanding of the magnitude and timing of regions' and provinces' responses to monetary policy actions can help the central bank to harmonize the unification and regional differences of monetary policy.

The implementation of monetary policy in China is made difficult due to the existence of regional effects of monetary policy. The analysis in this study has shown that a better design of monetary policy should account for regional data as the existence of different regional effects. Only considering national information together with regional information about real economic condition, monetary policy can be set optimally. Empirical evidence seems to support this view in the United States (Meade & Sheets, 2002; Heinemann & Hüfner, 2002; Schunk, 2005) and in European Union (De Grauwe, 2000; Arnold, 2001; Gros & Hefeker, 2002; Rodríguez-Fuentes & Dow, 2003).

To be successfully in conducting monetary policy, the PBC has to weigh the different consequences of monetary policy actions on different regions and reconcile the economic interests of different regions, thus it is very important to understand the regional effects of monetary policy. Given the different effects across regions of monetary policy, it may be better that regions with different economic and financial structures could have their own voices at the Central Bank in order to account their welfare interests.

1. 6. 2. 2 To Promote the Balanced Development of Regional Economies

As a large and diverse country, an analysis of regional effects of monetary policy is needed for China to find optimal stabilization policies reducing regional disparities. Obviously, there is a big gap among regions in China. Unified monetary policy is an important factor that causes the unbalanced economic development in China. Meanwhile, a proper monetary policy can also narrow the gap and promote balanced development across regions. This requests a better understanding of regional effects of monetary policy. Under the unified monetary policy, the PBC could assign its branch of each region a certain autonomous right, allowing them to make a fine adjustment according to their own characteristics. This is very helpful to promote regional economic development and make a harmonious society.

To reduce the regional effects of monetary policy, the PBC has introduced the DRRR policy. If it can be proved that the DRRR policy do can help the economy of less developed disaster area to gain more growth, the PBC can apply it to the less developed Middle and West to support their economic growth. This can not only reduce the regional effects of monetary policy, but also narrow the gap among regions and provinces.

1. 6. 2. 3 Help to Reinforce Cooperation of Monetary and Fiscal Policies

As macro-economic policies, a well coordination of monetary policy and fiscal policy is necessary. While fiscal policy can be tailored for a particular region or sector, the consequences of monetary policy are national by nature. However, the effects of monetary policy will not be uniform as countries are typically composed of diverse regions. Therefore, it is very helpful to understand regional effects of monetary policy, if one region experiences negative influence of monetary policy, it can be compensated by the fiscal policy. Monetary policy and fiscal policy can make a better coordination to stabilize and promote coordinated regional economic development.

1.7 Scope of Study

This study focuses on three regions (the East, the Middle and the West) as well as the 31 provinces in Mainland China, the period is from 1978 until 2011. There are 31 provinces, autonomous regions and municipalities in mainland China. The West Develop Strategy enacted in 2000 divided China into three regions: the East, the Middle and the West. The coastal areas refer to the East, the inland areas mean the Middle and the West.

This study also uses 31 provinces cross sectional data to examine the factors affecting the regional effects of monetary policy. The data contains the proportion of industry in each province, the percent of small and large banks and the proportion of small enterprises, stated-owned enterprises and state-holding enterprises in each province. This study averages the data of these variables from 2000 to 2011.

In the case study, panel data is used to analyze the effect of the DRRR policy on the earthquake-stricken areas (39 counties enjoying the DRRR policy and 39 counties without the DRRR policy in Sichuan province) from 2008 to 2011.

The data are obtained from the National Bureau of Statistics of China, the

Ministry of Commerce of China, the People's Bank of China, the China Banking Regulatory Commission (CBRC), China Statistical Yearbook (1980 – 2010), Sichuan Statistical Yearbook (2004 – 2012), Almanac of China's Finance and Banking (1986 – 2010), the Regional Financial Operation Report (2004 – 2010), the China Banking Regulatory Commission Annual Report (2006 – 2010), IMF Data and Statistics and World Bank Database.

1.8 Organization of Study

The remainder of this study is organized as follows: Chapter 2 provides historical economic background of China and describes the changes of all key economic variables in the past. Chapter 3 reviews the previous studies about the regional effects of monetary policy. Chapter 4 provides detailed information about (empirical) model specification as well as deals with the estimation techniques. Chapter 5 presents the results of the analysis and the discussion of the results. Chapter 6 provides the summary, policy implications, limitation of this study and the direction of future research suggestions.

Chapter 2

Economic Background

2. 1 Overview

This chapter focuses on the historical background of China's economy. China's economy is one of the highly performing world's economies and has also attracted large attention for its sustainable economic growth, especially during the period when world's economy is slowing down. On average, China's economy has experienced higher levels of economic growth than the other main economies in the world.

Figure 2. 1 shows the average annual growth rate of GDP achieved by China's economy was higher than main economies in the world. The average GDP growth rate in China has surpassed that in other economies by more than 2-fold from 2000 to 2010. During the financial crisis in 2008 – 2010, although a slight decline, China's GDP growth rate was still very high and recovered fast from the financial crisis.

As well known, China is in a transition from its planned economy to a socialist market economy. With the deepening of economic reform and opening up, and the establishment and development of the socialist market economic system, monetary policy has played a more and more important role in macro-eco-

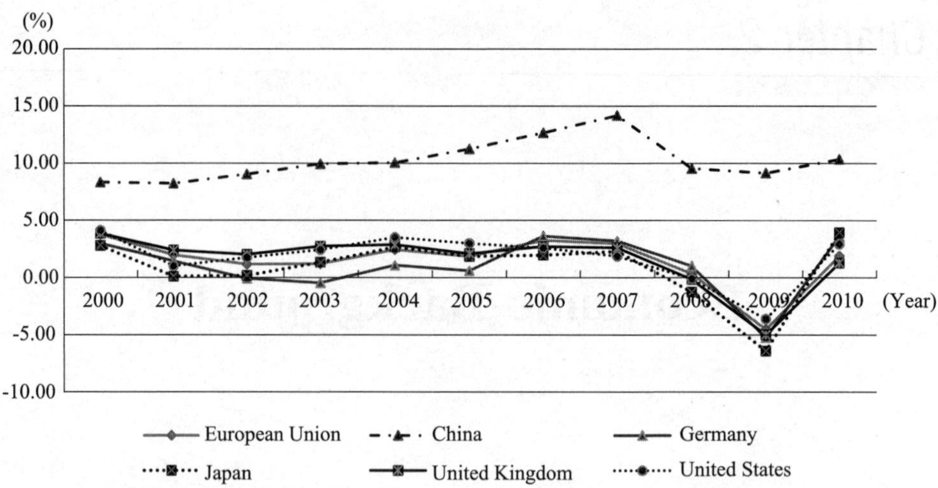

Figure 2. 1 Annual GDP Growth Rate at Market Price of Main Economies

Sources: The World Bank Database.

nomic regulation (Qin, Quising, He & Liu, 2005). Tong (2011) uses Structural Vector Auto-Regression (SVAR) to measure the national effects of monetary policy in China and concludes that monetary policy has been effective as a whole in China from 2000 to 2010, before the financial crisis, besides keeping the inflation rate, monetary policy stimulated the economic development; after the occurrence of financial crisis in 2008, monetary policy played an essential role in inhibiting the economic downturn, although with a lagged effect, and bringing about inflation.

To stimulate the economy, the PBC has adopted several types of monetary policy. After the occurrence of Asian economic crisis in 1997, the PBC has adopted prudent monetary policy from 1998 to 2006, which is the longest period of implementing certain type of monetary policy in China since the PBC began to perform the functions of central bank. In fact, during 1998 – 2002, monetary policy is prudent with a slight loose trend, with the purpose of getting out of the deflation since 1997. From 2003 to 2006, monetary policy is prudent with a slight tight trend in order to control local inflation and overheating of certain parts of the economy. During 2007. 01 – 2008. 08, the generalized inflation became clear, and the PBC carried out the moderately tight monetary policy to curb the inflation. In later 2008, facing global financial crisis, China has eased monetary policy stance from tight to moderately loose (actually extremely loose) until 2010. Since 2011, China has switched its monetary policy from relatively loose to prudent to slow rising inflation and keep economic growth at a sustainable pace. The prudent monetary policy meant compared with 2010, monetary policy was biased toward tightening. In together, monetary policy has played an increasingly important role in macro-economic regulation.

2.2 More Evidences on Regional Disparity

Although China has experience a sustainable high economic growth for a long time, the gap among regions has been widened since economic reform and opening up in 1978. A better understanding of regional economy is helpful to analyze the regional and provincial effects of monetary policy.

With regard to a developing country, it should not be surprise that uneven pattern happens across regions during the process of development (Fleisher & Chen, 1997; Barrios & Strobl, 2009; Habibullah, Dayang-Affizzah & Puah, 2012), especially in a large country like China. As a matter of fact, from a historical point of view, even well before 1949, the eastern coastal regions had been already more developed than the interior region① due to their geographical advantages. After the founding of the People's Republic of China, the government tried to give more substantial industrial support to the Middle and the West so as to reduce the development gap, however, their achievements were limited.

① Lu and Wang (2002) point out that the gap between the coastal and interior areas is due both to differences in regional characteristics, such as production factors, and to over 100 years of foreign colonial influence before 1949.

The problem of unbalanced regional development has been existed ever since the initiation of economic reform. At the expense of the interior regions, the economic reform shifted its concentration away from developing all regions in China to only encouraging the development of the coastal region, which traditionally had a relatively well-developed infrastructure and a strong economic base, with the purpose that the rich leads the poor, finally realizing the common prosperity. Nevertheless, forty years passed, this objective has not become the fact and furthermore, the gap between the coastal region and the inland region has been continued to widen (Fu, 2004).

Nowadays, China's regional disparity is the largest in the world. According to the Gini index, the emerging economies—China, the Russian Federation, India and Brazil—displayed the greatest regional disparity in GDP per capita in 2007 among the emerging economies. ①

According to the West Develop Strategy enacted in 2000, 31 provinces can be divided into three regions: the East, the Middle and the West. According to Figure 2.2, in 2010, the East accounted for 57.31% of the total GDP and 41.05% of the population in China, while at the same time it only occupies 11.26% of land. In stark contrast, despite holding more than 70% of land, the West only accounted for 18.63% of the total GDP.

Figure 2.3 displays the historical changes in GDP per capita for 31 provinces in China. The per capita GDP in each province has increased significantly since 1979. In 1979, the GDP per capita in majority of the provinces were similar, and only a few coastal provinces had a little higher per capita GDP. By 1992 the differences had grown. In 2003 and 2010, regional economic development was obviously unbalanced. In 2010, the per capita GDP of the richest province, Shanghai, was about as 6 times as that of the poorest province, Guizhou.

Generally speaking, China's FDI inflows and exports have made significant contributions to economic growth. However, FDI and exports have been largely

① Data sources: OECD library statistics, http://www.oecd-ilibrary.org/.

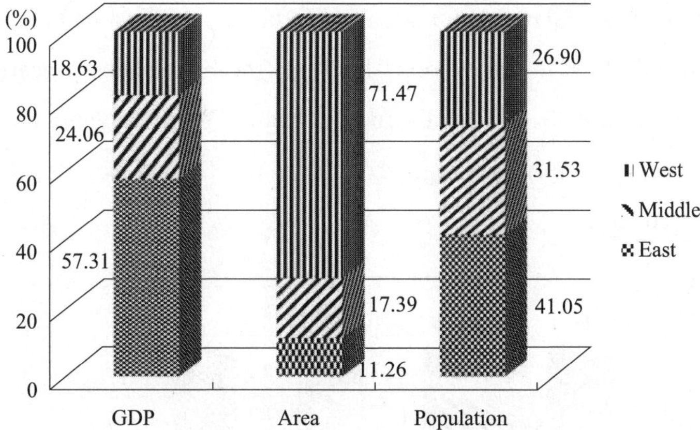

Figure 2. 2 Three Regions' GDP, Area and Population in 2010

Sources: The National Bureau of Statistics of China.

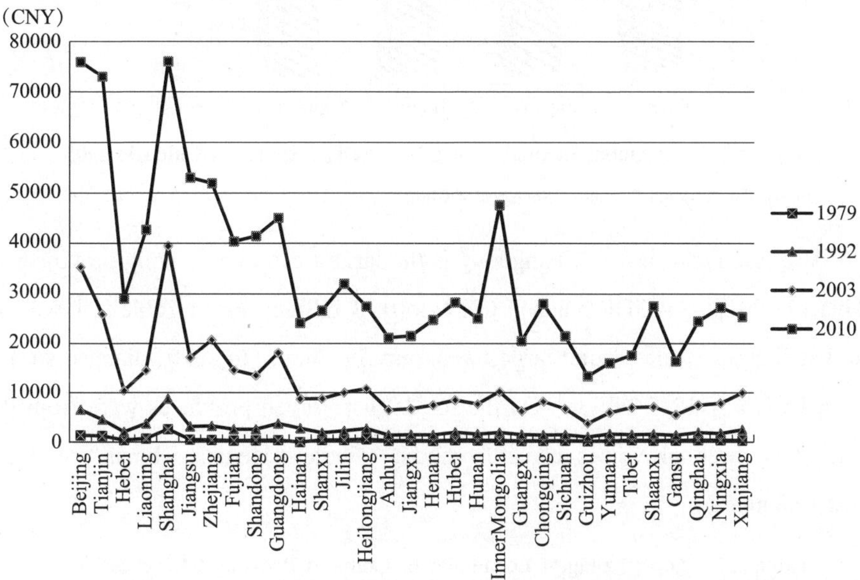

Figure 2. 3 The Changes of GDP Per Capita in Different Provinces

Notes: Units: The first 11 provinces belong to the eastern region, the second 8 provinces are from the middle region and the last 12 provinces belong to the western region.

Sources: The National Bureau of Statistics of China.

centered in the eastern coastal provinces and further exacerbated regional economic disparity. Figure 2. 4 reports the percentage of GDP, FDI and exports in each region in 2008. Given each region's population, the East had a considerable proportion of GDP, FDI and exports. In 2008, the East made up nearly 75% of FDI and more than 4/5 of China's foreign trade. While at the same time the Middle and the West only had negligible shares of FDI and exports, 8. 40% and 6. 36% respectively.

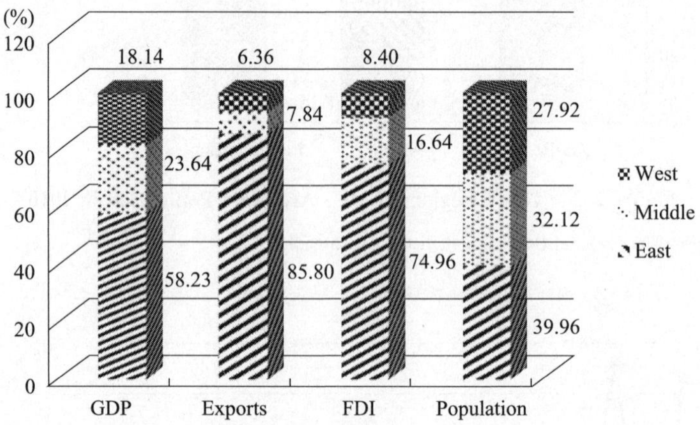

Figure 2. 4 Regional Inequality in GDP, FDI, Exports in China in 2008

Sources: The National Bureau of Statistics of China.

At a provincial level, Guangdong is the largest economy among provinces in China. In 2010, its GDP reached CNY 4601. 3 billion. From Table 2. 1 we can see that Jiangsu is the second largest economy in China. In 2010, Jiangsu's GDP reached CNY 4142. 5 billion. On the top 10 list, seven provinces were from the East. Only three provinces came from the Middle (Henan, Hunan) and the West (Sichuan).

Table 2. 1 Top 10 Biggest Economies in China at Provincial Level in 2010

Ranking	Province	GDP (billion CNY)	Region
1	Guangdong	4601. 31	East
2	Jiangsu	4142. 55	East
3	Shandong	3916. 99	East
4	Zhejiang	2772. 23	East
5	Henan	2309. 24	Middle
6	Hebei	2039. 43	East

continuous

Ranking	Province	GDP (billion CNY)	Region
7	Liaoning	1845. 73	East
8	Sichuan	1718. 55	West
9	Shanghai	1716. 60	East
10	Hunan	1603. 80	Middle

Sources: The National Bureau of Statistics of China.

2. 3 Sources of Regional Effects of Monetary Policy

As mentioned previously, monetary policy may have different impacts across regions on account of different economic and financial structures. Monetary transmission channels reveal three approaches through which monetary policy could affect regions differently. These include differences in regional industrial composition (interest rate channel), different distribution of small banks across provinces (bank lending channel) and provincial different firm size distributions (bank lending channel).

2. 3. 1 The Industrial Composition

Due to geography and location factors, different regions may have different industrial composition. According to interest rate channel, different industries display varying interest sensitivities. This different interest elasticity, in conjunction with the differing industry compositions across regions, may account for regional effects of monetary policy (Carlino & DeFina, 1998; Ibrahim, 2005; Peersman & Smets, 2005; Georgopous, 2009). For example, construction and industry have been more sensitive to interest rate changes than agriculture or services. Therefore, relatively industrialized regions or provinces tend to be more easily affected by monetary policy than the less industrialized counterparts.

As Table 2. 2 shows, there are large differences in industrial composition among provinces in China. For example, agriculture accounts for 26% in Hainan province, while in Beijing and Tianjin the number are less than 5%. Finance accounts for 13% in Beijing, while in Jilin and Gansu only 2%. In general, agriculture accounts more in the Middle and the West than that in the East, while finance and real estate are just the opposite.

Table 2. 2 GDP in Each Province Accounted for by Major Industry in 2010

Province	Agriculture	Industry	Construction	Finance	Real Estate	Services	Population
East							
Beijing	0. 01	0. 20	0. 04	0. 13	0. 07	0. 55	0. 01
Tianjin	0. 02	0. 48	0. 05	0. 06	0. 04	0. 36	0. 01
Hebei	0. 13	0. 47	0. 06	0. 03	0. 03	0. 28	0. 05
Liaoning	0. 09	0. 48	0. 06	0. 03	0. 04	0. 30	0. 03
Shanghai	0. 01	0. 38	0. 04	0. 11	0. 06	0. 40	0. 02
Jiangsu	0. 06	0. 47	0. 06	0. 05	0. 06	0. 30	0. 06
Zhejiang	0. 05	0. 46	0. 06	0. 08	0. 06	0. 29	0. 04
Fujian	0. 09	0. 43	0. 08	0. 05	0. 05	0. 30	0. 03
Shandong	0. 09	0. 48	0. 06	0. 03	0. 04	0. 29	0. 07
Guangdong	0. 05	0. 47	0. 03	0. 06	0. 06	0. 33	0. 08
Hainan	0. 26	0. 19	0. 09	0. 04	0. 09	0. 33	0. 01
Middle							
Shanxi	0. 06	0. 51	0. 06	0. 05	0. 02	0. 30	0. 03
Jilin	0. 12	0. 45	0. 07	0. 02	0. 02	0. 31	0. 02
Heilongjiang	0. 13	0. 44	0. 06	0. 03	0. 04	0. 31	0. 03
Anhui	0. 14	0. 44	0. 08	0. 03	0. 04	0. 26	0. 04
Jiangxi	0. 13	0. 45	0. 09	0. 03	0. 04	0. 27	0. 03
Henan	0. 14	0. 52	0. 06	0. 03	0. 03	0. 22	0. 07
Hubei	0. 13	0. 42	0. 07	0. 04	0. 04	0. 31	0. 04
Hunan	0. 14	0. 39	0. 06	0. 03	0. 03	0. 34	0. 05
West							
Inner Mongolia	0. 09	0. 48	0. 06	0. 03	0. 03	0. 30	0. 02
Guangxi	0. 18	0. 40	0. 07	0. 04	0. 04	0. 27	0. 03
Chongqing	0. 09	0. 47	0. 08	0. 06	0. 03	0. 27	0. 02
Sichuan	0. 14	0. 43	0. 07	0. 04	0. 03	0. 28	0. 06
Guizhou	0. 14	0. 33	0. 06	0. 05	0. 03	0. 39	0. 03
Yunnan	0. 15	0. 36	0. 09	0. 05	0. 03	0. 32	0. 03
Tibet	0. 14	0. 08	0. 24	0. 05	0. 03	0. 46	0. 00

continuous

Province	Agriculture	Industry	Construction	Finance	Real Estate	Services	Population
Shaanxi	0. 10	0. 45	0. 09	0. 04	0. 03	0. 30	0. 03
Gansu	0. 15	0. 39	0. 09	0. 02	0. 03	0. 32	0. 02
Qinghai	0. 10	0. 45	0. 10	0. 04	0. 02	0. 29	0. 00
Ningxia	0. 09	0. 38	0. 11	0. 06	0. 04	0. 32	0. 00
Xinjiang	0. 20	0. 40	0. 08	0. 04	0. 03	0. 26	0. 02
In Mainland China	0. 10	0. 40	0. 07	0. 05	0. 06	0. 32	—

Sources: The National Bureau of Statistics of China.

Table 2. 3 displays historical development of regional industrial composition in China. At the country level, the percent of primary industry and tertiary industry have been decreased gradually since 1978, while the percent of secondary industry remain almost the same. Three regions show the similar trends as the nation. On average, the secondary industry accounts for 50. 12 percent in the East and 40. 03 percent in the West. The percents of agriculture in the West are 10 percent more than the one in the East. The shares of industries in each province can be compared with an overall average in the nation.

Table 2. 3 Historical Development of Regional Industrial Mix in China (%)

Region	East			Middle			West			China		
Industry	PI	SI	TI	PI	SI	TI	PI	SI	TI	PI	SI	TI
1978	22. 09	58. 71	19. 20	35. 66	46. 45	17. 89	37. 12	43. 03	19. 85	28. 19	47. 88	23. 94
1979	25. 12	56. 17	18. 71	37. 86	45. 11	17. 03	38. 12	42. 07	19. 81	31. 27	47. 10	21. 63
1980	23. 97	56. 39	19. 64	35. 50	46. 21	18. 29	37. 97	41. 18	20. 85	30. 17	48. 22	21. 60
1981	24. 96	53. 95	21. 09	38. 69	42. 84	18. 47	40. 43	38. 13	21. 44	31. 88	46. 11	22. 01
1982	27. 05	51. 10	21. 85	38. 99	41. 72	19. 29	41. 16	37. 19	21. 65	33. 39	44. 76	21. 85
1983	27. 25	49. 95	22. 80	39. 14	41. 20	19. 65	40. 14	37. 47	22. 39	33. 18	44. 38	22. 44
1984	26. 71	49. 93	23. 37	37. 45	42. 18	20. 38	39. 09	37. 30	23. 61	32. 13	43. 09	24. 78
1985	24. 17	51. 16	24. 67	34. 47	43. 33	22. 20	36. 96	38. 07	24. 97	28. 44	42. 89	28. 67
1986	23. 68	49. 77	26. 55	33. 66	42. 58	23. 76	35. 69	37. 70	26. 60	27. 14	43. 72	29. 14
1987	22. 84	49. 85	27. 31	32. 69	42. 80	24. 50	34. 96	37. 07	27. 97	26. 81	43. 55	29. 64
1988	22. 39	48. 41	29. 19	30. 41	42. 87	26. 72	34. 00	37. 16	28. 84	25. 70	43. 79	30. 51
1989	21. 45	48. 22	30. 33	29. 57	42. 00	28. 43	32. 95	36. 82	30. 23	25. 10	42. 83	32. 06
1990	21. 79	46. 24	31. 97	32. 61	39. 49	27. 90	34. 79	34. 85	30. 36	27. 12	41. 34	31. 54
1991	20. 22	45. 79	33. 99	28. 58	40. 79	30. 63	32. 37	35. 62	32. 01	24. 53	41. 79	33. 69

continuous

Region	East			Middle			West			China		
Industry	PI	SI	TI	PI	SI	TI	PI	SI	TI	PI	SI	TI
1992	17. 50	48. 00	34. 49	26. 37	42. 43	31. 19	29. 87	36. 82	33. 31	21. 79	43. 45	34. 76
1993	15. 54	50. 47	33. 99	24. 50	44. 65	30. 85	26. 92	39. 97	33. 11	19. 71	46. 57	33. 72
1994	15. 53	50. 29	34. 18	26. 09	43. 11	30. 81	27. 25	40. 08	32. 66	19. 86	46. 57	33. 57
1995	15. 63	49. 28	35. 10	26. 85	41. 82	31. 33	27. 03	39. 50	33. 47	19. 96	47. 18	32. 86
1996	15. 11	48. 68	36. 20	26. 62	41. 62	31. 77	26. 93	39. 05	34. 02	19. 69	47. 54	32. 77
1997	13. 88	48. 59	37. 54	25. 19	41. 75	33. 06	26. 09	38. 87	35. 03	18. 29	47. 54	34. 17
1998	13. 12	48. 11	38. 77	23. 89	41. 69	34. 43	24. 89	38. 71	36. 40	17. 56	46. 21	36. 23
1999	12. 24	47. 75	40. 01	21. 75	41. 91	36. 34	23. 15	38. 42	38. 43	16. 47	45. 76	37. 77
2000	11. 01	48. 02	40. 97	19. 99	42. 25	37. 77	21. 57	38. 60	39. 83	15. 06	45. 92	39. 02
2001	10. 44	47. 32	42. 23	19. 21	42. 43	38. 36	20. 34	38. 41	41. 26	14. 39	45. 15	40. 46
2002	9. 67	47. 28	43. 05	18. 41	42. 55	39. 04	19. 42	38. 50	42. 07	13. 74	44. 79	41. 47
2003	8. 81	49. 18	42. 01	16. 57	44. 28	39. 15	18. 70	39. 81	41. 49	12. 80	45. 97	41. 23
2004	8. 81	50. 45	40. 73	17. 66	45. 18	37. 16	18. 90	41. 12	39. 99	13. 39	46. 23	40. 38
2005	8. 11	51. 41	40. 48	16. 21	47. 38	36. 41	17. 69	42. 79	39. 52	12. 12	47. 37	40. 51
2006	7. 49	51. 89	40. 62	14. 95	48. 88	36. 17	16. 18	45. 23	38. 58	11. 11	47. 95	40. 94
2007	7. 11	51. 58	41. 31	14. 44	49. 55	36. 01	15. 97	46. 32	37. 70	10. 77	47. 34	41. 89
2008	6. 93	50. 83	42. 24	14. 13	50. 50	35. 37	14. 73	47. 65	37. 62	10. 73	47. 45	41. 82
2009	6. 74	49. 53	43. 72	13. 58	49. 93	36. 49	13. 73	47. 46	38. 81	10. 33	46. 24	43. 43
2010	6. 49	49. 72	43. 79	12. 91	52. 16	34. 93	13. 15	49. 99	36. 87	10. 10	46. 75	43. 14
Average	16. 48	50. 12	33. 40	26. 20	44. 05	29. 75	27. 83	40. 03	32. 14	28. 19	47. 88	23. 94

Notes: PI: Primary Industry; SI: Secondary Industry; TI: Tertiary Industry①.

Sources: The National Bureau of Statistics of China.

2. 3. 2 The Role of Small Banks

Samolyk (1989, 1991, 1992) suggests that it is different financial structures across regions which really cause the regional impacts of monetary policy. Regional credit market segmentation due to imperfect information induces local

① Primary industry (PI) means agriculture. Secondary industry (SI) contains industry and construction. Tertiary industry (TI) consists of transports, storage and post; wholesale and retail trades; hotels and catering services; financial intermediation; real estate; other services.

small firms and other borrowers depend more on the local financial institution (mainly banks). Therefore, the development of banking system in varied regions will play a prominent role in the monetary transmission process (Rodríguez-Fuentes, 1998).

Kashyap and Stein (1995) indicate that monetary policy actions can have varied effects on different banks' abilities to make loans. They propose that bank size can affect their financing abilities. Large banks can always find external or non-bank funding easily and cheaply than small banks. Therefore, regions where most of loans are made by small banks might respond more to monetary policy actions than regions in which a majority proportion of loans come from large banks.

Regions' dependence on local banks will be reduced if borrowers can get loans from sources beyond local regions. However, some studies (Robert & Fishkind, 1979; Moore & Hill, 1982; Harrigan & Mcgregor, 1987) find evidence to support the segmented banking markets along borders of regions. Moore and Hill (1982) indicate as the existence of such kind of regional banking markets segmentation, small firms and households with no access to national credit market mainly depend on the regional credit market to raise funds. As local banks can identify and monitor local investment projects more efficiently than banks and investors outside, it would be less costly for households and small enterprises to borrow from local banks. Local banks also tend to provide favorable loan terms to local enterprises in anticipation of future deposit business. Summarizing, different distribution of small banks across provinces will affect the effectiveness of bank lending channel, leading to different effects of monetary policy across regions.

In China, indirect financing (mainly loan) accounts for an overwhelming part in funds financing. According to Figure 2.5, direct financing only accounts for less than 2.5% during 1992 – 2010. In 2010, this proportion of indirect financing in the East was 97.07%, while that in the Middle and the West was 98. 19% and 98. 63%. Then bank loan is the main channel for corporate financing and bank lending channel is the main channel of monetary transmission in China (Zhou & Jiang, 2002; Baek, 2005; Liu & Xie, 2006; Du, 2010).

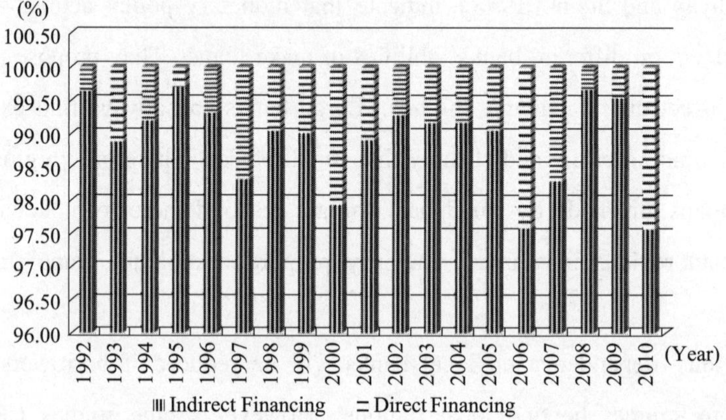

Figure 2. 5 Direct Financing and Indirect Financing in China from 1992 to 2010

Notes: Indirect (Direct) Financing = Loans (Raised Capital)/Total Financing.

Sources: The National Bureau of Statistics of China.

Kashyap and Stein (2000) find that the credit of small banks is easily affected by monetary policy actions than the credit of large banks. Thus if a province's banking system is mainly consisted of small banks, the shift in loan supply would be more easily. Figure 2. 6 reports the differences in the size distribution of banks across provinces. This study just selects five provinces in each region to make a comparison. In our definition, large banks contain five large commercial banks. Small banks mainly consist of city commercial banks and rural cooperative institutions. According to Figure 2. 6, the biggest proportion of small bank is 35. 83% in Ningxia (the West), the smallest one is 12. 33% in Beijing (the East). In general, the size distributions of large and small banks are very different across provinces in China. The proportion of small banks in the Middle and the West are bigger than the one in the East.

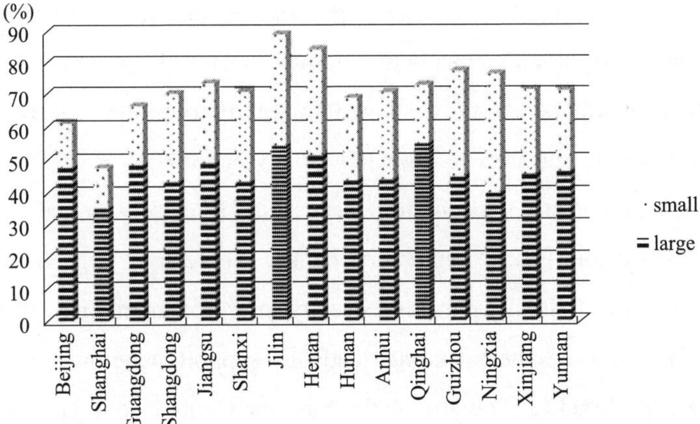

Figure 2. 6 The Distribution of Large versus Small Banks in Selected Provinces in 2011

Notes: The proportion of small bank = Assets of small banks/Total assets of all banks

The proportion of large bank = Assets of large banks/Total assets of all banks

The first five provinces are in the East, the second five ones are in the Middle and the last five ones are in the West.

Sources: Regional Financial Operation Report in China (2011).

2. 3. 3 The Structure and Size of Firms

Regional differences in the proportion of large and small borrowers and the sources of credit available to each could also cause provinces to respond differently to monetary policy actions. Considering the size of enterprises, Bernanke and Blinder (1988), Bernanke (1993), Gertler and Gilchrist (1993) point out that monetary policy can influence regional economies through affecting different banks' abilities of loan supply. To some extent firms (especially small firms with no access to national financial market) and individuals would largely depend on banks for financing due to imperfect information and external financing premiums (Kashyap & Stein, 1997; Arnold & Vrugt, 2004). Therefore, when banks cut loans, these borrowers cannot easily offset the reduction in bank loan supply. Furthermore, if they cannot obtain new funds quickly, their spending levels may fall. Then bank lending channel works. By comparison, large enterprises generally have more and varied channels to external, non-bank funding. As a consequence, the economy of one province with a large proportion of small enterprises could be particularly sensitive to monetary policy actions.

In China, monetary transmission mechanism is closely linked to the four large state-owned joint-stock commercial banks. These four large banks historically play the part of fiscal agents and occupy a large market share of loans and deposits. Furthermore, their lending tends to support state-owned enterprises (SOE) (Kong, 2003). The strong tie between China's four large banks and SOE is a prime example of the "soft budget constraint syndrome" introduced by Kornai (1986).

To some extent, the existence of soft budget constraint constrains the effectiveness of monetary policy. With a soft budget constraint, SOE have no incentive to operate efficiently and to respond appropriately to a tight monetary policy as the government stands ready with subsidies, easy credit, and bailouts (Phillips & Kunrong, 2005). Therefore, the provinces' responses to monetary policy actions may be negatively related to the proportion of SOE.

According to Table 2. 4, the percent of small enterprises (SE) across provinces are different. Tibet has the biggest proportion (93. 3%) of SE while Ningxia has the smallest percentage (80. 03%). Within each region, the highest percentage of SE is about 10 percentage points more than the lowest. The distribution of percent of state-owned and state-holding enterprises (SOHE) has a large disparity among both regions and provinces. The percent of the West is two times more than that of the East. The highest percent is 60. 39% of Tibet and the lowest is 3. 17% of Zhejiang. Generally speaking, the East has a bigger proportion of SE while the Middle and the West have a higher percentage of SOHE. According to bank lending channel and the soft budget constraint, the East will respond more than the Middle and the West to monetary policy shocks.

Table 2. 4 The Percent of SE and SOHE by Region and Province (%)

East	SE	SOHE	Middle	SE	SOHE	West	SE	SOHE
Beijing	89. 93	29. 32	Shanxi	81. 77	29. 76	Inner Mongolia	84. 29	26. 70
Tianjin	89. 65	23. 09	Jilin	86. 37	28. 15	Guangxi	86. 08	32. 26
Hebei	87. 26	16. 63	Heilongjiang	83. 65	30. 34	Chongqing	84. 68	20. 32
Liaoning	90. 34	16. 75	Anhui	88. 20	14. 20	Sichuan	85. 74	16. 69
Shanghai	88. 47	12. 73	Jiangxi	89. 82	28. 05	Guizhou	88. 40	38. 45
Jiangsu	90. 40	4. 72	Henan	88. 33	15. 45	Yunnan	80. 70	35. 12
Zhejiang	92. 36	3. 17	Hubei	88. 73	20. 36	Tibet	93. 30	60. 39
Fujian	89. 75	8. 91	Hunan	91. 26	20. 74	Shaanxi	84. 42	35. 72
Shandong	86. 51	8. 99				Gansu	88. 95	26. 45
Guangdong	87. 40	6. 92				Qinghai	85. 56	43. 86
Hainan	82. 78	41. 39				Ningxia	80. 03	26. 69
						Xinjiang	85. 78	44. 39
East	88. 62	15. 69	Middle	87. 27	23. 38	West	85. 66	33. 92

Notes: SE means small-sized enterprise①, SOHE refers to the state-owned and state holding enterprise. Percent = numbers of SE or SOHE by province/total numbers of enterprise. The percent is the average from 2000 to 2010.

Sources: The National Bureau of Statistics of China.

2. 4 Evolution of China's Banking System

After more than thirty year of reform and opening up, China's banking sector has turned to a new period of strong development. During past few years, marked acceleration of China's banking reform has been seen, particularly significant strengthening of the central bank's capacity for supervision and macroeconomic management, substantial improvement in the management of the commercial banks, and greater openness of the banking industry.

The People's Bank of China (PBC) was established in December 1948, just before the founding of the People's Republic of China. Before 1978, The PBC was the sole financial institution in China, and in accord with the highly planned

---

① The definition of small-sized enterprise: The numbers of employees below 300, Annual sales below 30 million CNY, Total assets below 40 million CNY.

economy, was part of the fiscal allocation system, it attached to the Ministry of Finance, acting as the role of cashier. The PBC is a mono-bank engaged in both policy and commercial banking operations in China at that time. In January 1978, the PBC separated from the Ministry of Finance, marking the beginning of reform of the banking system in China.

From 1979 to 1984, four large banks (the Industrial and Commercial Bank of China (ICBC), the Bank of China (BOC), the Agricultural Bank of China (ABC) and the China Construction Bank (CCB)) have been set up to take over the banking business from the PBC successively, allowing the PBC to concentrate on monetary policy and regulation in order to make the PBC act as a central bank. These four state-owned specialized banks undertook different special commercial banking activities in their specific area respectively.

In 1987, some joint-stock banks such as Bank of Communications, China Merchants Bank and Shenzhen Development Bank were allowed to establish in order to promote diversification of financial institutions. In 1994, the commercialization of four specialized banks was started, to make the four specialized banks real state-owned commercial banks, three policy banks (China Development Bank, China Agricultural Development Bank, China Export-Import Bank) were established in 1994 to separate the policy lending from commercial lending. By then, a banking system consisting mainly of the four state-owned commercial banks, joint-stock commercial banks and rural credit cooperative under the supervision of the PBC had initially taken shape.

Although functioned as the central bank since 1984, in fact, the PBC was not a full-fledged central bank because it did not own a clear legal status. In March 1995, the Law of the People's Bank of China stipulated that the main function of the PBC is to implement monetary policy and supervise the banking industry under the leadership of the State Council. The law strengthens the independence of the PBC through prohibiting it's financing of fiscal deficits and interference in the performance of its functions by any government agency.

Until 1998, the branch network of the PBC was based on China's administrative system, with 31 branch offices located at the provincial level. In 1998, the branches of the PBC underwent a major restructuring. The 31 provincial branches of the PBC were replaced by nine regional branches that are in a better position to conduct common monetary policy. The purpose is to further strengthen the independence of the PBC and to increase the effectiveness of monetary policy.

In 2003, the China Banking Regulatory Commission (CBRC) was established to take over the regulatory functions from the PBC. The purpose is to make a separation of the conduct of monetary policy and supervision of the banking system and to leave the PBC to focus on formulating and implementing monetary policy.

After years of a series of significant reforms in its banking system, now China's banking system is consisted of large commercial banks, joint-stock commercial banks, city commercial banks and rural cooperative institutions and so on.

Large commercial banks① contain the Industrial and Commercial Bank of China (ICBC), the Bank of China (BOC), the Agricultural Bank of China (ABC) and the China Construction Bank (CCB), and Bank of Communications. Today, in the banking business, the traditional four large banks are still the biggest players though their market shares decline gradually. Bank of Communications is actually a joint-stock commercial bank. It is attributed to large commercial bank because its total assets satisfy the standard of large commercial banks.

The second-tier commercial banks are joint-stock commercial banks. The existence of this type of banks increases the competition in the banking market and meets the diversified needs of banks. Most of these banks were set up to sup-

① According to China Banking Regulatory Commission, large commercial bank means total assets are equal or greater than two trillion CNY.

port the development of certain region and industry initially, but now many of them have nationwide branches and expand their business all over the country. Now joint-stock commercial banks contain 12 national or regional commercial banks, such as China Merchants Bank, China Minsheng Bank, Guangdong Development Bank, Pudong Development Bank and so on. Along with the competition and development of bank market, creating professional advantages and enhancing competitiveness by features have become a common strategy for these banks to make reforms.

The third significant group is city commercial banks. Many of them were founded on the basis of urban credit cooperatives. Since 2003, altogether 800 urban credit cooperatives have either been successfully transformed into city commercial banks or exited from the market. The development strategy of city commercial banks is "staying focused on localities of incorporation, serving small and micro enterprises". Now they play a pivotal role in underpinning the small and micro enterprises development and consumer finance business. At the end of 2011, the total outstanding balance of small enterprise loans amounted to CNY1. 55 trillion, taking up 47. 8% of their loans to all corporations. The aggregate assets of city commercial banks reached CNY9. 98 trillion, 6. 8 times that of the value in 2003, accounting for 8. 8% of the total assets of the banking industry.

Since their establishment in 1951, rural credit cooperatives (RCC) has been endeavoring to strengthen and improve rural financial services by sticking to the principles of serving the farmers, agricultural industry and rural development as their key purpose and target. At the end of 2011, the RCC opened 77000 outlets with 760000 employees, offering 77. 4 percent of farming household loans and covering 76 percent of the townships or villages that were previously not reached by any financial institutions or services. Generally speaking, RCC are the financial institutions in China that have the most widely distributed outlets in rural areas and play the most sufficient role in supporting rural areas.

Since the pilot reform of RCC was launched in 2003, substantial progress has been made on many fronts, including in-depth equity restructuring across the country and enhanced corporate governance, operational efficiency and business performance. As a result, the RCC have been gradually steered on the sound track of healthy development. At the end of 2011, there were altogether 2667 rural cooperative financial institutions, including 212 rural commercial banks and 190 rural cooperative banks. The scale of RCC balance sheet, including deposits and loans, was 5 times that of the pre-reform era.

2.5 Evolution of China's Monetary Policy

2.5.1 Reform of China's Monetary Policy

Today monetary policy is conducted by the PBC under the Law of the PRC on The People's Bank of China. The main objective of monetary policy is to keep the stability of currency and thereby promote economic growth. That is to say, the primary goal is to maintain the stability of the CNY value, and takes the stability of the currency value as the means to promote economic growth.

The PBC owns several kinds of monetary policy instruments which can be divided into direct and indirect instruments. The direct quantitative instruments, which are seldom used now, mainly contain credit plans, direct central bank lending and window guidance①. The indirect instruments are mainly consisted of reserve requirement ratio, administrated benchmark interest rates and open market operations. During the last three decades, along with the reform of economic

① Window Guidance is often termed "moral suasion", it has been used to persuade banks and other financial institutions to keep to official guidelines. The "moral" aspect comes from the pressure for "moral responsibility" to operate in a way that is consistent with furthering the good of the economy.

system, in order to deeply integrate into the global economy, the conduct and instruments of monetary policy have experienced lots of changes, which mainly happened in the middle of 1990s. During this period, the conduct of monetary policy has been transformed from direct quantitative control to a more indirect market-oriented structure.

In China prior to 1978, money was issued to satisfy the needs of the highly planned economy. Credit was extended on the basis of the production plan due to the absence of financial market. Money was simply channeled through the only state bank, the PBC, to finance the physical production plan. In such a system where production and the supply of money were planned, prices were determined by the state.

Before a series of reforms that took place in mid 1990s, the PBC took the total credit as the intermediate target, exhibiting the characteristics of a centrally planned economy. The common monetary tools used at that time contained credit plans, relending policies and administered interest rates.

Credit plans were used extensively in the 1980s and the 1990s. Based on its policy targets, the PBC directly regulated the quantity and direction of bank lending. It provided explicit official guidance on the loans made by the state-owned commercial banks (the four large banks). This "directed lending" supported lots of large SOEs which traditionally made a lot of contribution to employment (Goodfriend & Prasad, 2007).

Relending policy of the central bank was mainly used to fill the gaps between the available funding of four large banks through deposit and their assigned loan quota. The PBC provided direct lending to four large banks by this policy in the case of deposit shortfalls (Park & Sehrt, 2001). Meanwhile, other S&M sized banks (joint-stock commercial banks) had no responsibility to provide policy loans to SOEs. Thus they had problems in access to the central bank relending facility and cannot get the funds of the PBC as easily as four large banks. Although shouldering a large burden of policy lending, banks still had certain autonomy in allocating loans. The relending rate as the price of central bank relending funds was the marginal cost of providing loans, indicating that to some extent relending policy could have certain potential influences on banks' decision of making credit.

The series of financial reforms happened in 1994 – 1995 which contained: relaxation of binding credit plans; adoption of a new Commercial Bank Law to improve managerial incentives and prudential financial regulation; establishment of policy banks to separate policy lending from commercial lending; as well as the establishment of a national, unified inter-bank market. The purpose of the reform was to turn the state-owned commercial banks into independent commercial banks and to make the PBC truly independent.

In 1998, credit quotas were terminated. Instead, the PBC use "window guidance" to provide official guidelines which should be followed by banks (Geiger, 2008). Also since 1998, the PBC restarted to regard reserve requirement ratio as an important monetary policy instrument and used it constantly in the following years. After the reforms, Open Market Operations (OMO) was used as the primary tool to manage monetary base (Bennett & Dixon, 2001). At present, OMO are mainly used to adjust liquidity of banks (Liu & Xie, 2006).

With the purpose of dealing with an increasing pressure from foreign exchange market, central bank bills were initiated by the PBC from September 2002. Similarly, the rediscount rate was introduced in 2004, and the reserve requirement ratio was more frequently used. Moreover, in 2005, the reverse bond based repo was introduced to cope with foreign exchange inflows resulting from the trade surplus. However, despite such recent developments, Green (2005) states that the effectiveness of these instruments is limited due to lagged financial market reform in China. In result, credit policy remains an important instrument for the PBC even today.

Even after the enforcement of the Commercial Bank Law, four larges banks' lending decisions still remained seriously constrained and a majority of their loans flowed to SOEs should actually be sorted to policy lending, leading to the difficulty for S&M sized firms in obtaining credit. Forty years after China officially opened its economy, although the reform of monetary policy got a big progress, the interest rates are still regulated, the independence of the banking sector is still dubious and the banks remain relatively ineffective in financing the investment activities of the corporate sector, indicating further reform is needed along with economic development.

2.5.2 Instruments of Monetary Policy in China

The main monetary policy instruments used by the PBC include open market operations, the rediscount rate and reserve requirement ratio. Besides, several non-market approaches, such as credit policy, instructive credit plans, and "window guidance" are also used as supplementary instruments. Yi (2001), as well as Xie (2004) considers that interest rate policy is also the main frequently used instruments. Xie (2004) notes that the PBC has traditionally used monetary base as the operational target and used money supply as the intermediate target. More recently, the PBC has been employing growth rates of monetary aggregates and bank credit as specific intermediate targets.

In China, interest rates decisions are taken by the PBC, but only with prior approval of the State Council (He & Wang, 2012). The PBC administers two benchmark interest rates: one year lending rate and one year deposit rate. In 1993, the Communist Party of China (CPC) adopted by the Third Plenary Session of the 14th Central Committee of CPC "Decision on Several Issues Concerning the Establishment of Socialist Market Economy System". This decision initially established the basic tentative framework of interest rate liberalization. From then on, interest rate liberalization has been in process.

In 1996, a national, unified inter-bank market established and China inter-bank offered rate (CHIBOR) is the earliest market rate in China's currency market. The issue of national bonds by price biding marked the beginning of interest rate liberalization in bonds market. In 1998, the PBC reformed the formulation mechanism of discount rate and rediscount rate. The rediscount rate became the benchmark rate. The PBC allowed the lending rate to small business for commercial banks can rise by 20% and the lending rate for rural credit cooperative can rise by 50%.

In recent years, the PBC has provided more flexibility for banks to set the benchmark loan rates. Financial institutions can determine loan rates based on the borrower's risk and other characteristics. More recently, a floor on lending rates and a ceiling on deposit rates were scrapped successively. Banks were also given more freedom to determine the loan rate and deposit rate by their own.

Reserve requirement ratios were different according to different types of deposits when the PBC established in 1984. But in 1985, reserve requirement ratio was unified to 10%. From 1987 to 1988, the ratio was raised to 13% and has remained unchangeable until 1998. It was reduced from 13% to 8% in 1998 (see Figure 2.7). After 1998, reserve requirements have been used quite frequently (see Figure 2.8).

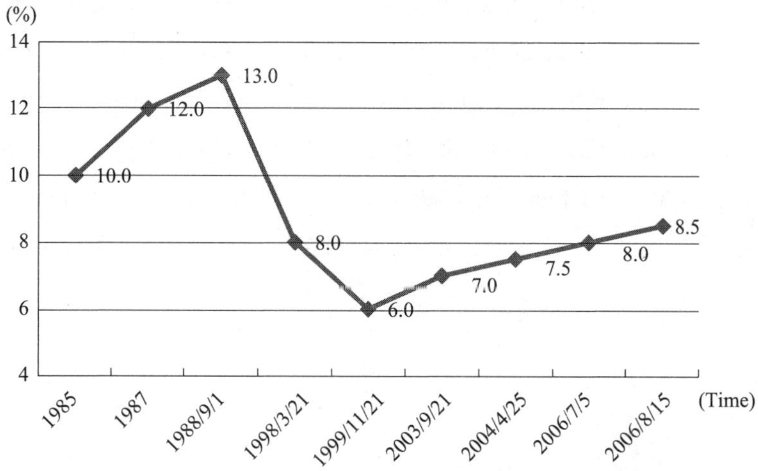

Figure 2.7 Reserve Requirement Ratio from 1985 to 2006

Sources: The People's Bank of China.

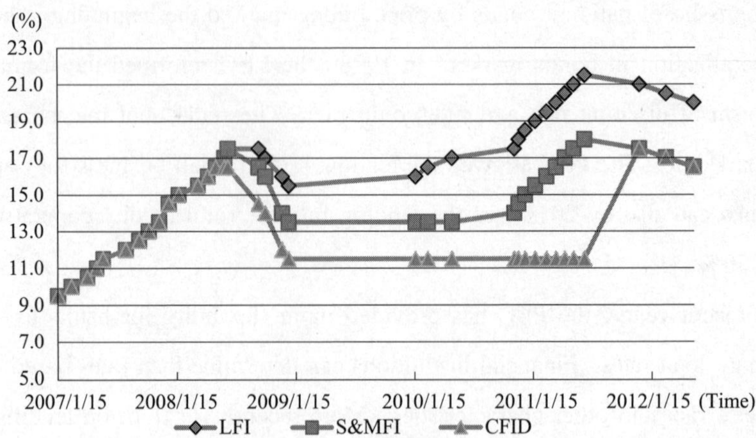

Figure 2.8 Reserve Requirement Ratio from 2007 to 2012

Notes: LFI: Reserve requirement ratio of Large Financial Institutions. S&MFI: Reserve requirement ratio of small and medium sized financial institutions. CFID: Reserve requirement ratio of corporate financial institutions in disaster area (39 counties).

Sources: The People's Bank of China.

In addition, the differentiated reserve requirement ratio (DRRR) was introduced on April, 2004. The DRRR means that financial institutions failing to satisfy certain standard would apply the DRRR 0.5% higher than normal level. To support the reconstruction of the disaster area, the PBC decided to apply the DRRR a little lower than normal level to corporate financial institutions in 39 counties in Sichuan province that suffered most in the earthquake on June 8th, 2008. On September 25th, 2008, the PBC applied DRRR to large financial institutions and S&M sized financial institutions. Large financial institutions applied the DRRR 1% higher than S&M sized financial institutions (see details in Chapter 1).

Chapter 3

Literature Review

3. 1 Theoretical Review

3. 1. 1 Introduction

This chapter is made up of two parts: theoretical review and empirical review. The theoretical review is consisted of monetary transmission mechanism theory, monetary transmission channels in China, the spillover effects, the role of small banks and the differentiated reserve requirement ratio (DRRR) policy. The empirical review contains model selection: the VAR model and other models, monetary transmission channels in China, monetary policy indicators and the factors affecting regional effects of monetary policy. The theoretical framework of this study is displayed in Figure 3. 1.

As Figure 3. 1 indicates, monetary policy has two influences on provinces (such as Province *A* and Province *B*): direct influence through monetary transmission mechanism and indirect influence by spillover effects. To our knowledge, most of previous literature tends to neglect the indirect effect (spillover effect). Carlino and DeFina (1998) argue that the spillover effect is an important factor which can affect the magnitude and timing of regional effects of monetary policy. This study will examine the impacts of monetary policy on regions and provinces when considering spillover effect.

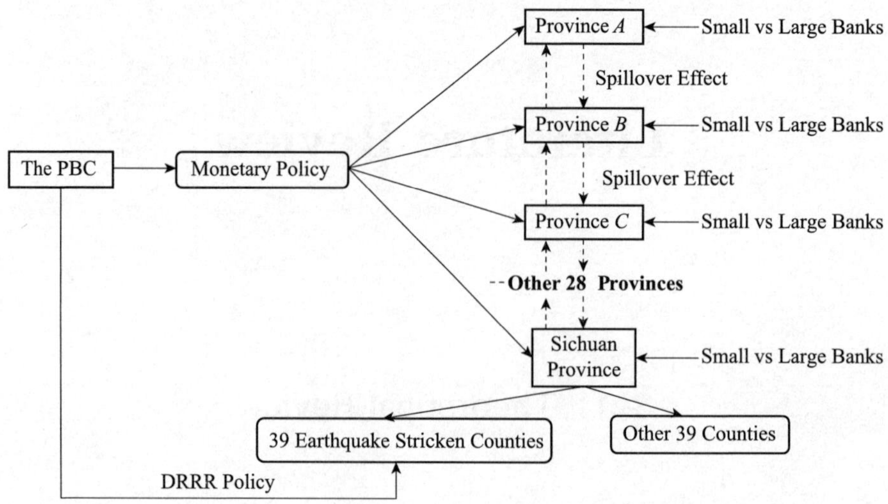

Figure 3. 1 Theoretical Framework of this Study

This study also emphasizes one factor: the different size distributions of small banks across provinces, to explain the regional effects of monetary policy. According to bank lending channel, if province *A* has a big proportion of small banks while province *B* has a small proportion of small banks, for example, a tight monetary policy would influence province *A* more than province *B*. Especially, if province *A* is a less developed area and province *B* is a more developed area, the gap between these two provinces would widen.

To narrow the gap across provinces, from a monetary policy perspective, this study introduces the DRRR policy as a case study in Sichuan province. The PBC has applied a lower DRRR to 39 earthquake-stricken counties in Sichuan province and a normal RRR to another 39 counties also in Sichuan province to see whether the DRRR can promote the economic growth of the disaster area more so as to narrow the gap among provinces and promote balanced regional economic development.

3. 1. 2 Monetary Policy Transmission Mechanism Theory

As well known, the main function of monetary policy focuses on macro-economic regulation and keeping the stability and sustainability of economic growth. Nevertheless, as the existence of time lags from adopting certain monetary policy instrument to going into effect and the different magnitude of regions' responses to this instrument, sometimes monetary policy may have unexpected consequences. Furthermore, these unexpected results are generally depended on the features of the propagation through which monetary policy affects macro-economic activity.

According to Christiano, Eichenbaum, and Evans (1998), monetary policy decisions and their subsequent economic consequences are the impacts of all the shocks to the economy. Therefore, to examine the regional effects of monetary policy is to evaluate the impacts of monetary policy shocks through a variety of channels. Monetary transmission mechanism describes how monetary policy actions work their way through certain channels, and finally trigger the changes in real economy (Taylor, 1995). Several literature, such as Gertler (1988), Gertler and Gilchrist (1993), Bernanke and Gertler (1995), Cecchetti (1995), Mishkin (1995), Christiano et al. (1998) offers a comprehensive overview on the monetary transmission mechanism. Below, this study briefly introduces several monetary transmission channels from a regional perspective.

3. 1. 2. 1 Interest Rate Channel

Conventional economic theory emphasizes the role of interest rate in the monetary transmission process and regards interest rate channel as the main monetary transmission channel. The basic point of the view of this channel emphasizes that how changes in interest rates affect the cost of capital, and further influence the investment, the consumption and the spending (Taylor, 1995). In short, the underlying meaning is that central bank can indirectly affect or adjust the economic behavior of micro-economic agents by modifying the capital (opportunity) cost relevant to the spending decisions of these agents.

An increase in interest rates will raise the cost of borrowing, reduce the investment of private-sector agencies and the expenditure of durable consumer goods, and therefore leading to a lower aggregate demand and real output. In this process, a key link is to what extent changes in interest rate can affect the investment and spending, which is largely related to interest rate sensitivity of different industries. At the regional level, different industrial compositions, together with varied interest sensitivities of different industries, would cause regions to respond differently to monetary policy shocks (Ganley & Simon, 1997; Carlino & DeFina, 1998; Hayo & Uhlenbrock, 1999).

3.1.2.2 Credit Channel

In recent years, another channel, credit channel has assumed increased prominence in the propagation process of monetary policy. Credit channel pays attention to the principal-agent problems in credit market. Due to the asymmetric information and the high cost in the enforcement of contracts, credit markets generally and continuously influence the real economy through credit channel (Bernanke, 1993). As a result, two basic channels can be identified: bank lending channel and balance sheet channel.

Actually, these two channels can be considered as complementary mechanisms amplifying or strengthening the conventional interest rate channel, not just an alternative (Bernanke & Gertler, 1995). Based on the view of credit channel, monetary policy can not only directly affect the consumption and the spending, but also can indirectly influence them through the endogenous changes in the external financial premium.

1) Bank Lending Channel

Bank lending channel relies on the credit market frictions, due to asymmetric information and costly enforcement of contracts, banks play a central role in the financial system as they are adept in coping with some borrowers such as small enterprises plagued by the information problem (Kashyap & Stein, 1997). The connections between small banks and small enterprises are of special importance to the propagation of monetary policy. To be more precise, facing a tight monetary policy, banks especially small banks with no access to alternative sources of funding for deposits cannot fully offset the decline of bank reserves to some extent, in consequence, they will reduce the availability of loans (Kashyap & Stein, 1995, 1997). As a result, closing bank credit will increase the external finance premium which constrains small firms dependent on bank financing (but not for large enterprises as they usually can easily get external, non-banking sources of funds), leading to the reduction of investment and other restrictive effects on the rest of non-financial sector.

As theory suggests, two crucial conditions must be satisfied for bank lending channel to smoothly operate: small banks cannot fully shield their loan portfolios and small firms lack other sources of funds besides bank loans. Therefore, at the regional level, the degree how small enterprises rely on bank loans (Bernanke & Blinder, 1988; Kashyap, Stein & Wilcox, 1993) and the ease with which banks can adjust their balance sheets (Kashyap & Stein, 1995) might affect the regional effects of monetary policy to some extent. Thus the different size distributions of small and large banks, together with the regional differences in the ability of banks to shield their loan portfolios may explain the differential regional effects of monetary policy (Carlino & DeFina, 1998).

2) Balance Sheet Channel

Balance sheet channel works through the impact of monetary policy on the net worth of enterprises which will affect the firms' ability to borrow (Bernanke & Gertler, 1995). It is based on the argument that external finance premium depends on the borrower's net worth. In this channel, assets prices are especially important in that they determine the value of the collateral that firm and individuals will have to present when obtaining a loan (Dornbusch, Favero & Giavazzi, 1998). A tight monetary policy will lower the assets prices of firms and subsequently reduce the net worth of firms, raising the external financing premium and in turn reducing the consumption and the investment. As firms' financing ability mainly rely on the value of collateral, raising interest rate will lower the value of collateral, and further affect the ability of firms to get bank loans, resulting in the reduction of lending and investment (Kashyap & Stein, 1997).

3.1.2.3 Exchange Rate Channel

Exchange rate channel tells that monetary policy can affect the real economy through the movements in the balance of payments (Menon, 1995). Under flexible exchange rates, movements in the exchange rate may cause changes in the relative prices of goods and services, and the level of spending of firms and individuals. This channel also involves interest rates effects, because when raising interest rates a little higher than the interest rate in foreign countries, domestic deposits become more attractive. Foreign capitals will flow in and cause appreciation of local currency. An appreciation of exchange rate makes the foreign goods and services relatively cheap, meanwhile makes exports more expensive to foreign buyers. This will reduce the net exports and the aggregate output. Therefore, if there exist regional differences in the importance of exports, regional effects of monetary policy might arise due to the different degree of openness across regions (Dornbusch, Favero & Giavazzi, 1998).

3.1.3 Monetary Transmission Channels in China

Jiang, Liu and Zhao (2005) consider that monetary policy transmission channels have important meaning to the effectiveness of monetary policy. Whether monetary policy is effective is decided by the smooth or unsmooth of monetary transmission channels. Monetary authority should understand when, to what extent and through which channel monetary policy affects the real economy, all of these refer to monetary transmission mechanism. The evaluation of these problems directly influences the achievement of final objectives of monetary policy.

Jiao, Sun and Liu (2006) point out that although monetary policy is effective as a whole in China, to some extent, the differential regional effects of monetary policy reduce the effectiveness of monetary policy. The sources of regional effects of monetary policy lie in the regional differences of monetary transmission channels, which cause regions to respond differently in the timing and magnitude to common monetary policy.

In China, monetary policy plays a role through both interest rate channel and bank lending channel (Zhou & Jiang, 2002), in comparison, as bank financial assets take a dominant position in the total financial assets and credit markets compose the main parts of China's monetary policy transmission (Liu & Xie, 2006). Therefore, the main monetary transmission channel is bank lending channel. As the main channel, the effectiveness of bank lending channel in China actually suffers some limitations as the PBC cannot totally control the credit behavior of commercial banks in the transition process.

The first limitation is that bank lending channel mainly affects the S&M sized enterprises which depend on external financing (bank loans). Large enterprises have a strong self-finance capacity and always have other sources of funds besides bank loans (Zhou & Jiang, 2002). Moreover, in China, there exists strong interdependence between large enterprises and large banks. On one side, state-owned enterprises have depended on four large banks (the Industrial and Commercial Bank of China, the Bank of China, the Agricultural Bank of China and China Construction Bank) for a long time, on the other side, with the establishment of credit risk management and promotion of credit rating, large enterprises especially listed companies and high quality enterprises in oligopoly industry are virtually the apples of banks' eye (Tong, 2005). Therefore, the extension and contraction of bank credit have a little influence on large enterprises. In addition, with the financial innovations and diversity of credit instruments, a lot of new emerging substitutes of bank credit reduce the effects of bank lending channel (Zhou & Jiang, 2002).

The second limitation is that the PBC has difficulties in directly affecting the credit behavior of commercial banks. Due to some political and historical reasons, the banking industry in China is not fully competitive and four large banks occupy a large market share, which enables them to arrive at consensus and agreement easily on certain issues. In fact, whether monetary policy actions adopted by the PBC could finally be applied to the whole economy to some extent depends on the four large banks' total assets, assets structures and the ways to employ them, since the four large banks' behavior may probably diverge from the direction of monetary policy (Liu & Xie, 2006). In China, four large banks occupy a big market share in the banking industry. Therefore, whether monetary policy can achieve its objectives or not, to a great extent, is decided by the reflection of four large banks to monetary policy actions. In some sense, four large banks are significant key links in monetary transmission channels (Jiao et al., 2006).

Four large banks adopt branch banking system, thus their branches in different regions have no difference essentially. However, due to the disparity of economic development, education, social habits, and so on, there are differences in the number of financial branches, business volumes, profits and level of service among branches of four large banks across regions. Business volumes are bigger in developed regions than that in less developed regions, and the assets quality in developed regions is also superior to these in less developed regions (Jiao et al., 2006).

The Research Group of Wuhan Branch of PBC (2002) considers that monetary policy transmission mechanism has some blocks especially in the less developed regions. In the current system, the credit supply of financial institutions fails to satisfy the needs of real economy in less developed regions where huge outflow of deposits induces that deposits cannot be translated into investment effectively. The expression of blocks are that deposits grow quickly while loan grow slowly, causing surplus of funds in these less developed regions which originally need lots of funds to support economic development. Deposit-loan gap continues to widening and a number of funds deposit into superior branches of banks.

3.1.4 The Spillover Effects

Spillover effect means how economic changes originated in one region affect other regions through interregional links. For example, monetary policy can directly affects the economy of province *A*, and through interregional links with province *B*, it can indirectly influences the economy of province *B*, and vice versa. Knowledge of interregional spillovers can help us to understand the regional growth dynamics. Carlino and DeFina (1995) document the importance of spillover effects among regions in the United States. They use Structural Vector Auto-Regressions (SVAR) model to explore the interregional links in regional income growth in the United States and find important and highly persistent interregional spillovers exist. Moreover, these spillovers tend to be geographically dispersed. Carlino and DeFina (1998) indicate that a shortcoming of existing literature which examines the regional effects of monetary policy (Beare, 1976; Garrison & Chang, 1979; Mathur & Stein, 1980, etc.) is their attempt to test the effects of monetary policy region by region with no consideration of spillover effects across regions.

Brun, Combes and Renald (2002) test the spillover effects from coastal provinces to inland provinces with panel data during 1981 – 1998 in China. They find regional growth spillover effects from coastal provinces to inland provinces and within coastal provinces do exist, but it is not enough to narrow the gaps among China's provinces in the short term (Fu, 2004). Ying (2000) examines provincial economic growth spillover effects between each province with those geographically near to it during 1978 – 1994 in China. Ying (2000) finds economic growths of nearby provinces are closely connected and both positive and negative spillovers exist, while the most developed province, Guangdong generates the strongest spillover effects to other provinces. Groenewold, Lee and Chen (2007) use vector auto-regressive (VAR) method to examine the spillover of output among three regions from 1953 to 2003 in China and find that there exist strong output spillovers from the East to the other two regions, from the Middle to the West, but no such effects spill from the West to the East and the Middle.

In short, the above-mentioned studies focus on spillover effect related to how economic growth or output changes in one region influence economies in other regions. Here "economic growth" can be induced by any factors such as FDI, fix asset investment, the increase of government expenditure, etc. Usually the spillover effect induced by economic growth is positive. This study emphasizes spillover effect of economic growth is induced by only one factor: monetary policy. Simply speaking, economic growth in one region is induced by the increase of money supply or credit. This study pays attention to the spillover effect of monetary policy. As for this type of spillover, it should be noticed that mobility of funds between regions may influence it as funds normally flow from less developed region to more developed region due to their profit-driven nature. To some extent this type of funds flow may offsets the positive spillover effects of monetary policy. This study will focus on this process.

Considering spillover effect, monetary policy has two types of effects on regional economy: direct effect through monetary transmission channels and indirect effect through spillover effect. To our knowledge, in China, the previous literature (Cortes & Kong, 2007; Kong et al., 2007; Jiang & Chen, 2009) fails to consider spillover effect when examining regional effects of monetary policy in China. This study will fully consider the influence of spillover effects among the three regions and their affiliated 31 provinces on the regional effects of monetary policy and regard this point as our contribution.

3. 1. 5 The Role of Small Banks

Samolyk (1989, 1991, 1992) develops a regional credit channel and emphasizes the role of local banks in funding small local borrowers. He finds that since information problem induces certain degree of regional credit segmentation, regional banking conditions can affect real economy of local region which mainly depends on local banks to satisfy the needs of investment.

Kashyap and Stein (1995, 1997) analyze the bank lending channel in detail and highlight the role of banks in monetary transmission process. In their explanation, a reduction in the supply of reserves pushes the banks toward a more costly form of financing. Because of the extra premium, the banks would make fewer loans after the reserve outflow. If the borrowers who lose their loans cannot obtain new funds quickly, their spending levels may fall. They examine the loan supply responses to monetary policy and find that compared with the banks which can easily raise uninsured external funds, banks in difficulty of obtaining external financing are more likely to be affected by a tight monetary policy. Kashyap and Stein (1995) argue that banks of different sizes use varied forms of financing. Large banks could more easily get non-deposit financing. They find that the loan supply of small banks is more sensitive to a monetary policy tightening than large banks. Therefore, regional differences in the abilities of banks to alter their balance sheets may explain the regional effects of monetary policy to some extent.

In China, corporate financing depends highly on indirect financing, mainly bank loans (Baek, 2005). So bank lending channel is the main monetary transmission channel in China (Zhou & Jiang, 2002; Liu & Xie, 2006). In China, four large banks occupy a big market share in the banking industry. There exists strong interdependence between large enterprises and large banks. SOEs have depended on four large banks for a long time (Tong, 2005). Therefore, four large banks and SOEs are significant key links in monetary transmission channels (Jiao et al., 2006).

The main limitation of bank lending channel is that this channel mainly affects small enterprises which depend on bank loans (Zhou & Jiang, 2002). Large enterprises have a strong self-finance capacity and always have other sources of financing besides bank loans. Considering most of loans made by small banks flow to small sized enterprises in China (China Banking Regulatory Commission Annual Report 2011)①, regional differences of the distribution of small banks may to some extent explain the regional effects of monetary policy.

3.1.6 Differentiated Reserve Requirement Ratio

The traditional description of monetary policy generally emphasizes the reserve requirement constraint on banks. In this story, banks are an important link in the transmission of monetary policy as changes in bank reserves affect the quantity of reservable deposits held by banks (Peek & Rosengren, 1995). Higher reserve requirement can restrict the growth of monetary aggregate and squeeze excess reserves if not fully neutralized, negatively affecting banks' ability to provide loans (Ma, Yan & Liu, 2013).

It is widely acknowledged that reserve requirement acts as a tax on banks, to some extent constrain their profits and raising the cost of credit, possibly further widening the loan-deposit rate spread (Borio & Disyatat, 2010; Montoro & Moreno, 2011). To keep their profits, banks would tend to transfer the cost added by reserve requirement through attempting to either pay depositors less or charge borrowers more or both—by widening the loan-deposit rate spread (Montoro & Moreno, 2011). This rests on the implicit assumption that the burden can be passed through.

① Available on the website of China Banking Regulatory Commission, http://www.cbrc.gov.cn/english/index.html

Hein and Jonathan (2002) point out that along with the widely accepted view that reserve requirement acts as a tax on banks, there is widespread disagreement that as to who bears the tax and who benefits when the tax is reduced. Black (1975), Fabozzi and Thurston (1986) argue that the reserve requirement tax is passed on to depositors of reservable instruments in the form of lower yields. Cargill and Mayer (2006) find that banks do not respond to the changes in reserve requirements essentially by changing their excess reserves, instead, banks meet a substantial part of their increased reserve requirements by reducing their earning assets, including loans. They prove that the increase in reserve requirements reduces the availability of bank credit.

There exist several evidences suggesting that at least a portion of the tax is not passed on to borrowers or depositors but rather is passed on to, or absorbed by, bank shareholders. Some authors (Osborne & Zaher, 1992; Cosimano & McDonald, 1998; Stewart & Hein, 2002) provide evidences suggesting that increases (reductions) in reserve requirement lead to lower (higher) bank stock prices.

According to bank lending channel, monetary policy can affect bank loan supply by changing bank reserves, and thus on the real economy (Kashyap & Stein, 1995). By lowering bank reserves, a tight monetary policy would reduce the core deposit funding of bank loans (Van Den Heuvel, 2002). If some banks (especially small banks) cannot get other financing to keep lending, loan supply will be reduced and certain borrowers (small firms) will be affected. Reduction in either loan supply or loan demand would result in decreasing investment and spends (Kishan & Opiela, 2000).

Ma, Yang and Liu (2011) argue that the PBC finds it easier to reach consensus on reserve requirement than interest rate decisions and enjoys greater discretion in applying this tool in recent years. The effects of reserve requirement should be explored in conjunction with other policy actions. Depending on the policy mix, higher reserve requirement tends to signal a tightening bias, to squeeze excess reserves of banks, to push market interest rates higher, and to help widen net interest spreads, thus tightening domestic monetary conditions. It is well known that reserve requirement is seemed as a tax burden on banks. Banks appear to pass through a big part of the burden to their customers, mostly depositors and the small and mediumsized enterprises (SMEs). Yet bank shareholders may also bear part of the burden, if wider margins and spreads in part reflect increased risk premia.

In all, most of the literature analyzes the function of reserve requirement and the link between reserve requirement ratio and bank loans. Only Gray (2011) gives a simple description of differentiated reserve requirement ratio. Gray (2011) indicates that most of countries uses a single reserve requirement rate for all reservable liabilities, a few countries use differentiated reserve requirement ratio with clear and achievable goals. Historically, some central banks have applied differential reserve requirement ratio to different types of banks (such as the United States set reserve requirement ratio based on location factors across member banks and the level of deposits during 1966 – 1972). This would appear to reflect the taxation aspect of unremunerated reserves, and imply a subsidy to those banks which have a lower reserve requirement.

To our knowledge, no literature tests the effects of the DRRR policy on different regions in China. This study will examine the effects of the DRRR policy on the disaster region in China. The effect, if significant, may have strong implication on future China's monetary policy structure, particularly with regards to China's efforts to reduce regional disparities across China.

3.2 Empirical Review

3.2.1 The VAR Model

Sims (1980) has developed the first generation of vector auto-regressive

(VAR) model to test how the real economy is influenced by unexpected shocks in economic policy and other factors. Sims claims that it is possible that we can estimate a reduced form model which is named unconstrained VAR, treating all variables as endogenous, instead of large scale structural model. VAR typically relies on a small number of variables expressed as past values of the dependent variables and past values of the other variables in the model. Though normalization, one estimates a VAR instead of an identified large scale structural model to analyze the variables' responses to certain unexpected shocks. The shocks are positive residuals of one standard deviation unit in each equation of the system.

After Sims' seminal work, many scholars have employed this model to measure the regional effects of monetary policy in different countries. Carlino and DeFina's series papers (1998, 1999) firstly estimate the regional impacts of monetary policy in the United States using VAR method and impulse response functions (IRF). Their analyses goes a further step in this area on the methods.

Carlino and DeFina (1998) use a quarterly Structural VAR (SVAR) to testify different effects of monetary policy across the eight Bureau of Economic Analysis regions during 1958: 01 – 1992: 04 in the United States. The VAR model specification is as follows:

$$AZ_t = B(L)Z_{t-I} + u_t \tag{3.1}$$

$$Z_t = [\Delta y_{1,t}, \Delta y_{2,t}, \cdots, \Delta y_{n-1,t}, \Delta p_{e,t}, m_t]' \tag{3.2}$$

Where $\Delta y_{i,t}$ is the growth rate of real personal income in region i at time t, $\Delta p_{e,t}$ is the growth rate of the relative price of energy, and m_t is a monetary policy variable. A is an $n \times n$ matrix of coefficients presenting the simultaneous relationship among the variables; $B(L)$ is an $n \times n$ matrix of polynomials in the lag operator L; and u_t is an $n \times 1$ vector of structural errors.

The results show that regions respond differently to monetary policy shocks. Some regions' responses are rather similar to those of the national economy, while other regions respond quite differently from that of the national economy.

De lucio and Izquierdo (1999) examine the regional effects of monetary policy in Spain and explain that it is the varied local characteristics causing the different responses across Spanish regions. They estimate a structural VAR model using seemingly unrelated regression (SUR) techniques to characterize regional responses. Different from Carlino and DeFina (1998), De lucio and Izquierdo (1999) indicate that the estimation of their regional VAR model is more accurate by reducing the standard deviation, since they use the SUR techniques to jointly estimate the regional model due to the possibly correlated residuals of equations (the probable correlation among regions).

Di Giacinto (2003) indicates Carlino and DeFina's (1998, 1999) assumption of no contemporaneous spillover across regions might be too restrictive in reality, particularly when they use quarterly data instead of monthly data in the model. Di Giacinto (2003) employs a modified SVAR model which considering the simultaneous relationship among regions based on geographical information through using spatial econometrics. Di Giacinto estimates a single VAR model for each state in the United States and employs information on spatial proximity to identify and estimate contemporaneous spatial spillover effects. However, considering the simultaneous spatial dependence structure makes the parameter estimation rather complicated and needing extra parameter constraints.

Comparing with monetarist reduced form model and Neo-Keynesian large scale macro-economic model (see details of these two model in the following section), the VAR method is undoubtedly a big progress in research technique. while the monetarists and Neo-classical Keynesians suppose the dichotomy of money, which means money supply has been considered exogenous at the national level and endogenous at the regional level, the New Keynesians argues that the capital is not fully mobile at the regional level, the Post Keynesians consider that money is endogenous at both levels. The VAR is rather neutral to the endogeneity or exogeneity problem. In a VAR system, all endogenous variables are determined contemporaneously, VAR treats monetary policy variable as an endogenous variable affected by the lagged values of all endogenous variables. Moreover, impulse response functions generated by VAR model can show the response of other variables to an unexpected change or shock in monetary policy variable. The monetary policy shock which means an unanticipated change of monetary policy is, of course, an exogenous shock. Therefore, it clearly isolates the exogenous component from its endogenous response to the economy (Ridhwan, Nijkamp, Rietveld & de Groot, 2008).

3.2.2 Other Models

Before 1990s, empirical literature frequently uses several other models to examine the regional effects of monetary policy. These models are reduced form model used by Monetarists who claim that monetary policy causes the business cycle directly at the regional level and large scale structural model used by Neoclassical Keynesians who emphasize that monetary policy influences the regional economic activities in a rather indirect way through the interest rate (Rodríguez-Fuentes & Dow, 2003; Rodríguez-Fuentes, 2006).

3.2.2.1 Reduced Form Model

Based on the work of Friedman & Schartz (1963) and Andersen & Jordan (1968), Beare (1976) employs a St. Louis reduced form model to test the monetarist's view that the business cycle is mainly due to monetary shocks, but he applies it at the regional level. Due to data problem at the regional level, Beare uses a small reduced form model to substitute the large scale structural model, the equation is as follows:

$$E_i = \alpha_0 + \alpha_1 M + \alpha_2 A_i \quad (3.3)$$

Where E_i stands for expenditure on products of the i-th region, M for money supply, and A_i for autonomous expenditure on products of the i-th region. Beare used personal income before taxes as a measure of E_i, total net income of farm operators from farming operations as a proxy for A_i. The empirical testing uses annual data both in nominal and real terms extending from 1965 to 1971 for the Prairie province of Canada. Beare concludes his model confirms the monetarist hypothesis.

Mathur and Stein (1980) pay attention to the bias problem of the reduced form models. The model specification they develop is a little similar as that of Beare (1976):

$$\Delta Y_{it} = \gamma_{i0} + \gamma_{i1}\Delta G_t + \gamma_{i2}\Delta T_t + \gamma_{i3}\Delta M'_t + e_{it} \quad (3.4)$$

Where Y is total personal income, G is high-employment government expenditure, T is high-employment receipts, M' is national current deposits plus currency in circulation, e is random error. The subscripts i is region. The estimation is for eight US regions during the period 1952: 01 – 1968: 04 and 1952: 01 – 1976: 04.

The results suggest that the coefficients of monetary and fiscal variables are not stable over time at the regional level. According to their results, Mathur and Stein doubt the validity of reduced form model to get reasonable results.

The advantage of reduced form model is its simplicity to some extent can avoid the data limitation at the regional level. But the reduced form model cannot reflect the causal linkages by which fiscal and monetary actions influence regional output. Moreover, Mathur and Stein (1980) notice that estimated coefficients of policy variables are unstable over time, thus they indicate the bias problem may plague the regional reduced form models and make its results not convincing. Garrison and Chang (1979) also point out "In short, the two independent variables in Beare's model may not really be independent". Though there is a debate about the bias problem, no definite answer give to this question and leave it open.

3.2.2.2 Large-Scale Structural Model

Fishkind (1977) employs H-O trade theory as an analytical framework and develops a structural model. The Indiana large scale structural model is a short-run, dynamic macro-economic system consisted of 34 simultaneous equations and

17 stochastic equations. The model is estimated by two stages least square using annual data. The first of these 17 stochastic equations is presented in their paper, the other are not presented.

$$QB_t = f(GNP_t, YCB_t) \tag{3.5}$$

Where *QB* is the state's basic output, *GNP* is the gross national product, and *YCB* is the yield on corporate bonds.

They simulate and compare the behavior of the Indiana economy with that of the nation in periods of tight and loose monetary policy using their model. And the results show significant differences exist between them for those two period (1969 – 1970, easy money; 1971 – 1972, hard money). Furthermore, this different influence appears to be asymmetrical.

Chase Econometric Associates (1981) estimate a regional model for four rural regions and four urban regions in the United States to test the regional effects of monetary policy. Their results are similar to Garrison and Chang (1979). The model is consisted of 164 equations, 114 identities and 38 exogenous variables. The results show that urban regions seem to be more easily influenced by restrictive monetary policy than rural regions, because of differences in elasticity across different economic sectors.

The large structure economic model actually is a dynamic model made up of simultaneous equations reflecting the relationship of important macro-economic variables. Therefore, estimation of the coefficients of these equations can make it clear the relationship of the macro-economic variables. There are different forms of the large structure economic model based on different economic theories. But the large structure model faces the well-know data limitations at the regional level. Thus fewer and fewer studies have used the large structure economic model for an empirical test since 1990s.

3.2.3 Monetary Policy Transmission Channels in China

In China, some literature employs monetary transmission channels to explain the regional effects of monetary policy. They test the effectiveness of several monetary transmission channels: bank lending channel, interest rate channel, balance sheet channel and exchange rate channel.

As for bank lending channel, Du (2010) indicates that in China, considering the importance of indirect financing by bank loans, bank lending channel plays a vital role in monetary policy transmission process. Sun, Ford and Dickinson (2010) argue that monetary policy mainly influence the behavior of macroeconomy through the change of bank loan supply in China. As now China's stock market and bond market are underdeveloped where direct financing is rather difficult especially for the S&M sized firms. Therefore, the main financing sources of firms in China are retained earnings and indirect bank loans (Gunji & Yuan, 2010; Sun et al., 2010). Bank lending channel plays an important role in the propagation of monetary policy to real economy (Bennett & Dixon, 2001). Cortes and Kong (2007) also find that the proportion of bank loans in industrial enterprises is an important variable influencing the provincial effects of monetary policy, lending some supports to the importance of bank lending channel.

There are some limitations in the bank lending channel in China. Gunji and Yuan (2010) find that monetary policy has a weak impact on loan supply for large banks or banks with less liquidity, and how banks respond to monetary policy actions do not necessarily depend on their capital adequacy. Banks with more profitability tend to be less affected by monetary policy shocks. The reason may be that while restrictive monetary policy reduces the deposits of banks, profitable banks can find other sources of funds more easily for the short of liquidity.

Different from the proposition of the traditional bank lending channel, Sun, Ford and Dickinson (2010) find that four large banks react quickly to a monetary policy tightening. The possible reason for this may be that four large banks often follow the signals of the PBC quickly due to political factors, such as window guidance still plays a key role in the conduct of monetary policy and the top leaders in four large banks are appointed by government in China (Sun et al. , 2010).

In terms of interest rate channel, although interest rate liberalization has made lots of progress in recent years, the current price-based instruments are still subject to heavy government intervention. All benchmark interest rates are still administrated by the PBC. The monetary transmission channel thus deviated greatly from the textbook traditional interest rate channel (Du, 2010).

However, Koivu (2009) points out that despite the interest rate channel is rather weak in China, in recent years, given the wide and deepen reforms in the financial sector, interest rates may have gained some influence in the last few years. Song and Zhong (2006) confirm that interest rate channel works in China. They find that among the three industries①, Secondary Industry shows the most sensitive response to interest rate innovations.

As for the balance sheet channel, capital market is not well functioned in China (Agenor & Montiel, 2008). Most of Chinese enterprises tend to rely largely on bank loans for external finance. Chinese customers are traditionally more accustomed to holding deposits in banks rather than stocks or bonds. A policy-induced change in asset prices cannot significantly influence the value of the collateral. The effect of balance sheet channel are thus severely undermined (Du, 2000).

Referring to the exchange rate channel, Du (2010) points out that as China has kept a de facto peg of the nominal exchange rate of the CNY to the USD for a long time, although after 2005 the regime went to a crawling peg, the exchange rate channel is actually blocked (Song & Zhong, 2006; Mehrotra, 2007).

① Three industries contain the Primary Industry, Secondary Industry and Tertiary Industry. Primary Industry means agriculture, Secondary Industry contains industry and construction, Tertiary Industry consists of transport, storage and post; wholesale and retail trades; hotels and catering services; financial intermediation; real estates; other services.

3. 2. 4 Monetary Policy Indicators

3. 2. 4. 1 The Monetary Policy Indicators in Foreign Country

It is of great importance for policy makers to measure the impacts of monetary policy on real economy accurately. In the empirical research of the effects of monetary policy, a considerable literature employs the VAR method to identify and examine the influences of monetary policy shocks on real economy. This identification is very important, as in empirical studies, inferences are very sensitive on the different monetary policy indicators (Eichenbaum, 1992). Different identifications of monetary policy innovations could cause varied inferences about the magnitude and timing of the responses of real economic variables (Bernanke, Boivin & Eliasz, 2005). Therefore, to best pursue the regional effects of monetary policy, one should select a proper indicator of monetary policy stance. Bernanke and Blinder (1992) argue that as the interest rate on Federal funds can sensitively reflect shocks to the supply of bank reserves, it is particularly informative about the future developments in real economy. Therefore, the funds rate is a good measure of changes in monetary policy.

Sims (1992) uses the innovations in short term interest rate to measure the stance of monetary policy, he just gives a simple qualitative description about the possible contamination to interest rate innovation by the non-policy parts. Although to some extent short term interest rate is a better monetary policy indicator than money stock, in empirical study, it always generates the so-called "price puzzle" which says that raising interest rate frequently fails to decrease the price level.

Christiano and Eichenbaum (1992) suggest using the quantity of non-borrowed reserves to represent the monetary policy stance (also see Eichenbaum, 1992). Strongin (1995) also indicates that monetary authorities can reduce the non-borrowed reserves by implementing a tight monetary policy, and the reduction of non-borrowed reserves would prompt banks to borrow more from the central bank through discount window. Thus he proposes the portion of non-borrowed reserve growth as a policy indicator.

Authors like Christiano (1991), Christiano and Eichenbaum (1995) assume that all movements in money stock reflect exogenous movements in monetary policy. Christiano (1991) argues that when the Federal Reserve System (Fed) surprises financial market by suddenly increasing the growth rate of money supply, the nominal interest rate falls, and employment and output rise, at least in the short run. However, if we regard the money stock innovation as a monetary policy shock, it will bring about some puzzling problems when explaining the subsequent changes of economic variables to a monetary policy shock, such as the "liquidity puzzle" which tells that a monetary policy tightening fails to make interest rates increase (Sims & Zha, 1995).

Bernanke and Mihov (1998) point out that monetary aggregated is not a good monetary policy indicator as in practice its growth rate is subjected to the influences of a lot of non-policy changes, such as changes in the demand of money and money supply (Reichenstein, 1987; Leeper & Gordon, 1992; Strongin, 1995). Long term changes in velocity caused by the reforms of financial market, deregulation of financial institutions, and so on, can potentially affect the growth rate of money stock, making it not a good indicator of monetary policy stance (Bernanke & Mihov, 1998). Based on their empirical results, Bernanke and Mihov (1998) suggest that the variables which can best measure the changes in monetary policy have varied over time: Federal funds rate prior to 1979; non-borrowed reserves from 1979 to 1982; Federal funds rate in recent years.

3.2.4.2 The Monetary Policy Indicators in China

In the existing literature concentrating on the effects of monetary policy in China, monetary aggregate and benchmark bank lending rate are usually used as monetary policy variable. The PBC has always regarded M2 as intermediate targets in recent years (Xie, 2004; Burdekin & Siklos, 2008; Koivu, 2009). Among the previous studies in China, Song and Zhong (2006), Jiang and Chen (2009), Cortes and Kong (2007) adopt M2 as monetary policy variable. Cortes and Kong (2007) also use bank lending rate to represent monetary policy variable. In China, the one year deposit and loan rate are the benchmark interest rates regulated by the central bank as primary monetary policy instruments. Cortes and Kong (2007) examine the influences of monetary policy represented by M2 or bank lending rate on regional economies using a VAR model. They find that as a monetary policy indicator, the influence of bank lending rate is bigger than that of M2, so they conclude that bank lending rate is better than M2 as a monetary policy variable.

As a measurement of monetary policy indicator, M2 is not very good as it is likely to be contaminated by the demand shocks, since the variations in monetary aggregates are partly caused by the changes of foreign exchange reserves. Although a portion of increased M2 is sterilized through the issuance of the central bank bill by the PBC, the correlation between broad money and monetary policy actions is still complicated. Moreover, as the growth rate of monetary aggregates is only announced annually by the PBC, and cannot adjust in time with the changes in macro-economic activities (He & Pauwels, 2008), in fact, M2 is not a very good measure of monetary policy stance.

Changes in the interest rate also cannot fully measure shifts in monetary policy actions due to the administrated benchmark interest rate, uncompleted interest rate liberalization, the on-going reforms of banking system and the relative less sensitive response of enterprise to the cost of capital. Xie and Luo (2002) apply the Taylor rule into China's monetary policy conduct and find that to some extent the formulation and implementation of monetary policy follow the Taylor rule. However, their results cannot be fully convincing on account of the potential limitations of interest rate and the pegged exchange rate system.

He and Pauwels (2008) point out that the PBC has adopted a wide range of varied monetary policy instruments during the past forty years, furthermore, along with the monetary policy reforms, some old instruments are no longer used by the PBC and some new ones appear over time. Therefore, only one single instrument cannot fully describe the shifts in monetary policy. He and Pauwels (2008) develop a policy stance index similar to Gerlach & Svensson (2002) and Gerlach (2004) and take multiple instruments together at the same time to measure the changes in monetary policy actions during 1997 – 2007. Their multiple instruments contain changes in reserve requirement ratio, benchmark bank lending and deposit rates, open market operations. They assume these instruments share the same weight in determining the monetary policy stance and subsequently construct a monetary policy index. The results show that this index can be a good measure of monetary policy actions.

Following Gerlach (2004), He and Pauwels (2008), Xiong (2012) employs an ordered probit model to construct a new policy stance index, which incorporates the changes in a variety of monetary policy instruments used by the PBC since 1986, and declare that this index can be seemed as a comprehensive measurement of monetary policy shifts.

3.2.5 The Factors Affecting Regional Effects of Monetary Policy

Previous literature generally employs two monetary transmission channels, interest rate channel and bank lending channel, to explain the regional effects of monetary policy. Interest rate channel reveals that a region which concentrates on interest sensitive industries might respond more to monetary policy actions. When industries have different interest rate sensitivities and industrial compositions are different across regions, monetary policy would have different impacts across regions (Carlino & DeFina, 1998).

Bank lending channel sheds lights on that different percent of large and small firms across regions, in conjunction with regional differences in banks' abilities to adjust their balance sheets to some extent are able to explain the regional effects of monetary policy (Carlino & DeFina, 1998). Based on the credit channel (Bernanke & Blinder, 1988; Bernanke, 1993; Gertler & Gilchrist, 1993), monetary policy actions can influence the real economy through affecting different banks' ability to make loans. To the extent some borrowers, especially small borrowers such as small firms with no access to sources of external, nonbank funds, largely depend on bank credit (Kashyap, Stein & Wilcox, 1993). By contrast, large firms can always easily get funds from other non-bank sources. As a result, monetary policy will have larger impacts on the regions with a high proportion of small borrowers (small firms).

Kashyap and Stein (1995) point out monetary policy actions can exert different impacts on varied banks' ability to provide loans. They consider that bank size to some extent can explain the differences in financing abilities. Comparing with small banks, large banks always have more options to raise funds besides deposits in order to argument liquidity. Thus regions with a heavy percent of loans provided by small banks might be more sensitive to monetary policy actions than regions with a big proportion of bank loans made by large banks.

Carlino and DeFina (1998, 1999) also test the factors which cause monetary policy to have different impacts across regions by resorting to interest rate channel and bank lending channel. They find that regions concentrating on interest sensitive industries respond more to monetary policy shocks, lending supports to interest rate channel. But they do not find evidences of bank lending channel at the regional level. Regional differences in the proportion of small firms have no significant correlation to the magnitude of regions' responses to monetary policy shock. Moreover, regions with a large percent of small banks are found to respond less to monetary policy shock. These findings are inconsistent with the idea of bank lending channel. Thus Carlino and DeFina (1998) conclude that bank lending channel is rather weak at the regional level.

Regarding the factors affecting the regional effects of monetary policy, De lucio and Izquierdo (1999) argue that the links between financial structure and the real sector in the monetary transmission channels can lead to regional different impacts of monetary policy. They emphasize the regional differences in macro-structure and micro-structure, together with varied financial structures across regions induce regions to respond differently to common monetary policy innovations. In detail, these factors are economic compostion, the structure of financial sector, the process of wage determination and international openness. De lucio and Izquierdo (1999) estimate a structural VAR model using the SUR techniques to characterize regional responses in Spain. They find that the importance of interest sensitive industries, the degree of nominal indexation and international openness are factors that enhance the regional impacts of monetary policy. In addition, regions characterized by a more important presence of less credit constrained firms respond less to monetary policy shocks. These findings are similar to those of Carlino and DeFina (1998).

Nachane, Ray and Ghosh (2002) employ the VAR method to test whether monetary policy has similar impacts across regions in India during 1969 – 1999. The results reveal that two sets of states respond differently to the monetary shock: a core of states that respond to monetary policy in a significant fashion, and others whose responses are less significant. They also examine the reasons for the differential responses of these two sets of states: regional differences in the proportion of interest sensitive industries, varied mixtures of large enterprise versus small enterprise across states, and the differential financial deepening across states. The results indicate that those states which have a greater concentration of manufacturing units or are relatively intensively banked tend to be more responsive to monetary policy shocks, lending support to interest rate channel and broad credit channel.

Weber (2006) argues that there exist different economic specializations across states in Australia, such as the inland and the north are rich in oil and mining, while the south-eastern seaboard focuses on manufacture and services. Monetary policy affects varied states differently as they go through different business cycles at the same time. Weber considers that Australia is a small open economy with highly dependence on exports, naturally the main monetary transmission channel is exchange rate channel. As a result, monetary policy exerts much stronger impacts on the interior and the north, while at the same time relatively slight influences on the south-eastern seaboard. The results support Weber's previous argument and give evidence to the existence of interest rate channel and exchange rate channel in Australia.

Georgopoulos (2009) examines three factors which can lead to regional differential impacts of monetary policy in Canada: regional differences in the share of interest sensitive industries, in the importance of exports and in the percent of large and small enterprises. Georgopoulos highlights that as a small open country, exchange rate channel plays a key role in the propagation of monetary policy in Canada. Thus regional difference in the proportion of exports is a major factor affecting the regional impacts of monetary policy. The results also prove his arguments.

Cortes and Kong (2007) employ the VEC model to examine the regional effects of monetary policy across provinces in China during 1980 – 2004. They also develop two VEC models, one focuses on the whole nation and the other one deals with Chinese provinces. According to the results of the national VEC model, they find that comparing with M2, bank lending rate is a better monetary policy indicator in China. The findings of their provincial VEC model show that different proportion of loans flowed to all industrial enterprises and varied percent of primary sector across provinces are responsible for the different regional responses to monetary policy shocks. But the share of state-owned enterprises is negatively, but not significantly related to the responses of provinces to monetary policy innovations.

Kong, Cortes and Qin (2007) (in Chinese) also use VAR method to study the influences of monetary policy on the real output of 29 provinces (except Tibet and Chongqing) in the mainland China. They test their provincial VAR model and confirm the different regional effects of monetary policy. They use the proportion of loan to all industrial enterprises to represent the bank lending channel and confirm the role of this channel at the regional level. An important shortcoming of this study is that actually the proportion of loan to all industrial enterprises cannot describe the bank lending channel, according to Kashyap and Stein (1995), there should be the proportion of loan to small enterprises. The findings of Kong, Cortes and Qin (2007) are more or less the same as that of Cortes and Kong (2007).

Jiang and Chen (2009) (in Chinese) employ the SVAR method to examine the regional effects of monetary policy. Their regional SVAR system contains M2, real regional GDP, loans of financial institutions, GDP deflator from 1978 to 2006. The differences are that they divide China into eight regions according to the reports "The Strategy and Policy of Coordinated Regional Development" published by Development Research Center of the State Council. Their findings confirm the regional effects of monetary policy. They also find that the correlation coefficient of the proportion of second industry and the magnitude is very small. Thus they conclude that the proportion of second industry cannot explain the regional effects of monetary policy to some extent, indicating that the relative weakness of interest rate channel in China.

As China is a transition economy, the factors analyzed above may be not very applicable. But they can provide a simple framework. In China, the previous literature pursues the factors affecting the regional effects of monetary policy based on monetary transmission channels. For example, Song and Zhong (2006) check the sensitivity of three industries to interest rate and find the second industry is most sensitive. Therefore, regional differences in the shares of second industry to some extent can explain the regional effects of monetary policy. They also check the balance-sheet channel. They use the ratio of industrial output value of small enterprises as an influencing factor and find that it is positive to the responses of provinces to monetary policy shock. Cortes and Kong (2007) select primary sector GDP share to represent the industry mix and find it is positive in statistical significant level to the response. Liu (2010) checks the responses of overall industrial production and find that heavy industry responds more than light industry to monetary policy actions. Liu also checks the responses of state-owned enterprises versus privately-owned enterprises and find that the output of privately-owned enterprises responds more strongly to monetary policy actions. He (2009) just considers two provinces' responses to monetary policy actions and indicates that the differences in structure of industry explain the regional effects of monetary policy.

In China, the exchange rate has maintained a crawling peg to USD for a long time. On July, 2005, China improved the managed floating exchange rate regime by moving into a managed floating exchange rate regime based on market supply and demand with reference to a basket of currencies. Song and Zhong (2006) find that exchange rate channel has no explanation about the regional effects of monetary policy.

In China, monetary transmission mechanism is closely linked to the four large state-owned joint-stock commercial banks. These four large banks historically play the part of fiscal agents and occupy a large market share of loans and deposits. Furthermore, their lending tends to support state-owned enterprises (SOEs) (Kong, 2003). The strong link between China's four large banks and SOEs is a prime example of the "soft budget constraint syndrome" introduced by Kornai (1986). As Kong (2003) indicates that four large banks traditionally provide lots of quasi-fiscal loans to such SOEs which have problem in keeping normal operation. So much lending has been insensitive to quality and risk for too long and this leads to the high ratio of non-performing loans (Kong, 2003).

To some extent, the existence of soft budget constraint constrains the effectiveness of monetary policy. With a soft budget constraint, SOEs have no incentive to operate efficiently and to respond appropriately to a tight monetary policy as the government stands ready with subsidies, easy credit, and bailouts. Therefore, the provinces' responses to monetary policy actions may be negatively related to the proportion of SOEs. This study also uses the proportion of large commercial banks and the proportion of state-owned and state-holding enterprises in each province as proxies to describe this monetary transmission process in each province.

Chapter 4

Methodology

This chapter will focus on the model specification and the estimation procedure. In this chapter, this study will present three models specification in detail used to solve the three research questions listed in Chapter 1 and discuss about the estimation procedure of these models.

4.1 Model Specification for Spillover Effect

The first model is used to solve the first research question. The first objective is to measure the regional and provincial effects of monetary policy in China with accounting for spillover effects across regions or provinces. To achieve this objective, this study should examine the regions' and provinces' responses to monetary policy actions. Therefore, the first model actually contains two models: regional model and provincial model. To emphasize the spillover effects, this study also develops the model for each region and the model for each province without spillover effects so as to compare the results with the regional model and provincial model.

According to monetary policy transmission channels, monetary policy can influence the output and price level. According to the Taylor (1993) rule and the McCallum (1988) rule①, the formulation of monetary policy is determined by the output level and inflation level. The spillover effects say that regions and provinces can affect each other through interregional links (Carlino & DeFina, 1995). Therefore, the first regional model contains five endogenous variables: monetary policy variable, the price level, the outputs of the East, the Middle and the West. It is assumed that these five variables can be influenced by each other.

Since economic reform and opening up, China's economy has become more and more open. Being the largest trading nation and the largest FDI recipient among the developing countries, China has actively taken part in the process of globalization and played an important role during the past forty years. Thus China's regional economy might be influenced by the world economy (Zhang & Zhang, 2003). According to this point of view, this study adds world economy as an exogenous variable and assumes that world economy can affect the domestic endogenous variables.

In sum, based on monetary transmission mechanism theory and monetary policy rule, this study sets the regional SVAR (structural vector auto-regressive) model. Compared with the VAR and VECM, the main advantage of SVAR is that it can measure the contemporaneous influences among the variables while the VAR and VEC cannot do.

4.1.1 The Proxy for Monetary Policy

In the empirical study, how to properly measure the stance of monetary policy is very important as the validity of the measure of monetary policy would influence the accuracy of the estimation of regional effects of monetary policy. As China is a transition country, all the benchmark interest rate are regulated by the

① The Taylor (1993) rule refers to the target interest rate set by the central bank is changing with the expected output gap and the inflation gap. The McCallum (1988) rule indicates the money supply growth targets the expected output gap and the inflation gap.

PBC and interest rate liberalization is still in proceeding, the change of interest rates cannot precisely reflect the supply and the demand of funds. Monetary aggregates also is not a best indicator of monetary policy, as they are subject in practice to a wide variety of other disturbances, including shifts in the demand for money, which often dominate the information they contain about changes in the state of policy. Although these two variables cannot best measure the stance of monetary policy, there are no other variables which are better monetary policy indicators than these two. As the empirical period in this study is 1978 – 2011, the policy stance index approach may be not appropriate due to short of the needed data. Therefore, in this study, considering the potential shortcoming of each monetary policy instrument alone, as well as the characteristics of the PBC's monetary policy operations, the choice might be suboptimal. In this study, monetary aggregates (M1 and M2), one year bank lending rate (BLR) are used as measurements of monetary policy variable to check which one can properly represent the monetary policy stance during the empirical periods.

4. 1. 2 The Inter-Regional SVAR Model for Each Region with Spillover Effect

Since Sims' (1980) pioneering work, the VAR method has become one of the leading approaches employed in analysis of dynamic economic system, especially in research of the interactions between monetary policy and macro-economy. Following Carlino and DeFina (1998), SVAR model is employed to measure the regional effects of monetary policy in China in this study. The specification of the benchmark inter-regional SVAR model for each region with spillover effect is as follows:

$$MP_t = \alpha_0 + \sum_{i=0}^{k} \alpha_{1i} Price_{t-i} + \sum_{i=0}^{k} \alpha_{2i} MP_{t-i} + \sum_{i=0}^{k} \alpha_{3i} EGDP_{t-i} + \sum_{i=0}^{k} \alpha_{4i} MGDP_{t-i} + \sum_{i=0}^{k} \alpha_{5i} WGDP_{t-i} + \alpha_6 WDGDP_t + e_{1t} \quad (4.1)$$

$$EGDP_t = \beta_0 + \sum_{i=0}^{k} \beta_{1i} Price_{t-i} + \sum_{i=0}^{k} \beta_{2i} MP_{t-i} + \sum_{i=0}^{k} \beta_{3i} EGDP_{t-i} + \sum_{i=0}^{k} \beta_{4i} MGDP_{t-i} + \sum_{i=0}^{k} \beta_{5i} WGDP_{t-i} + \beta_6 WDGDP_t + e_{2t} \quad (4.2)$$

$$MGDP_t = \gamma_0 + \sum_{i=0}^{k} \gamma_{1i} Price_{t-i} + \sum_{i=0}^{k} \gamma_{2i} MP_{t-i} + \sum_{i=0}^{k} \gamma_{3i} EGDP_{t-i} + \sum_{i=0}^{k} \gamma_{4i} MGDP_{t-i} + \sum_{i=0}^{k} \gamma_{5i} WGDP_{t-i} + \gamma_6 WDGDP_t + e_{3t} \quad (4.3)$$

$$WGDP_t = a_0 + \sum_{i=0}^{k} a_{1i} Price_{t-i} + \sum_{i=0}^{k} a_{2i} MP_{t-i} + \sum_{i=0}^{k} a_{3i} EGDP_{t-i} + \sum_{i=0}^{k} a_{4i} MGDP_{t-i} + \sum_{i=0}^{k} a_{5i} WGDP_{t-i} + a_6 WDGDP_t + e_{4t} \quad (4.4)$$

$$Price_t = b_0 + \sum_{i=0}^{k} b_{1i} Price_{t-i} + \sum_{i=0}^{k} b_{2i} MP_{t-i} + \sum_{i=0}^{k} b_{3i} EGDP_{t-i} + \sum_{i=0}^{k} b_{4i} MGDP_{t-i} + \sum_{i=0}^{k} b_{5i} WGDP_{t-i} + b_6 WDGDP_t + e_{5t} \quad (4.5)$$

MP is monetary policy variable represented by M2, M1 and BLR. *Price* is the national price level measured by the CPI (Consumer Price Index, 1978 = 100). Price level is added into the model to examine the effects of monetary policy on inflation and control the price puzzle①. *EGDP*, *MGDP* and *WGDP* are the real GDP of the East, the Middle and the West. *WDGDP* is real World GDP, an exogenous variable. This SVAR system treats these five variables (except *WDGDP*) as endogenous. It relies on these variables expressed as past values of the dependent variable and past values of the other variables in the model. This SVAR model can be estimated to analyze the system's responses to monetary policy shocks. This shock is positive residual of one standard deviation unit in monetary policy equation of the system.

We can express (4.1) – (4.5) as the form of vector, let vector Y_t

① When monetary policy shocks are identified with innovations in interest rates, the responses of output and money supply are correct as a monetary tightening (an increase in interest rates) is associated with a fall in the money supply and output. However, the response of the price level is wrong as monetary tightening is associated with an increase in the price level rather than a decrease (see Sims, 1992).

$$Y_t = [MP_t, EGDP_t, MGDP_t, WGDP_t, Price_t]'$$

Then we get

$$CY_t = A(L)Y_{t-1} + H(L)WDGDP_t + u_t \qquad (4.6)$$

Where C is a 5×5 matrix of coefficients, which represents the simultaneous relationship among the variables; $A(L)$ and $H(L)$ are 5×5 matrix of polynomials in lag operator; u_t is a 5×1 vector of structural residuals. This study will use annual data to estimate the model during 1978 – 2011.

$$u_t = [u_{mt}, u_{1t}, u_{2t}, u_{3t}, u_{pt}]'$$

For explicitly, transform (4.6) as a reduced-form VAR:

$$Y_t = Z(L)Y_{t-1} + G(L)WDGDP_t + e_t \qquad (4.7)$$

where $Z(L) = C^{-1}A(L)$ and $G(L) = C^{-1}H(L)$ are infinite-order lag polynomials, and $e_t = C^{-1}u_t$ and $u_t = Ce_t$ describe the relationship between the structural residuals and reduced-form residuals. We can transform $u_t = Ce_t$ as $A - B$ SVAR specification in order to estimate the model: $Ae_t = Bu_t$. How to identify the structural shocks u_t from the VAR reduced-form residuals e_t and their variances will be discussed later. The solution relies on identification restrictions placed on the A and B matrices and on the variance-covariance matrix of structural errors.

4.1.3 The Inter-Regional SVAR Model for Each Region without Spillover Effect

The main advantage of the benchmark inter-regional SVAR model is that it considers the spillover effects among three regions. This study argues that when examining the regional effects of monetary policy, we should emphasize the influence of spillover effects and the shortcoming of previous studies is that they neglect this effect. As the previous studies without accounting for the spillover effects use different control variables, different estimation period and different region division, especially most of them do not give the exact size of monetary policy shock, direct comparison of the results is impossible and unmeaning. Therefore, this study also estimates SVAR models for each region with no consideration of the spillover effect to make the comparison and highlights the importance of spillover effect.

The specification of inter-regional SVAR model for each region without spillover effect is as follows:

$$RMP_t = \alpha_0 + \sum_{i=0}^{k} \alpha_{1i} RPrice_{t-i} + \sum_{i=0}^{k} \alpha_{2i} RMP_{t-i} + \sum_{i=0}^{k} \alpha_{3i} RGDP_{t-i} + \alpha_4 WDGDP_t + e_{1t} \quad (4.8)$$

$$RGDP_t = \beta_0 + \sum_{i=0}^{k} \beta_{1i} RPrice_{t-i} + \sum_{i=0}^{k} \beta_{2i} RMP_{t-i} + \sum_{i=0}^{k} \beta_{3i} RGDP_{t-i} + \beta_4 WDGDP_t + e_{2t} \quad (4.9)$$

$$RPrice_t = \gamma_0 + \sum_{i=0}^{k} \gamma_{1i} RPrice_{t-i} + \sum_{i=0}^{k} \gamma_{2i} RMP_{t-i} + \sum_{i=0}^{k} \gamma_{3i} RGDP_{t-i} + \gamma_4 WDGDP_t + e_{3t} \quad (4.10)$$

RGDP represents the real GDP of the East, the Middle or the West. *RMP* is regional monetary policy variable (measured by the best monetary policy variable selected by the regional SVAR model). *RPrice* is the regional price level measured by the CPI index of the East, the Middle or the West (1978 = 100). *WDGDP* is real World GDP, an exogenous variable. This study will estimate this model for each region: the East, the Middle and the West.

We can also express (4.8) – (4.10) as the form of vector, let vector Y_t

$$Y_t = [RMP_t, RGDP_t, RPrice_t]'$$

Then we get

$$CY_t = A(L) Y_{t-1} + H(L) WDGDP_t + u_t \quad (4.11)$$

Where C is a 3×3 matrix of coefficients describing the contemporaneous correlation among the variables; $A(L)$ and $H(L)$ are 3×3 matrix of polynomials in the lag operator; u_t is a 3×1 vector of structural residuals. We will use annual data to estimate the model during 1978 – 2011.

$$u_t = [u_{mt}, u_{rt}, u_{pt}]'$$

4.1.4 The Inter-Regional SVAR Model for Each Province with Spillover Effect

The inter-regional SVAR model for each province with spillover effect is to examine the provinces' responses to monetary policy actions. The specification is as follows:

$$MP_t = \alpha_0 + \sum_{i=0}^{k} \alpha_{1i} Price_{t-i} + \sum_{i=0}^{k} \alpha_{2i} MP_{t-i} + \sum_{i=0}^{k} \alpha_{3i} P_j GDP_{t-i} + \sum_{i=0}^{k} \alpha_{4i} R_{1-pj} GDP_{t-i} + \sum_{i=0}^{k} \alpha_{5i} R_2 GDP_{t-i} + \sum_{i=0}^{k} \alpha_{6i} R_3 GDP_{t-i} + \alpha_7 WDGDP_t + u_{1t} \quad (4.12)$$

$$P_j GDP_t = \beta_0 + \sum_{i=0}^{k} \beta_{1i} Price_{t-i} + \sum_{i=0}^{k} \beta_{2i} MP_{t-i} + \sum_{i=0}^{k} \beta_{3i} P_j GDP_{t-i} + \sum_{i=0}^{k} \beta_{4i} R_{1-pj} GDP_{t-i} + \sum_{i=0}^{k} \beta_{5i} R_2 GDP_{t-i} + \sum_{i=0}^{k} \beta_{6i} R_3 GDP_{t-i} + \beta_7 WDGDP_t + u_{2t} \quad (4.13)$$

$$R_{1-pj} GDP_t = \gamma_0 + \sum_{i=0}^{k} \gamma_{1i} Price_{t-i} + \sum_{i=0}^{k} \gamma_{2i} MP_{t-i} + \sum_{i=0}^{k} \gamma_{3i} P_j GDP_{t-i} + \sum_{i=0}^{k} \gamma_{4i} R_{1-pj} GDP_{t-i} + \sum_{i=0}^{k} \gamma_{5i} R_2 GDP_{t-i} + \sum_{i=0}^{k} \gamma_{6i} R_3 GDP_{t-i} + \gamma_7 WDGDP_t + u_{3t} \quad (4.14)$$

$$R_2 GDP_t = \delta_0 + \sum_{i=0}^{k} \delta_{1i} Price_{t-i} + \sum_{i=0}^{k} \delta_{2i} MP_{t-i} + \sum_{i=0}^{k} \delta_{3i} P_j GDP_{t-i} + \sum_{i=0}^{k} \delta_{4i} R_{1-pj} GDP_{t-i} + \sum_{i=0}^{k} \delta_{5i} R_2 GDP_{t-i} + \sum_{i=0}^{k} \delta_{6i} R_3 GDP_{t-i} + \delta_7 WDGDP_t + u_{4t} \quad (4.15)$$

$$R_3 GDP_t = a_0 + \sum_{i=0}^{k} a_{1i} Price_{t-i} + \sum_{i=0}^{k} a_{2i} MP_{t-i} + \sum_{i=0}^{k} a_{3i} P_j GDP_{t-i} + \sum_{i=0}^{k} a_{4i} R_{1-pj} GDP_{t-i} + \sum_{i=0}^{k} a_{5i} R_2 GDP_{t-i} + \sum_{i=0}^{k} a_{6i} R_3 GDP_{t-i} + a_7 WDGDP_t + u_{5t} \quad (4.16)$$

$$Price_t = b_0 + \sum_{i=0}^{k} b_{1i}Price_{t-i} + \sum_{i=0}^{k} b_{2i}MP_{t-i} + \sum_{i=0}^{k} b_{3i}P_jGDP_{t-i}$$
$$+ \sum_{i=0}^{k} b_{4i}R_{1-pj}GDP_{t-i} + \sum_{i=0}^{k} b_{5i}R_2GDP_{t-i} + \sum_{i=0}^{k} b_{6i}R_3GDP_{t-i}$$
$$+ b_7WDGDP_t + u_{6t} \qquad (4.17)$$

MP is the monetary policy variable measured by the best monetary policy variable selected by the regional SVAR model (M2, M1 or BLR). *Price* is the national price level measured by national CPI index (Consumer Price Index, 1978 = 100). P_j is one province in R_1 region. R_1 represents one region (the East, the Middle or the West), R_2 and R_3 are the other two regions①. P_jGDP is the real GDP of the P_j province (j = 1, 2, ···, 31). $R_{1-pj}GDP$ is the real GDP in region R_1 containing province P_j less the real GDP of the province P_j. R_2GDP and R_3GDP are real GDP of the R_2 region and R_3 region. These four variables measure the regional level economic activity. *WDGDP* is real World GDP, an exogenous variable to isolate exogenous economic changes. u_i are structural residuals.

We can express (4.12) – (4.17) as the form of vector, let vector Y_t

$$Y_t = [MP_t, P_iGDP_t, R_{1-pi}GDP_t, R_2GDP_t, R_3GDP_t, Price_t]'$$

Then we get

$$CY_t = A(L)Y_{t-1} + H(L)WDGDP_t + u_t \qquad (4.18)$$

Where C is a 6 × 6 matrix of coefficients describing the contemporaneous correlation among the variables; $A(L)$ and $H(L)$ are 6 × 6 matrix of polynomials in the lag operator; u_t is a 6 × 1 vector of structural residuals. This study will use annual data to estimate the model during 1978 – 2011.

$$u_t = [u_{1t}, u_{2t}, u_{3t}, u_{4t}, u_{5t}, u_{6t}]'$$

4.1.5 The Inter Regional SVAR Model for Each Province without Spillover Effect

The same as the inter-regional SVAR model for each region, to highlight

① For example, if P_j province is Shanxi province, the R_1 is the Middle, R_2 is the East and R_3 is the West. If P_j province is Tibet Gutonomous Region, the R_1 is the West, R_2 is the East and R_3 is the Middle.

the importance of the spillover effects, this study also estimates the inter-regional SVAR model for each province without spillover effect to make a comparison. The specification is as follows:

$$P_jMP_t = \alpha_0 + \sum_{i=0}^{k} \alpha_{1i} P_jPrice_{t-i} + \sum_{i=0}^{k} \alpha_{2i} P_jMP_{t-i} + \sum_{i=0}^{k} \alpha_{3i} P_jGDP_{t-i} + \alpha_4 WDGDP_t + e_{1t} \quad (4.19)$$

$$P_jGDP_t = \beta_0 + \sum_{i=0}^{k} \beta_{1i} P_jPrice_{t-i} + \sum_{i=0}^{k} \beta_{2i} P_jMP_{t-i} + \sum_{i=0}^{k} \beta_{3i} P_jGDP_{t-i} + \beta_4 WDGDP_t + e_{2t} \quad (4.20)$$

$$P_jPrice_t = \gamma_0 + \sum_{i=0}^{k} \gamma_{1i} P_jPrice_{t-i} + \sum_{i=0}^{k} \gamma_{2i} P_jMP_{t-i} + \sum_{i=0}^{k} \gamma_{3i} P_jGDP_{t-i} + \gamma_4 WDGDP_t + e_{3t} \quad (4.21)$$

P_jGDP represents the real GDP of each province (31 provinces, $j = 1, 2, \cdots, 31$). P_jMP is provincial monetary policy variable (measured by the best monetary policy variable selected by the regional SVAR model). P_jPrice is the price level of each province measured by the CPI of each province (1978 = 100). *WDGDP* is real World GDP, an exogenous variable. We will estimate this SVAR model separately for 31 provinces in the mainland China.

We can also express (4.19) – (4.21) as the form of vector, let vector Y_t

$$Y_t = [PMP_t, PGDP_t, PPrice_t]'$$

Then we get

$$CY_t = A(L)Y_{t-1} + H(L)WDGDP_t + u_t \quad (4.22)$$

Where C is a 3×3 matrix of coefficients describing the contemporaneous correlation among the variables; $A(L)$ and $H(L)$ are 3×3 matrix of polynomials in the lag operator; u_t is a 3×1 vector of structural residuals. This study will use annual data to estimate the model during 1978 – 2011.

4.1.6 Identification Problems

To estimate the SVAR models, firstly this study should transform the structural VAR into the reduced form VAR. For A-B SVAR model, $A\varepsilon_t = Bu_t$ describes the relationship between the reduced-form residuals and the structural residuals. u_t is seemed as the structural shocks. The structural shocks are supposed to be economically meaningful, genuine primary shocks, exogenous to everything else in the model, including each other. Hence their variance-covariance matrix is supposed to be diagonal. This exogeneity property allows one to analyze their effects on the model variables without having to bother with simultaneity considerations.

For A-B SVAR model, $A\varepsilon_t = Bu_t$, A and B are invertible matrices of order n, the distributional assumption is: $E(u_t) = 0$, $E(u_t u'_t) = I_n$, Σ is the unrestricted variance-covariance matrix of the reduced form. For n order A-B SVAR model, $2n^2$ parameters need to estimate. The condition $A\Sigma A' = BB'$ naturally induces $n(n+1)/2$ restrictions on the parameters, then you should at least add $2n^2 - n(n+1)/2$ restrictions so as to identify the SVAR model.

To be simplicity, B is assumed to be the diagonal matrix. Then you should add $n(n+1)/2$ restrictions on A to identify the model. Traditionally, the usual (indeed, almost mechanical) procedure is to assume a recursive contemporaneous structure, i. e. assume A to be triangular. One of the most commonly used identification strategies is the Cholesky decomposition (recursive identification strategy).

Based on the assumption above, we can get the identification matrix A and matrix B①. For the regional SVAR model:

$$A = \begin{bmatrix} 1 & 0 & 0 & 0 & 0 \\ a_{21} & 1 & 0 & 0 & 0 \\ a_{31} & a_{32} & 1 & 0 & 0 \\ a_{41} & a_{42} & a_{43} & 1 & 0 \\ a_{51} & a_{52} & a_{53} & a_{54} & 1 \end{bmatrix} \tag{4.23}$$

① For SVAR model for each region and each province, 3 order matrix A and matrix B are used. For the provincial SVAR model, 6 order matrix A and matrix B are used.

$$B = \begin{bmatrix} b_{11} & 0 & 0 & 0 & 0 \\ 0 & b_{22} & 0 & 0 & 0 \\ 0 & 0 & b_{33} & 0 & 0 \\ 0 & 0 & 0 & b_{44} & 0 \\ 0 & 0 & 0 & 0 & b_{55} \end{bmatrix} \tag{4.24}$$

A widely recognized problem with SVAR is that the results are sensitive to the model's identification scheme (Sims & Zha, 1995). Thus seemingly small changes in the identifying assumptions can lead to substantial changes in the estimated effects of the shocks and in their relative importance over the sample period. This sensitivity has led many researchers to informally test the results against over-identifying restrictions. A popular restriction, used to identify monetary policy shocks and advocated by Bernanke and Blinder (1992), is that monetary policy has no instantaneous impacts on output and inflation. This assumption is appealing given the broadly held view that the effects of monetary policy take a considerable time to be felt. Moreover, Fan, Yu and Zhang (2011) prove that the formulation of China's monetary policy follows the Taylor rule and McCallum rule. Therefore, this study adopts the restriction suggested by Bernanke and Blinder (1992). For the regional SVAR model, the first order of the five endogenous variables is *EGDP*, *MGDP*, *WGDP*, *Price*, *MP*.

Subsequently, matrix *A* and matrix *B* can be explained. Matrix *A* reflects the contemporaneous relationship of the five endogenous variables. It is assumed that monetary policy has no instantaneous impact on *EGDP*, *MGDP*, *WGDP*, and *Price*. Within one period, *EGDP* can affect *MGDP*, *WGDP*; *MGDP* can affect *WGDP*, but *MGDP*, *WGDP* cannot affect *EGDP*; *WGDP* cannot affect *MGDP* (Groenewold, Lee & Chen, 2007). As the East is the more developed region while the Middle and the West are less developed regions, this assumption is in line with reality. This study also assumes the structural residuals have unit variances, thus we treat matrix *B* as a diagonal matrix. The elements in the main diagonal are simply the estimated standard deviation of the structural shocks.

In the first SVAR order of endogenous variables, this study adopt the assumption that that monetary policy has no instantaneous impact on output and inflation suggested by Bernanke and Blinder (1992), thus monetary policy variable ranks last in the first order of identification scheme. However, the use of restrictions advocated by Bernanke and Blinder (1992) has been associated with a number of puzzles, notably the prize puzzle, the exchange rate puzzle and the liquidity puzzle. ① These puzzles shed some doubts on whether the identified shocks are pure monetary policy shocks. Moreover, the assumption that monetary policy shocks do not affect prices within one year might be hard to defend in more open economies where the link between monetary policy, the exchange rate, imports and consumer prices is quite immediate.

Di Giacinto (2003) also points out this assumption is likely to be too restrictive in practice, especially when monthly time series are not available and the model is fitted using quarterly data. This study uses annual data, so this assumption is hardly to stand. Thus this study changes the identification scheme, assuming that monetary policy can affect the outputs of three regions and the price level simultaneously. So in the second order of identification scheme, the variables are arranged like this: *MP*, *EGDP*, *MGDP*, *WGDP*, *Price*. This study will compare the results of SVAR models using these two identification schemes to check which order is better.

All the restrictions used above are short-run restrictions. Short-run restrictions also suffer another pitfall. They usually depend more on heuristic arguments than theoretical considerations (Kieler & Saarenheimo, 1998). Sometimes certain heuristic propositions used are not consistent with the theoretical results. For

① The price puzzle is the tendency of prices to increase temporarily after a contractionary monetary policy shock. For a discussion see Sims (1992). The liquidity puzzle is the tendency of interest rates to fall after a decrease in the money supply. See Christiano and Eichenbaum (1992). The exchange rate puzzle is the tendency of exchange rates to depreciate temporarily after a contractionary monetary policy shock. See Grilli and Roubini (1993). As in China, exchange rate and interest rate are not totally liberalized, we don't check the liquidity and exchange rate puzzle in this research.

instance, the widely used hypothesis that monetary policy has no short-run (contemporaneous) impacts on output is contradicted with the neoclassical view that monetary policy only has short-run effects on output.

Some Studies have used long-run restrictions to identify the SVAR. Keating (1992) and Walsh (1993) use the restriction that monetary policy actions have no long-run effects on real variables such as real output, the real interest rate or the real money stock. While many economists would find a long-run dichotomy between nominal and real variables plausible, it is not clear that the exclusive use of long-run restrictions pins down monetary policy shocks, as, for example, temporary demand shocks are likely to satisfy identical long-run restrictions. As the sample period is not very long, this study does not add long-run restrictions on the models.

As for the SVAR model for each region, the provincial SVAR model and the SVAR model for each province, this study uses the best variable order selected by the regional SVAR model and the similar n order matrix A and matrix B to achieve identification.

4.2 Estimation Procedure for the Inter-Regional SVAR Model

4.2.1 Unit Root Tests—Stationary Test

The existence of trend is a major concern in the analysis of time series. Before running the model, firstly we should determine which form of trend the data exhibit. There are two types of variable trend, namely deterministic linear time trend and the stochastic trend (Stock & Watson, 1998). Trended data need certain kind of approach to remove their trend, as the presence of variable trends in time series data can lead to misleading inferences by using the conventional econometric methodologies. One of the popular procedures being used to remove trend is first differencing which is especially proper when time series is I (1). Unit root tests can be employed to determine whether the data should be made stationary by first differencing.

In time series model estimation, the variables should be stationary so that the standard theory applies. Unit root tests are the widely acceptance method to test whether variables are stationary or non-stationary (Gujarati, 2004). In this study, unit root tests are applied to test the stationarity. There are two most popular used unit root tests: the Augmented Dickey-Fuller (ADF) test (Dickey & Fuller, 1981; Said & Dickey, 1984) and the Philip-Perron (PP) test (Phillip & Perron, 1988), whose null hypothesis are both that a unit root exists in the time series.

The ADF procedure requires homoscedastic and uncorrelated errors in the underlying structure. Meanwhile, PP test is a non-parametric test that generalizes the ADF procedure and allows for less restrictive assumption. Hence, it will be eliminating any nuisance parameters. A major drawback of the ADF tests and the PP tests is that they have low statistical power in distinguishing between true unit root processes and near unit root processes (Campbell & Perron, 1991). Also, several authors have shown that the ADF test tends to reject the non-stationarity hypothesis far too often, when the series have large (long-run) moving average processes. If there is evidence or doubt about such cases then it is recommended to introduce an additional unit root test to justify the integration order of the series by using the mean stationary test developed by Kwiatkowski, Phillips, Schmidt, and Shin (1992) which is also known as KPSS test.

4.2.2 Lag Length Selection

In SVAR estimation process, a critical problem is the choice of lag lengths, as the statistic of interest are functions of the order of the auto-regressive lag polynomial, estimates of a VAR whose lag length differs from the true lag length are inconsistent as the impulse response functions and variance decompositions are derived from the estimated VAR (Braun & Mittnik, 1993). Lütkepohl (1993) indicates that over-fitting (selecting a higher order lag length than the true lag length) causes an increase in the mean-square-forecast errors of the VAR and that under-fitting the lag length often generates auto-correlated errors.

In this study, the lag length is determined by several explicit statistical criterions such as the general-to-specific sequential Likelihood Ratio (LR) test, the Final Prediction Error (FPR), the Akaike Information Criterion (AIC), the Schwarz Criterion (SC) and the Hannan-Quinn (HQ) Information Criterion. In this study, the optimal lag length is determined with the AIC and the SC criterions. If there is a contradiction between the AIC and the SC, then we refer to the LR standard. Meanwhile, the SVAR must satisfy the conditions for stationarity.

4.2.3 Impulse Response Functions and Robustness Test

The VAR model is hard to analyze simply. It is not meaningful to just focus on the coefficients in the equations themselves. These coefficients are often likely to oscillate and always have complicated cross-equation feedbacks. The common econometric practice of summarizing distributed lag relations in terms of their implied long run equilibrium behavior is quite misleading in these systems (Sims, 1980).

Impulse response functions are a good tool to analyze the variables' responses to monetary policy shocks. The impulse response functions can trace out the impacts of monetary policy shocks on other variables in the equations over time and can offer reasonable economic interpretation. The "monetary policy shocks" are positive residuals of one standard deviation unit in the money equation of the model, it is sometimes referred to as the "money innovation", since it is the component of money which is "new" in the sense of not being predicted from past values of variables in the system.

Impulse response functions track the impact of a one standard deviation innovation to monetary policy variable on current and future values of the endogenous variables in the VAR system. Monetary policy shocks will cause a chain reaction of all variables over time in the VAR system. A shock in monetary policy variable amounts to one standard deviation calculated from the variance-covariance matrix. A monetary policy shock would directly influence monetary policy variable, and is also transmitted to other endogenous variables through the dynamic structure of the VAR. A change in monetary policy variable will immediately change the current values of other variables. It will also change the future values of all the variables considered in the model since lagged variables appear in all the equations. If the innovations are uncorrelated, interpretation of the impulse response is straightforward. The impulse response function measures the effect of a one standard deviation shock on current and future values of the variables concerned.

To examine the regional and provincial effects of monetary policy in China, this study will estimate the impulse responses of all SVAR models. This study will use the SVAR models generated impulse responses and cumulative impulse responses to measure the magnitude and timing of regions' and provinces' responses to monetary policy shock.

To check the robustness of the results, alternative specifications are estimated to examine the sensitivity of the results to alternative measures of monetary policy (M1, one year lending rate), this study will change the identification schemes and compare the results to run the robustness tests.

4.3 The Sizes of Banks as One of the Determinants for the Regional Effects of Monetary Policy

The second model is mainly to solve the second research question. This study will explore the factors explaining the regional effects of monetary policy in

China. According to interest rate channel, a province which has a bigger proportion of interest rate sensitive industry would respond more to monetary policy shock. Therefore, this study uses the secondary industry in one province/GDP of this province to measure the industrial mix. Bank lending channel (Kashyap & Stein, 1995; Carlino & DeFina, 1998) says that regional differences in the mix of large firms versus small firms, and large banks versus small banks can explain the regional effects of monetary policy. A province's concentration of small firms and small banks would have a bigger response to monetary policy shock. So this study uses the proportion of small firms and the proportion of small banks in each province to represent bank lending channel. This study uses the number of small enterprises/total enterprises in each province to measure the proportion of small firms in each province. As the banks in China adopt branch banking system, we cannot employ the number of small banks to measure the proportion of small banks, according to Kashyap and Stein (1995), this study uses total assets of small banks/total assets of all banks in each province as a proxy.

The monetary transmission process in China is closely tied to the four large banks. They occupy a big market share. These large banks historically function as fiscal agents and account for a majority of all deposits. More importantly, their lending is biased in favor of state-owned enterprises (Kong, 2003). The strong tie between China's state-owned banks and state-owned firms is a prime example of the "soft budget constraint syndrome" introduced by Kornai (1986). An important implication is that the effectiveness of monetary policy is questionable in the presence of a soft budget constraint. Therefore, the sensitivity of provinces to monetary shocks may be negatively related to the percentage of firms that are state-owned.

Therefore, this study also uses the proportion of large commercial banks and the percentage of state-owned and state-holding enterprises in each province as proxies to describe this monetary transmission process in each province. According to bank lending channel, a province with a big proportion of large banks would respond less to monetary policy innovations. This study uses total assets of large banks/total assets of all banks in each province as a proxy for the proportion of large commercial banks. This study employs the number of state-owned and state-holding enterprises/total enterprises in each province to represent the proportion of small firms in each province.

This study will use long-run (6 years) cumulative impulse responses① as the dependent variable to represent the magnitude of regional effects of monetary policy. To show the robustness of the results, long-run (10 years) cumulated responses and maximum cumulated responses are also chosen as alternative dependent variables. The model has two sets of independent variables. The first set of independent variables describes the interest rate channel and the traditional bank lending channel. The second set of variables describes the interest rate channel and the bank lending channel with soft budget constraint. As the impulse responses represent average behavior during the sample period, averaging data for independent variables is appropriate. Data availability limited averaging to the period from 2000 to 2011.

The second model specification is as follows:

$$Impulse_i = \alpha_0 + \alpha_1 IndustryMix_i + \alpha_2 Smallbank_i + \alpha_3 Smallfirm_i + e_i \quad (4.25)$$

$$Impulse_i = \beta_0 + \beta_1 IndustryMix_i + \beta_2 Largebank_i + \beta_3 SOE_i + \varepsilon_i \quad (4.26)$$

Where i represents province i (31 provinces), $Impulse_i$ is the provincial SVAR model generated long-run stable (6 years or 10 years) cumulative impulse response or maximum cumulated impulse response of province i. $IndustryMix_i$ is the proportion of interest sensitive industries in each province (measured by the output of Secondary Industry② in province i/ the GDP of province i). *Small-*

① At this level (6 years), the cumulated impulse responses of most of provinces go to stable.

② In China, industry mix contains three industries: Primary Industry, Secondary Industry and Tertiary Industry. Primary Industry means agriculture, Secondary Industry contains industry and construction, Tertiary Industry consists of transports, storage and post; wholesale and retail trades; hotels and catering services; financial intermediation; real estate; other services.

bank$_i$ is the proportion of small banks in province i (measured by the assets of small banks① in provinces i/ total assets of all banks in province i). $Largebank_i$ is the percent of large commercial banks② in each province (measured by the assets of large commercial banks in provinces i/ total assets of all banks in province i). $Smallfirm_i$ is the percent of small enterprises in province i (measured by the number of small enterprises③ in province i/total number of all enterprises in province i). SOE_i is the proportion of state-owned and state-holding enterprises in province i (measured by the number of state-owned and state-holding enterprises in province i/total number of all enterprises in province i). e_i and ε_i are the residuals. This study runs multiple linear regressions using cross-sectional data for 31 provinces in the mainland China to check the relationship between these independent variables and dependent variables.

4.4 Does the DRRR Contribute to Eliminate the Regional Effects of Monetary Policy: A Case Study

The third model is used to solve the research question three. In objective three, this study wants to do a case study to examine whether or not the differentiated reserve requirement ratio (DRRR) policy has some effects on the outputs of the earth quake-stricken areas. If we try to reduce the regional effects of monetary policy from the perspective of monetary policy itself, a possible feasi-

① According to the People's Bank of China, the small bank means city commercial bank, rural commercial banks, rural cooperative banks and rural credit cooperatives.

② According to the People's Bank of China, large commercial banks contain the Industrial and Commercial bank of China, the Bank of China, China Construction Bank, the Agricultural Bank of China and Bank of Communications.

③ According to the standards to divide large-size, medium-size, small-size and micro-enterprises in statistics (promulgated by the ministry of industry and information technology of china), small enterprise is: 20≤number of employees <300, 3 million CNY≤operating income <2000 million CNY.

ble way is that the PBC can attempt to implement differentiated monetary policy instruments across regions based on their characteristic and economic development. The PBC can apply some preferential monetary policy instruments to the poor region and provinces to stimulate the economic growth so as to narrow the gap among regions.

In fact, the PBC has already done some attempts in recent years. An outstanding example is that the DRRR policy has been implemented in the earth quake-stricken area in Sichuan province by the PBC. So in the third model, this study will check the role of DRRR policy on the outputs of the earth quake-stricken areas. In May, 2008, a big earthquake happened in Sichuan province and made a lot of damages. To help the recovery of the earthquake-stricken areas, the PBC decided to implement a preferential DRRR policy to corporate financial institutions in 39 most badly hurt counties. Financial institutions in other counties which suffer relatively small losses still apply the normal RRR. As we expect a preferential DRRR can promote a more quickly economic recovery than the normal RRR, this study also randomly selects 39 counties in Sichuan province from the other 142 counties which do not enjoy the DRRR policy as cases. This study will examine the role of the DRRR policy on the 39 earthquake-stricken counties and that of the normal RRR on the other 39 counties to make a comparison in order to check whether or not the DRRR policy can promote the GDP growth more in the earth quake-stricken 39 counties than the normal RRR policy implemented in the other 39 counties. The estimation period is the implementation period of the DRRR policy during 2008 – 2011. If the positive role of the DRRR policy can be confirmed, it can be extended to a great range in order to reduce the regional effects of monetary policy. For example, the PBC can use it to support the development of the West or less developed provinces to narrow the gap among regions.

This study constructs the model mainly based on the expenditure approach of GDP. As well known, GDP mainly contains four parts: government expenditure, investment, consumption and net exports. As these 78 counties in Sichuan province belong to the less developed western region, far from the coastal areas, there are very little or even no exports in these counties. Thus net export is neglected in this model. This study divides investment into two parts: in the first part, the funds of investment are from bank loans, in the second part, the funds are from other sources. According to bank lending channel, reserve requirement ratio can affect loans and the change of loans can influence investment, and finally will affect the real economy. It is assumed that the DRRR can affect investment through loans, thus this study introduces an interaction item: DRRR × Loans, into GDP equation. We assume that the interaction item mainly affects the real economy and want to measure the influence of this interaction item on the GDP. Therefore, the third model like this:

$$GDP_{it} = a_i + b_i GOV_{it} + c_i LOAN_{it} + \alpha_i DRRR_{it} \times LOAN_{it}\text{①}$$
$$+ \beta_i OI_{it} + \gamma_i CONS_{it} + e_{it} \quad (4.27)$$

Where GDP_{it} is the real GDP of 39 counties in Sichuan province, t = 2008, 2009, 2010 and 2011, $i = 1, 2, \cdots, 39$. The $LOAN_{it}$ is a proxy for the funds of investment which are mainly from bank loans measured by the total loan of each county. GOV_{it} is government expenditure measured by the local government intra-budgetary ordinary expenditure of each county. OI_{it} donates the investment whose funds are from other sources (except bank loans) measured by total investment in fixed assets (minus bank loans) of each county. $CONS_{it}$ represents consumption measured by total retail sales of consumer goods in each county. These variables are real variables adjusted by the CPI index (2008 = 100) in logarithm except $DRRR_{it}$ and RRR_{it}. $DRRR_{it}$ is the differentiated reserve requirement ratio. RRR_{it} is the reserve requirement ratio. As the counties in Sichuan province are less developed areas located in inland China with no or very little FDI, this study does not include FDI as an independent variable in the equation. e_{it} are

① For 39 earthquake-stricken counties, the interaction part is $DRRR \times LOAN$. For the other 39 counties, the interaction part is $RRR \times LOAN$.

residuals.

This study will use panel data model to estimate this equation. The data cover 78 counties in Sichuan province from 2008 to 2011. Firstly this study will estimate the model for the 39 earthquake badly hurt counties enjoying the DRRR policy in Sichuan province, and then estimate the model for the other 39 counties with the normal RRR policy in Sichuan province. This study will compare the coefficients α_i to check the effects of the DRRR (RRR) policy on the outputs in the counties with the preferential DRRR policy and counties with normal RRR policy.

4.5 Estimation Procedure of the Panel Data Model

4.5.1 Pooled Regression Model

$$GDP_{it} = a + bGOV_{it} + cLOAN_{it} + \alpha DRRR_{it} \times LOAN_{it} + \beta OI_{it} + \gamma CONS_{it} + e_{it} \quad (4.28)$$

This model is called pooled regression model as we just simply put all the observations together and assume that the coefficients (including the intercepts) do not change with different individuals over time. In fact, due to these assumptions, pooled regression model is equal to simple linear regression model and we can use the pooled ordinary least squares (POLS) to estimate the model.

The pooled regression model is usually seemed as a rough and ready way of analyzing the data. It just provides a simple and quick benchmark which can be compared with more sophisticated regressions. As a matter of fact, the pooled OLS regression is subject to lots kinds of errors. Since the pooled regression model neglects the distinction among individuals, this heterogeneity across individuals would be contained in residuals. Then the independent variables will be correlated with the residuals and the OLS estimator will be biased and inconsistent.

4.5.2 Fixed Effect Model

The fixed effects models pay attention to the individual characteristics and assume these county specific effects might affect the independent variables. "Least Squares Dummy Variable" method is adopted by fixed effects model to control for county differences. It assumes invariable coefficients for explanatory variables and constant variance across groups. In this study, the fixed effects model is as follows:

$$GDP_{it} = a_i + bGOV_{it} + cLOAN_{it} + \alpha DRRR_{it} \times LOAN_{it} + \beta OI_{it} + \gamma CONS_{it} + e_{it} \tag{4.29}$$

For fixed effects model, the intercepts may be distinct across counties. Due to the heterogeneity between individuals, each county is allowed to have its own intercept value in the fixed effects model. "Fixed effects" refers to that though intercepts may differ across counties, they are time-invariant. The fixed effects model is based on this assumption:

$$E(e_{it} \mid Govexp_{it}, DRRR_{it}, GDP_{it}, Loan_{it}, Othinvest_{it}, Consum_{it}, a_i) = 0$$

Hence the exogeneity assumption is satisfied.

In the fixed effects model, we have to pay attention to two assumptions. The first one is it is assumed that county specific characteristic is likely to affect the variables and should be control in the equations. Therefore, in the fixed effects model, each county has a different a_i, leaving the coefficients measuring the net effects of independent variables. Another one is that this county specific effect is unique to each county and is uncorrelated with other counties. Thus the error term and intercept of each county are independent. If the residuals are correlated, fixed effects no longer applied and random effects may be proper.

The least squares dummy variable (LSDV) model is often used to estimate fixed effects model because the LSDV use dummy variables as the individuals in panel data and it can be easily interpreted. In fact, it is simply the OLS estimator with enough dummy variables. We should notice that only when the residuals are independent across time and individual, the LSDV generates consistent and unbiased estimates.

Within estimator is also frequently used to estimate fixed effects model. It eliminates unobserved heterogeneity of fixed effects model by taking deviations from individual means. It is called the within estimator because it relies on variations within individuals rather than between individuas. Within estimator avoids using dummies by mean-centering all modeled variables, including the dependent, thus increasing degrees of freedom.

Another alternative estimator called first-differences estimator which attempts to eliminate the fixed effects. The first-differences estimator firstly transforms the baseline fixed effects model into the first-differences model and then runs a pooled OLS on the first-differences model. Through transformation, time invariant omitted variables are wiped out. Wooldridge (2012) shows that under a strict exogeneity assumption on the explanatory variables, the fixed effects estimator is unbiased. The fixed effects estimation is always much more convincing that random effect estimation for policy analysis using aggregate data (Wooldridge, 2012).

4.5.3 Random Effect Model

In the random effects model, the unobserved difference among counties is assumed to be random and uncorrelated with any of the explanatory variables. Therefore, this study treats a_i as random variable in the random effects model:

$$\begin{aligned} GDP_{it} = a_0 + b_i GOV_{it} + c_i LOAN_{it} + \alpha_i DRRR_{it} \times LOAN_{it} \\ + \beta_i OI_{it} + \gamma_i CONS_{it} + a_i + e_{it} \end{aligned} \tag{4.30}$$

In this model, the residuals are independent with the explanatory variables. However, the residuals for counties are correlated with each other and show certain degree of heteroskedasticity. If variations among counties would affect dependent variable, then the random effects model applies.

In order to determine which model is preferred for the equation estimation, the Hausman test will be used. The null hypothesis of the Hausman test is the estimated model should be the random effects model unless the Hausman test is rejected. A rejection of the Hausman test is taken to mean that the key random effects assumption is false, and then the fixed effect estimates are used (Wooldridge, 2012).

The generalized least squares (GLS) is the appropriate estimator for random effects model. The GLS estimator is efficient as it can correct the serial correlation problem and adjust the parameter estimates for heteroskedasticity. Moreover, it can get the most out of the panel data and reduce the residuals as far as possible. For more detail about the estimation of fixed effects and random effects model, please refer to Hsiao (2003), Cameron and Trivedi (2005). This study does not consider dynamic panel data model and use the generalized method of moments (GMM) estimator, as the panel data only cover four years from 2008 to 2011.

4.6 Data Collection

The data are obtained from the National Bureau of Statistics of China, The Ministry of Commerce of China, The People's Bank of China, China Banking Regulatory Commission (CBRC), China Statistical Yearbook (1980 – 2012), Sichuan Statistical Yearbook (2004 – 2012), Almanac of China's Finance and Banking (1986 – 2010), The Regional Financial Operation Report (2004 – 2012), China Banking Regulatory Commission Annual Report (2006 – 2012), IMF Data and Statistics and World Bank Database. The first model uses annual data from 1978 to 2011. The second model uses cross-sectional data with the information of 31 provinces in the mainland China. The third model uses panel data of 78 counties in Sichuan province during 2008 – 2011. For the detail information, please see Table 4. 1.

Table 4. 1 Variables, Description and Data Sources

Variable	Description	Sources
GDP	real GDP of three regions: the East, the Middle and the West; real GDP of 31 provinces; real GDP of 78 counties in Sichuan province	National Bureau of Statistics of China; China Statistical Yearbook (1980 – 2012); Sichuan Statistical Yearbook (2004 – 2012)
WDGDP	real world GDP	IMF Data and Statistics
Price	CPI of the nation; CPI of three region; CPI of 31 provinces (1978 = 100)	National Bureau of Statistics of China; China Statistical Yearbook (1980 – 2012); Statistical Yearbook of Each province (2000 – 2012)
MP	M2, M1 and BLR	National Bureau of Statistics of China
Industry Mix	the proportion of Secondary Industry	National Bureau of Statistics of China
Small bank	the proportion of small bank	Almanac of China's Finance and Banking (1986 – 2010)
Large bank	the percent of large bank	Almanac of China's Finance and Banking (1986 – 2010)
Small firm	the proportion of small firm	National Bureau of Statistics of China
SOE	The percent of state-owned and state-holding enterprises	National Bureau of Statistics of China
GOV	government expenditure measured by the local government intra-budgetary ordinary expenditure of each county	Sichuan Statistical Yearbook (2004 – 2012)
LOAN	total loan of each county	Sichuan Statistical Yearbook (2004 – 2012)
OI	total investment in fixed assets minus bank loans	Sichuan Statistical Yearbook (2004 – 2012)
CONS	consumption measured by total retail sales of consumer goods in each county	Sichuan Statistical Yearbook (2004 – 2012)
DRRR RRR	differentiated reserve requirement ratio; reserve requirement ratio	National Bureau of Statistics of China

Notes: As the dependent variable cumulative impulse response represent average behavior during the sample period, the variables: Industry Mix, Small bank, Large bank, Small firm and SOE are averaging data from 2000 – 2011.

Chapter 5

Results and Discussions

5.1 Introduction

This Chapter addresses the results of statistical analysis described in Chapter 4 and discussion of the estimation of the research. EViews 6.0 statistical software package is used to analyze the data. This chapter begins with the presentation of the results of the first model, the magnitude and timing of regions' and provinces' responses to monetary policy. In this part, this chapter firstly provides the descriptive statistics of data in order to grasp the first impression of the basic features of the variables. Following that, unit roots tests are employed to measure the stationarity of the data series. Then the results and discussion of the first model are presented. As the first model is divided into the regional model and the provincial model, in the first place, this chapter describes and discusses the impulse responses of regions to monetary policy. To emphasize the importance of the spillover effects, it also provides the results of the model by each region and makes a contrast with that of the regional model. Next, this chapter presents and analyzes the results of the provincial model using the same procedure as the regional model. Later, this chapter presents and discusses the results of the second model, the factors affecting regional effects of monetary policy in China.

Finally, this chapter addresses the results and discussion of the third model, the role of the DRRR policy on the earthquake-stricken counties.

5.2 The Responses of Regions and Provinces to Monetary Policy

5.2.1 Descriptive Statistics

Descriptive statistics are used to describe the basic features of the data in the study. They provide simple summaries about the variables. Before getting into a more detail econometric analysis, the variations of data are analyzed to provide initial view on how the variables behave. Descriptive statistics of selected macro-economic variables are presented in Table 5.1 – Table 5.4.

Table 5.1 Descriptive Statistics for Regional and National Variables

Item	EGDP	MGDP	WGDP	WDGDP	CPI	M2	M1	BLR
Mean	179.60	70.97	52.28	87620.34	317.15	1562.76	577.43	0.08
Median	104.69	43.91	32.24	112885	367.95	538.37	222.64	0.07
Max.	678.01	260.44	199.10	152122.6	565.00	8515.91	2898.48	0.12
Min.	17.44	10.07	7.22	13322.16	100.00	11.80	8.59	0.05
S. D.	187.27	68.00	51.43	52277.56	161.27	2219.44	785.18	0.02
Skewness	1.26	1.33	1.39	−0.23	−0.10	1.73	1.65	0.46
Kurtosis	3.51	3.80	4.02	1.37	1.39	5.19	4.83	2.15
Jarque-Bera	9.42 [0.01]	10.92 [0.00]	12.49 [0.00]	4.08 [0.13]	3.74 [0.15]	23.86 [0.00]	20.21 [0.00]	2.20 [0.33]

Notes: For Mean, Median, Max., Min., S. D., the unit of variables (except the CPI and BLR) is 10 billion CNY. EGDP, MGDP and WGDP are the real GDP of the East, the Middle and the West. WDGDP is the real GDP of the world. CPI is the national consumer price index (1978 = 100). M2 and M1 are monetary aggregates. BLR is bank lending rate, the benchmark one year bank lending rate. Max. refers to Maximum and Min. is Minimum. S. D. is Standard Deviation.

According to Table 5.1, the average GDP during 1978 – 2011 in the East is bigger than the sum of the Middle and the West, with the maximum of 6780.1 billion CNY and the minimum of 174.4 billion CNY. The average GDP during

1978 – 2011 in the World is 876203. 4 billion CNY (constant 1978). The average CPI is 317. 15 (1978 = 100) being used as a measure of country's inflation. And the average BLR (bank lending rate) for the past 34 years is 8% with the maximum of 12% and the minimum of 5%.

Table 5. 2 – Table 5. 4 present the real GDP of each province in three regions. In the East, Hainan has the smallest average GDP (15. 6 billion CNY). Besides Hainan, the range of the average GDP is 65 billion – 320 billion CNY. The biggest average GDP is 318. 0 billion CNY flowed to Jiangsu province. The range of average GDP in the Middle is 58 billion – 150 billion CNY. Henan has the biggest average GDP. The 8 provinces in the Middle share the similar situation of economic development and no big differences measured by the real GDP.

Table 5. 2 Descriptive Statistics for Provincial GDP Variables in the East

Item	Beijing	Tianjin	Hebei	Liaoning	Shanghai	Jiangsu	Zhejiang	Fujian	Shandong	Guangdong	Hainan
Mean	8. 45	6. 51	14. 92	14. 34	19. 38	31. 80	18. 01	8. 99	24. 74	30. 90	1. 56
Median	5. 14	3. 28	9. 02	9. 22	11. 22	17. 89	10. 42	5. 35	14. 14	17. 87	1. 15
Max.	29. 08	28. 40	53. 72	52. 86	66. 69	125. 2	66. 72	35. 12	95. 61	118. 92	5. 70
Min.	1. 09	0. 83	1. 83	2. 29	2. 73	2. 49	1. 24	0. 66	2. 25	1. 86	0. 16
S. D.	8. 14	7. 23	14. 76	13. 67	18. 83	34. 54	19. 04	9. 55	26. 35	33. 79	1. 51
Skew.	1. 18	1. 60	1. 19	1. 39	1. 17	1. 31	1. 19	1. 28	1. 30	1. 22	1. 23
Kurt.	3. 22	4. 67	3. 33	3. 99	3. 15	3. 66	3. 24	3. 65	3. 61	3. 36	3. 64
Jarque -Bera	7. 97 [0. 02]	18. 47 [0. 00]	8. 14 [0. 02]	12. 31 [0. 00]	7. 72 [0. 02]	10. 37 [0. 01]	8. 07 [0. 02]	9. 86 [0. 01]	10. 14 [0. 01]	8. 64 [0. 01]	9. 22 [0. 01]

Notes: For Mean, Median, Max., Min., S. D., the unit of variables is 10 billion CNY. Skew. is Skewness. Kurt. is Kurtosis. GDP of each province is in real terms.

Generally speaking, the West has the smallest average GDP, among the 12 provinces, only Sichuan has an average GDP more than 100 billion CNY. The other 11 provinces show the average GDP between 4 billion – 65 billion CNY. Qinghai, Ningxia and Tibet display the average GDP below 10 billion CNY. From the data of GDP, it is clear that the provinces in the East are more developed and that in the Middle and the West are less developed. The regional economies are unbalanced in China.

Table 5. 3　Descriptive Statistics for Provincial GDP Variables in the Middle

Item	Shanxi	Jilin	Heilongjiang	Anhui	Jiangxi	Henan	Hubei	Hunan
Mean	6. 00	5. 81	8. 23	8. 99	6. 20	14. 88	11. 83	9. 04
Median	3. 52	3. 52	5. 32	5. 58	3. 89	9. 03	7. 42	5. 63
Max.	21. 47	22. 23	27. 77	33. 45	22. 77	55. 03	44. 36	33. 37
Min.	0. 88	0. 82	1. 75	1. 14	0. 87	1. 63	1. 51	1. 47
S. D.	5. 78	5. 71	7. 10	8. 71	5. 93	14. 81	11. 44	8. 56
Skew.	1. 25	1. 44	1. 29	1. 32	1. 35	1. 28	1. 36	1. 39
Kurt.	3. 43	4. 16	3. 68	3. 83	3. 86	3. 61	3. 96	4. 02
Jarque-Bera	9. 15 [0. 01]	13. 60 [0. 00]	10. 13 [0. 01]	10. 88 [0. 00]	11. 31 [0. 00]	9. 85 [0. 01]	11. 73 [0. 00]	12. 39 [0. 00]

Notes: For Mean, Median, Max. , Min. , S. D. , the unit of variables is 10 billion CNY. Skew. is Skewness. Kurt. is Kurtosis. GDP of each province is in real terms.

5. 2. 2　Unit Root Tests

In this sub-section, the preliminary analysis to determine the existence of unit root problem (non-stationarity) is conducted to test stationarity of variables. Unit root tests have little power due to small sample. Thus three tests, namely Augmented Dickey-Fuller (ADF) test, Phillips-Perron (PP) test and Kwiatkowski, Phillips, Schmidt and Shin (KPSS) test are provided. The analysis with unit root tests as outlined in the previous chapter in order to discriminate the conclusion of stationarity and non-stationarity for all series under investigation. For ADF test, the lag length selection is based on Akaike Information Criteria (AIC) and Schwarz Criterion (SC), while for PP and KPSS tests, we allow for Newey-West bandwidth to be automatically choosing the optimal lag length for us.

5. 2. 2. 1　Augmented Dickey-Fuller (ADF) Tests

The results for the ADF test in determining the presence of unit roots of all variables in the sample is reported in the following Table 5. 5.

Table 5. 4 Descriptive Statistics for Provincial GDP Variables in the West

Item	Inner Mongolia	Guangxi	Chongqing	Sichuan	Guizhou	Yunnan	Tibet	Shaanxi	Gansu	Qinghai	Ningxia	Xinjiang
Mean	6. 03	5. 07	5. 06	12. 93	2. 99	4. 72	0. 49	6. 35	3. 95	0. 74	0. 84	3. 12
Median	2. 77	3. 33	3. 12	8. 10	1. 97	3. 29	0. 26	3. 60	2. 54	0. 46	0. 53	2. 27
Max.	27. 80	18. 95	20. 22	49. 01	10. 59	16. 04	1. 82	25. 16	13. 60	2. 68	2. 98	10. 25
Min.	0. 58	0. 76	0. 67	1. 85	0. 47	0. 69	0. 07	0. 81	0. 65	0. 14	0. 13	0. 39
S. D.	7. 28	4. 95	5. 09	12. 51	2. 69	4. 16	0. 49	6. 52	3. 62	0. 68	0. 78	2. 75
Skew.	1. 68	1. 36	1. 47	1. 39	1. 32	1. 17	1. 30	1. 46	1. 18	1. 40	1. 30	1. 09
Kurt.	4. 76	3. 91	4. 38	4. 06	3. 84	3. 47	3. 60	4. 20	3. 37	3. 99	3. 72	3. 17
Jarque-Bera	20. 30 [0. 00]	11. 60 [0. 00]	14. 98 [0. 00]	12. 57 [0. 00]	10. 93 [0. 00]	8. 05 [0. 02]	10. 0 [0. 01]	14. 10 [0. 00]	8. 14 [0. 02]	12. 49 [0. 00]	10. 29 [0. 01]	6. 77 [0. 03]

Notes: For Mean, Median, Max. , Min. , S. D. , the unit of variables is 10 billion CNY. Skew. is Skewness. Kurt. is Kurtosis. GDP of each province is in real terms.

Table 5. 5 shows the results of the ADF tests for all the 70 variables at levels and first differences of the natural log values with the exception of the BLR. At level, the null hypothesis of the presence of unit root cannot be rejected for all the 70 variables with the exception of only three variables (Hebei, Jiansu and Tibet) in the test with trend. At first difference, the null hypothesis can be rejected for 46 variables at conventional significance levels in all cases both with trend and without trend. 22 variables are stationary either with trend or without trend. Only for two variables (Jiangxi and Chongqing), the null hypothesis of unit root cannot be rejected with or without trend.

5. 2. 2. 2 Phillips-Perron (PP) Tests

PP unit root tests have also performed for all the variables, and similar to ADF, the test is conducted with trend and without trend. From the results as shown in Table 5. 6, the null hypothesis of unit root cannot be rejected for all the variables except two variables (lnHebei and lnGansu) with trend at level.

At first difference, the null hypothesis can be rejected for 42 variables at conventional significance levels in all cases both with trend and without trend. 14 variables are stationary only when tested without trend. One variable (lnWyunnan) is stationary when tested with trend only. The unit root null cannot be rejected with trend or without trend for 13 variables, indicating these variables may not be stationary.

5. 2. 2. 3 Kwiatkowski, Phillips, Schmidt and Shin (KPSS) Tests

The results for the KPSS tests for unit roots of all variables in the sample are reported in the Table 5. 7. At level, the null hypothesis of stationarity is rejected for most of variables, suggesting that these variables are not stationary. One variable (BLR) is found to be stationary without trend. 10 variables are found to be stationary with trend.

Table 5.5 Unit Root Tests—ADF Tests

Variables	Level		First Difference		Variables	Level		First Difference	
	C	C&T	C	C&T		C	C&T	C	C&T
lnEGDP	0. 67	−2. 76	3. 49**	3. 49*	lnGansu	5. 01	1. 50	−4. 90***	−6. 90***
lnMGDP	4. 85	1. 24	−2. 41	−5. 89***	lnQinghai	2. 99	−0. 76	−7. 71***	−2. 53
lnWGDP	2. 04	3. 08	−2. 91*	−3. 70**	lnNingxia	2. 29	0. 22	−1. 57	−3. 28*
lnWDGDP	−2. 19	0. 17	−4. 30***	−5. 41***	lnXinjiang	−0. 22	−2. 12	−3. 25**	−3. 15
lnCPI	−1. 08	−1. 07	−3. 16**	−3. 24*	lnEbeijing	0. 66	−2. 88	−3. 55**	−3. 55*
lnM2	−2. 52	−0. 92	−3. 30**	−1. 90	lnEtianjin	0. 52	−2. 91	−3. 52**	−3. 47*
lnM1	−1. 29	−1. 41	−5. 31***	−5. 41***	lnEhebei	0. 65	−2. 85	−3. 54**	−3. 53*
BLR	−2. 42	−2. 91	−3. 88***	−3. 97**	lnEliaoning	0. 49	−2. 95	−3. 50**	−3. 44*
lnBeijing	1. 09	−2. 65	−4. 28***	−4. 34***	lnEshanghai	0. 45	−3. 09	−3. 54**	−3. 48*
lnTianjin	2. 77	0. 53	−0. 02	−3. 26*	lnEjiangsu	1. 87	−2. 03	−3. 33**	−3. 35*
lnHebei	1. 24	−5. 22***	−2. 91*	−2. 55	lnEzhejiang	0. 86	−2. 50	−3. 81***	−3. 92**
lnLiaoning	1. 55	−0. 09	−3. 50**	−2. 61	lnEfujian	0. 73	−2. 65	−3. 50**	−3. 51*
lnShanghai	0. 66	−2. 29	−2. 98**	−3. 05	lnEshandong	0. 65	−2. 85	−3. 81***	−3. 85**
lnJiangsu	0. 60	−4. 24**	−4. 06***	−4. 03**	lnEguangdong	0. 95	−2. 34	−3. 40**	−3. 52*
lnZhejiang	−0. 82	−2. 35	−4. 29***	−4. 30**	lnEhainan	0. 68	−2. 75	−3. 51**	−3. 51*
lnFujian	−0. 63	−2. 34	−4. 21***	−4. 12**	lnMshanxi	4. 10	1. 15	−3. 15**	−5. 08***
lnShandong	0. 74	−2. 31	−3. 64**	−3. 72**	lnMjilin	5. 43	1. 16	−0. 81	−6. 54***
lnGuangdong	−1. 29	−1. 78	−2. 80*	−2. 24	lnMheilongjiang	3. 78	0. 75	−3. 56**	−5. 12***
lnHainan	−0. 38	−2. 86	−4. 02***	−3. 94**	lnManhui	5. 27	1. 66	1. 14	−6. 24***
lnShanxi	1. 20	−2. 05	−3. 68***	−4. 66***	lnMjiangxi	4. 95	1. 10	−2. 38	−6. 03***
lnJilin	1. 69	−0. 71	−3. 97***	−4. 89***	lnMhenan	5. 06	2. 27	−2. 51	−4. 95***
lnHeilongjiang	6. 37	0. 67	−3. 38**	−2. 92	lnMhubei	4. 63	1. 27	−2. 47	−5. 52***

continuous

Variables	Level		First Difference		Variables	Level		First Difference	
	C	C&T	C	C&T		C	C&T	C	C&T
lnAnhui	2. 44	−2. 25	−3. 86***	−3. 93**	lnMhunan	4. 91	1. 16	−2. 54	−6. 16***
lnJiangxi	1. 70	−0. 49	−2. 26	−2. 91	lnWInner-Mongolia	1. 99	2. 20	−3. 11**	−3. 84**
lnHenan	2. 02	−0. 17	−5. 52***	−5. 92***	lnWguangxi	1. 24	4. 37	0. 95	−3. 66**
lnHubei	4. 96	0. 22	−4. 01***	−6. 67***	lnWchongqing	2. 05	3. 19	−3. 13**	−3. 90**
lnHunan	3. 29	1. 27	−2. 60	−3. 53**	lnWsichuan	1. 90	2. 89	−3. 11**	−3. 78**
lnInner-Mongolia	1. 76	−0. 67	2. 84*	−3. 52*	lnWguizhou	2. 09	2. 51	−2. 96**	−3. 80**
lnGuangxi	1. 73	−1. 55	−2. 30	−3. 47*	lnWyunnan	2. 06	3. 09	−2. 67*	−3. 51*
lnChongqing	2. 09	−0. 10	−2. 24	−2. 78	lnWtibet	2. 02	3. 05	−2. 90*	−3. 67**
lnSichuan	2. 34	−0. 20	−2. 85*	−3. 83**	lnWshaanxi	1. 92	2. 50	−2. 78*	−3. 50*
lnGuizhou	1. 67	0. 09	−3. 53**	−3. 08	lnWgansu	2. 03	2. 92	−2. 80*	−3. 59**
lnYunnan	1. 01	−1. 89	−5. 63***	−5. 55***	lnWqinghai	2. 04	2. 96	−2. 87*	−3. 66**
lnTibet	1. 57	−3. 44*	−3. 07**	−3. 10	lnWningxia	2. 05	2. 95	−2. 92*	−3. 71**
lnShaanxi	2. 73	−0. 40	−3. 98***	−4. 58***	lnWxinjiang	2. 16	3. 24	−2. 95*	−3. 81**

Notes: 1. Asterisk *, ** and *** indicates the rejection of the null hypothesis at level of confidence 10%, 5% and 1% respectively, critical values are from Davidson and Mackinnon (1993). The null and alternative hypothesis are respectively H_0 = unit root (series is non-stationary) and $H_1 > 0$ (series is stationary). The selection of lag length is based on the Akaike Information Criterion (AIC) and Schwarz Criterion (SC), considering the degree of freedom.

2. C refers to Constant. C&T represents constant & trend. EGDP, MGDP, WGDP and WDGDP represent the real GDP of the East, the Middle, the West and the World (1978 = 100). "ln" indicates variables are expressed in logs. CPI is the national consumer price index (1978 = 100). M2 and M1 are monetary aggregates. BLR is the one year bank lending rate. The name of each province represents the real GDP of each province. The names "E + name of province i", "M + name of province i", "W + name of province i" represent the real GDP of region (the East, the Middle or the West) minus the real GDP of province i.

Table 5.6 Unit Root Tests—PP Tests

Variables	Level		First Difference		Variables	Level		First Difference	
	C	C&T	C	C&T		C	C&T	C	C&T
lnEGDP	0.99	−2.76	−2.87*	−2.66	lnGansu	1.82	−3.78**	−5.14***	−5.54***
lnMGDP	2.95	−0.52	−2.37	−2.55	lnQinghai	3.60	−0.83	−6.91***	−8.00***
lnWGDP	3.16	−0.02	−2.83*	−3.71**	lnNingxia	1.72	−0.97	−3.38**	−3.57**
lnWDGDP	−2.19	−0.25	−4.28***	−7.01***	lnXinjiang	−0.78	−1.66	−3.36**	−3.28*
lnCPI	−1.19	−0.95	−2.43	−2.46	lnEbeijing	1.02	−2.77	−2.90*	−2.73
lnM2	−1.83	−0.84	−3.31**	−3.60**	lnEtianjin	0.85	−2.84	−2.91*	−2.68
lnM1	−1.29	−1.53	−5.30***	−5.41***	lnEhebei	0.92	−2.71	−2.88*	−2.67
BLR	−1.76	−2.19	−3.68***	−3.73**	lnEliaoning	0.85	−2.67	−2.98**	−2.86
lnBeijing	2.33	−1.92	−4.14***	−5.89***	lnEshanghai	0.84	−2.86	−2.95*	−2.71
lnTianjin	4.05	0.15	−2.08	−3.09	lnEjiangsu	1.13	−2.72	−3.10**	−2.93
lnHebei	1.81	−3.42*	−2.93*	−2.97	lnEzhejiang	1.21	−2.76	−2.94*	−2.75
lnLiaoning	2.29	−1.25	−2.91*	−3.26*	lnEfujian	1.03	−2.75	−2.81*	−2.61
lnShanghai	1.60	−2.00	−3.03**	−3.05	lnEshandong	0.98	−2.78	−2.83*	−2.64
lnJiangsu	0.68	−2.80	−4.01***	−3.96**	lnEguangdong	1.23	−2.54	−2.77*	−2.62
lnZhejiang	−0.72	−2.30	−3.23**	−3.22*	lnEhainan	1.00	−2.75	−2.86*	−2.65
lnFujian	−0.01	−2.03	−4.40***	−4.33***	lnMshanxi	2.35	−0.43	−2.41	−2.75
lnShandong	0.99	−2.61	−3.67***	−3.45*	lnMjilin	2.31	−0.55	−2.40	−2.84
lnGuangdong	−0.50	−1.59	−3.63**	−3.66**	lnMheilongjiang	2.35	−0.80	−2.55	−2.79
lnHainan	0.11	−1.94	−3.68***	−3.75**	lnManhui	2.56	−0.41	−2.43	−2.61
lnShanxi	1.89	−1.56	−3.40**	−4.10**	lnMjiangxi	2.30	−0.58	−2.35	−2.66
lnJilin	2.89	−0.89	−3.78***	−5.04***	lnMhenan	2.68	−0.25	−2.56	−3.21
lnHeilongjiang	9.66	1.54	−3.39**	−5.46***	lnMhubei	3.16	−0.11	−2.16	−2.26

continuous

Variables	Level		First Difference		Variables	Level		First Difference	
	C	C&T	C	C&T		C	C&T	C	C&T
lnAnhui	0. 84	−1. 78	−3. 84***	−3. 95**	lnMhunan	2. 64	−0. 19	−2. 36	−2. 59
lnJiangxi	2. 74	−0. 12	−4. 22***	−5. 22***	lnWInner-Mongolia	3. 17	−0. 05	−3. 04**	−3. 84**
lnHenan	0. 74	−1. 93	−5. 52***	−5. 49***	lnWguangxi	3. 01	0. 19	−2. 82*	−3. 66**
lnHubei	1. 22	−1. 13	−4. 13***	−4. 44***	lnWchongqing	3. 13	−0. 09	−3. 13**	−3. 90**
lnHunan	3. 65	0. 28	−2. 15	−3. 08	lnWsichuan	3. 09	−0. 28	−3. 03**	−3. 77**
lnInner-Mongolia	2. 64	−0. 25	−2. 88*	−3. 62**	lnWguizhou	3. 27	−0. 10	−2. 97**	−3. 81**
lnGuangxi	2. 43	−1. 38	−3. 13**	−3. 38*	lnWyunnan	3. 31	0. 22	−2. 60	−3. 51*
lnChongqing	3. 02	0. 11	−2. 26	−3. 11	lnWtibet	3. 15	−0. 04	−2. 81*	−3. 68**
lnSichuan	2. 93	0. 34	−2. 92*	−3. 85**	lnWshaanxi	3. 04	−0. 10	−2. 71*	−3. 53*
lnGuizhou	1. 35	−0. 43	−3. 53**	−3. 87**	lnWgansu	2. 98	0. 21	−2. 80*	−3. 59**
lnYunnan	0. 97	−2. 31	−5. 63***	−5. 54***	lnWqinghai	3. 13	−0. 01	−2. 78*	−3. 67**
lnTibet	1. 09	−1. 15	−4. 62***	−4. 72***	lnWningxia	3. 17	−0. 02	−2. 83*	−3. 73**
lnShaanxi	2. 55	−0. 60	−3. 91***	−4. 59***	lnWxinjiang	3. 37	0. 05	−2. 86*	−3. 80**

Notes: C refers to Constant. C&T represents constant & trend. Asterisk *, ** and *** indicates the rejection of the null hypothesis at level of confidence 10%, 5% and 1% respectively. The null and alternative hypothesis are respectively H_0 = unit root (series is non-stationary) and $H_1 > 0$ (series is stationary). The selection of lag length is based on the Newey-West bandwidth to be automatically choosing the optimal lag length.

Table 5.7 Unit Roots Test—KPSS Tests

Variables	Level		First Difference		Variables	Level		First Difference	
	C	C&T	C	C&T		C	C&T	C	C&T
lnEGDP	0. 68**	0. 13*	0. 28	0. 06	lnGansu	0. 68**	0. 18**	0. 36*	0. 08
lnMGDP	0. 68**	0. 18**	0. 37*	0. 07	lnQinghai	0. 68**	0. 19**	0. 58**	0. 07
lnWGDP	0. 68**	0. 18**	0. 51**	0. 09	lnNingxia	0. 68**	0. 14*	0. 29	0. 09
lnWDGDP	0. 61**	0. 20**	0. 49**	0. 14*	lnXinjiang	0. 68**	0. 15**	0. 14	0. 10
lnCPI	0. 67**	0. 16**	0. 22	0. 12*	lnEbeijing	0. 68**	0. 121*	0. 27	0. 07
lnM2	0. 68**	0. 18**	0. 31	0. 09	lnEtianjin	0. 68**	0. 113*	0. 24	0. 06
lnM1	0. 68**	0. 14*	0. 22	0. 07	lnEhebei	0. 68**	0. 125*	0. 17	0. 05
BLR	0. 22	0. 16**	0. 22	0. 11	lnEliaoning	0. 68**	0. 11	0. 24	0. 07
lnBeijing	0. 68**	0. 19**	0. 31	0. 25***	lnEshanghai	0. 68**	0. 10	0. 15	0. 06
lnTianjin	0. 68**	0. 20**	0. 55**	0. 11	lnEjiangsu	0. 68**	0. 139*	0. 31	0. 07
lnHebei	0. 68**	0. 14*	0. 32	0. 17**	lnEzhejiang	0. 68**	0. 142*	0. 35*	0. 06
lnLiaoning	0. 68**	0. 16**	0. 42*	0. 07	lnEfujian	0. 68**	0. 136*	0. 29	0. 06
lnShanghai	0. 68**	0. 18**	0. 34	0. 10	lnEshandong	0. 68**	0. 127*	0. 28	0. 06
lnJiangsu	0. 68**	0. 08	0. 12	0. 08	lnEguangdong	0. 68**	0. 158**	0. 35*	0. 05
lnZhejiang	0. 68**	0. 06	0. 07	0. 04	lnEhainan	0. 68**	0. 130*	0. 28	0. 06
lnFujian	0. 68**	0. 09	0. 07	0. 08	lnMshanxi	0. 69**	0. 171**	0. 37*	0. 08
lnShandong	0. 68**	0. 13*	0. 18	0. 05	lnMjilin	0. 68**	0. 176**	0. 36*	0. 07
lnGuangdong	0. 679**	0. 127*	0. 12	0. 10	lnMheilongjiang	0. 69**	0. 161**	0. 30	0. 11
lnHainan	0. 68**	0. 11	0. 06	0. 07	lnManhui	0. 68**	0. 181**	0. 42*	0. 07
lnShanxi	0. 68*	0. 18**	0. 28	0. 06	lnMjiangxi	0. 68**	0. 174**	0. 36*	0. 07
lnJilin	0. 69**	0. 16**	0. 34	0. 13*	lnMhenan	0. 68**	0. 181**	0. 42*	0. 08
lnHeilongjiang	0. 68**	0. 21**	0. 70**	0. 10	lnMhubei	0. 68**	0. 180**	0. 407*	0. 10

continuous

Variables	Level		First Difference		Variables	Level		First Difference	
	C	C&T	C	C&T		C	C&T	C	C&T
lnAnhui	0.69**	0.11	0.14	0.05	lnMhunan	0.68**	0.170**	0.359*	0.10
lnJiangxi	0.68**	0.18**	0.50**	0.12*	lnWInner-Mongolia	0.69**	0.173**	0.48**	0.08
lnHenan	0.68**	0.12	0.11	0.05	lnWguangxi	0.68**	0.176**	0.49**	0.10
lnHubei	0.69**	0.13*	0.21	0.08	lnWchongqing	0.68**	0.178**	0.50**	0.09
lnHunan	0.68**	0.19**	0.51**	0.07	lnWsichuan	0.68**	0.176**	0.50**	0.08
lnInner-Mongolia	0.68**	0.18**	0.43*	0.09	lnWguizhou	0.68**	0.180**	0.52**	0.08
lnGuangxi	0.68**	0.15**	0.38*	0.06	lnWyunnan	0.68**	0.183**	0.53**	0.09
lnChongqing	0.69**	0.17**	0.44*	0.08	lnWtibet	0.68**	0.177**	0.51**	0.09
lnSichuan	0.69**	0.18**	0.48**	0.09	lnWshaanxi	0.68**	0.177**	0.49**	0.08
lnGuizhou	0.69**	0.13*	0.30	0.15**	lnWgansu	0.69**	0.177**	0.46**	0.09
lnYunnan	0.69**	0.09	0.15	0.09	lnWqinghai	0.68**	0.178**	0.50**	0.09
lnTibet	0.68**	0.18	0.22	0.08	lnWningxia	0.68**	0.179**	0.51**	0.09
lnShaanxi	0.68**	0.17**	0.43*	0.09	lnWxinjiang	0.68**	0.183**	0.54**	0.09

Notes: C refers to constant. C&T represents constant & trend. Asterisk *, ** and *** indicates the rejection of the null hypothesis at level of confidence 10%, 5% and 1% respectively. The null and alternative hypothesis are respectively H_0 = series is stationary and H_1 = unit roots (series is non-stationary). The selection of lag length is based on the Newey-West bandwidth to be automatically choosing the optimal lag length.

At first difference, the null hypothesis cannot be rejected for 29 variables at conventional significance levels in all cases both with trend and without trend. 34 variables are stationary only when tested with trend. 5 variables are stationary when tested without trend only. Only 2 variables (lnWDGDP and lnJiangxi) are found to be non-stationary according to the KPSS tests.

In summary, among these tests, at least two tests find that most of these variables are stationary with trend or without trend at first difference. Only one variable (Chongqing) passes one test (Only the KPSS tests find it stationary, the other two tests prove it non-stationary). Combining the results of unit root tests, it is concluded that all variables are stationary at first difference. Thus first-differences of all variables (growth rates) are used to estimate the models.

If variables are I (1), it is clear that Johansen cointegration test should be performed before selecting the appropriate model. If variables are not cointegrated, the VAR model can be estimated in first differences of the variables. If cointegration exists among the variables, meaning there exist longrun economic relationships between variables, then the modeling should be in the VECM form, which includes the error correction term.

However, this study does not perform Johansen cointegration test and directly estimate the SVAR model in first difference. The reasons are as follows.

First, in fact, the data in this study is not ideal to use asymptotically valid VECM. The small sample sizes (only 34 years) together with the low data frequency (annual data) are likely insufficient to identify meaningful long-run relationships in the data. Furthermore, Bewley, Orden, Yang and Fisher (1994) indicate that small sample problems of bias and kurtosis obscure the appropriate method for estimating cointegrated systems. Johansen and Juselius (1990) also point out that cointegration test does not generally lead to a unique determination of cointegrating relationships. This is meaningless from an economic point of view as interpreting estimated cointegrated variables can be difficult when more than two cointegrating relationships exist.

Second, the purpose of this study is to examine the regional effects of monetary policy. Impulse response function is an essential tool to evaluate the effectiveness of a policy change. Therefore, impulse response analysis is the main focus of this study. This approach has been commonly used in the literature on measuring the effects of monetary policy shocks, such as Carlino and DeFina (1998, 1999) and Di Giacinto (2003). SVAR model has some advantages in interpreting impulse response function. It provides a framework for incorporating identifying restrictions (contempaneous and short-term relationships) derived from economic theory for the innovations to be traced out in an impulse response function and may convey useful information on the relations of variables (Lütkepohl, 2006). Benkwitz, Lütkepohl and Wolters (2001) point out that adding restrictions based on economic theory to the shortrun dynamics of a system can improve the precision of estimated impulse response, leading to a more informative picture of the dynamic interactions between the concerned variables.

As annual data are used in this study, the contemporaneous relationship of variables is of special importance. Failing to account for this could lead to underestimation of the responses of variables to monetary policy. The main advantage of the SVAR model comparing with the VAR and the VECM is that it can measure the contemporaneous relationship of variables. Thus first-differences of all variables are used to estimate the SVAR models.

In addition, at short horizon, VECM estimates are known to be perform poorly relative to those from a SVAR, this property will affect impulse response function (Naka & Tufte, 1997). Faust and Leeper (1997) also prove that relying on long-run restrictions to derive short-run and medium-run implications can be highly misleading. Moreover, the impulse response derived from the VECM may show the variables not returning to their original levels given that they are integrated. As some shocks may have permanent effects, the impulse response may not converge to zero, the total cumulative impulse response will generally not exist (Lütkepohl & Krätzig, 2004). For this reason, this study may not be able to make conclusive statements on the dynamics of outputs in response to a temporary monetary shock (Georgopoulos, 1999). In addition, while Johansen cointegration test does not specifically reject an unrestricted VAR, it does indicate that imposing a cointegrating restriction will offer an efficiency improvement (Naka & Tufte, 1997).

Third, China is a transition economy. The estimation period in this study is properly the time of China's economic reform and opening up, switching from a centrally planned economy to a market system. During this period, there happen a lot of changes related to the price mechanism (artificially low price to market price), the central government development strategies and large regional disparity, the reform of monetary instruments and monetary policy, and so on. For mature market economies, there may exists a long time period of data with relatively stable regimes (Elbourne & de Haan, 2006). But for China' only 34-year (1978 – 2011) economic reform and opening up, due to comprehensive changes in the economic area, we would not expect the data to show a stable long-run relationship. In short, in this study, the SVAR model in first difference is directly estimated to measure the regional effects of monetary policy.

5.2.3 Impulse Responses of the Inter-Regional SVAR Model for Each Region with Spillover Effect

In the inter-regional SVAR model for each region with spillover effect, this section will compare the impulse responses of all variables to different monetary policy variables (M2, M1, BLR) in order to select the proper monetary policy indicator. In the identification scheme analyzed in Chapter 4, two assumptions are raised: one is that monetary policy affects the real economy with one period lag. The other one is that for annual data, monetary policy can affect the real economy within one period. Different assumptions produce different orders of variables. Therefore, for the first assumption, the identification order is *EGDP*,

MGDP, *WGDP*, *Price*, *MP*. Monetary policy variable ranks the last. For the second assumption, the identification order is *MP*, *EGDP*, *MGDP*, *WGDP*, *Price*. Monetary policy variable ranks the first. Firstly M2 is used as monetary policy variable in the first regional SVAR model. This section also examines which order is more proper for all the endogenous variables: the first order (*EGDP*, *MGDP*, *WGDP*, *Price*, *MP*) or the second order (*MP*, *EGDP*, *MG-DP*, *WGDP*, *Price*).

In the SVAR estimation process, a critical problem is the choice of lag lengths, as the statistic of interest are functions of the order of the autoregressive lag polynomial. EViews 6.0 provides five criteria for lag order selection: the general-to-specific sequential Likelihood Ratio Test (LR), the Final Prediction Error (FPR), the Akaike Information Criterion (AIC), the Schwarz Criterion (SC) and the Hannan-Quinn Information Criterion (HQ). The FPE and the AIC are asymptotically equivalent (Lütkepohl, 2005). In small samples, the AIC and the FPE may have better properties (choose the correct order more often) than the HQ and the SC (Lütkepohl, 2005). Thus, in small as well as large samples, models based on the AIC and the FPE may produce superior forecasts although they may not estimate the orders correctly. But if consistency is the yardstick for evaluating the criteria, the SC and the HQ are superior than the AIC and the FPE. Lütkepohl (2005) indicates that for lower order the VAR processes, the most parsimonious the SC criterion is found to do quite well in terms of choosing the correct VAR order and providing good forecasting models. Therefore, in this study, the optimal lag length is mainly determined with the AIC criteria and the SC criteria. If there is a contradiction between the AIC and the SC, then the LR standard is checked. Meanwhile, the other criteria are also referred to and the SVAR must satisfy the conditions of stationarity.

5.2.3.1 Impulse Responses to M2 (Rank Last)

First of all, M2 is used as monetary policy variable. The order of endogenous variables is the first order: *EGDP*, *MGDP*, *WGDP*, *Price*, *MP*. The first inter-regional SVAR model is run in EViews 6. 0, the lag length is one. The identification matrices are five order matrix *A* and matrix *B*. All inverse roots lie inside the unit circle, showing that the estimated regional SVAR model is stable. The model is just identified through structural factorization with matrix *A* and matrix *B*. Impulse response functions are employed to investigate the dynamic impact of monetary policy shocks on the SVAR system. They are the plots of the effects of one shock on current and all future variables. They show how endogenous variables react to monetary policy shock. Cumulative impulse response is the sum over impulse response functions. Long-run cumulated response is the stable level of cumulative impulse response as time goes on. Then the first inter-regional SVAR generated impulse response graphs can be seen in Figure 5. 1 and Figure 5. 2. Please notice that in this model, M2 ranks at the last place.

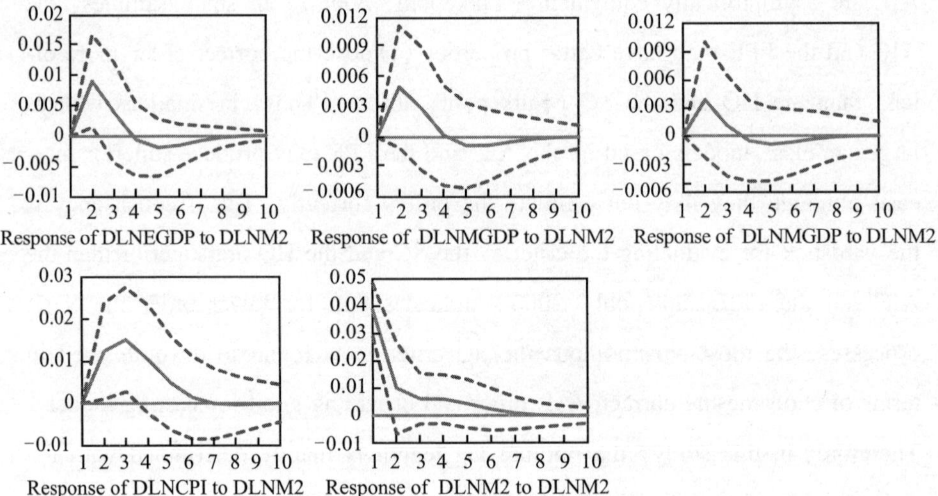

Figure 5. 1 Response to Structural One S. D. Innovations ± 2 S. E. (M2 rank last)

Figure 5. 1 displays the impulse responses to structural one-standard-deviation (3. 8752%) unanticipated increase in M2 Change. The solid lines represent the point estimate of variables' impulse responses. The dashed lines show plus/minus two standard error bands (analytic). As this study assumes monetary policy affects other variables with one period lag, the responses of three regions' GDP growth begin to increase after one year, reach the peak at the second year and then decline gradually and finally die out to zero. The impulse responses indicate that monetary policy shocks have their maximum impacts on real GDP growth of the East, the Middle and the West at the 2nd year. But the magnitudes of the responses are very different. The *EGDP* growth shows a maximum 0.9139% increase at the 2nd year, while the growth of *MGDP* and *WGDP* increase maximum 0.5082% and 0.3855%. The response of price increase reaches its peak at the 3rd year, later decreases gradually to zero. The response of *EGDP* growth is significant within 2 years, while that of *MGDP* growth and *WGDP* growth are insignificant during the whole period.

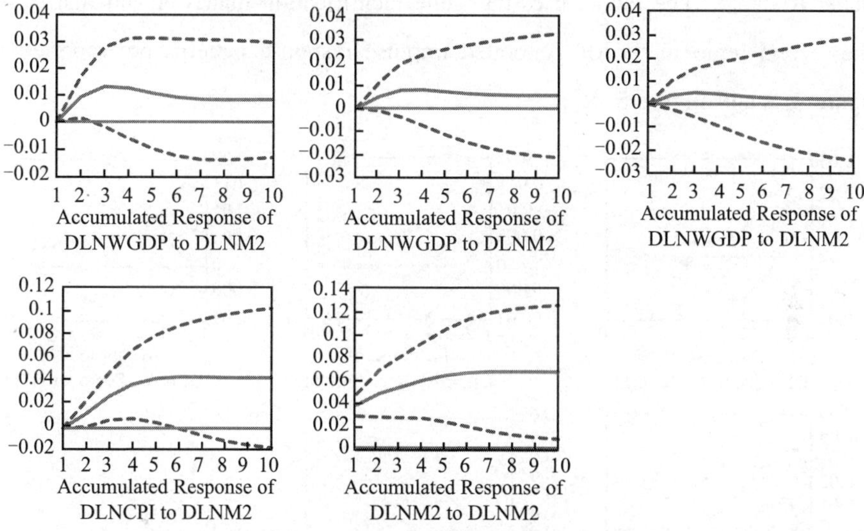

Figure 5.2 Accumulated Response to Structural One S. D. Innovations ±2 S. E. (M2 rank last)

Figure 5.2 shows accumulated responses to structural one S. D. (3.8752%) unanticipated increase in M2 Change. The cumulative maximum increase of the *EGDP* growth is 1.3080% at the 3rd year. After 6 years, it remains stable and approaches to 0.8301% at the 10th year. The growth of *MGDP* reaches its cumulative peak (0.8166%) at the 3rd year. Then the response decreases gradually and after 6 years it remains stable (0. 5756% at the 10th year). The maximum cumulative increase of *WGDP* growth is 0. 4947% at the 3rd year. Then the response decreases gradually and finally it remains stable at 0. 2299% at the 10th year. The responses of *M*2 and *CPI* increase gradually and remain stable after 6 years.

5. 2. 3. 2 Impulse Response to M2 (Rank First)

The second order of the variables is like this: *MP*, *EGDP*, *MGDP*, *WGDP*, *Price*. Here M2 ranks first, indicating that monetary policy can affect the real economy within one year. The second inter-regional SVAR model is estimated using the second order of variables. The lag length is one and this SVAR model is stable. The model uses the same identification matrix *A* and matrix *B*. The second regional SVAR generated impulse response patterns are reported in Figure 5. 3 and Figure 5. 4.

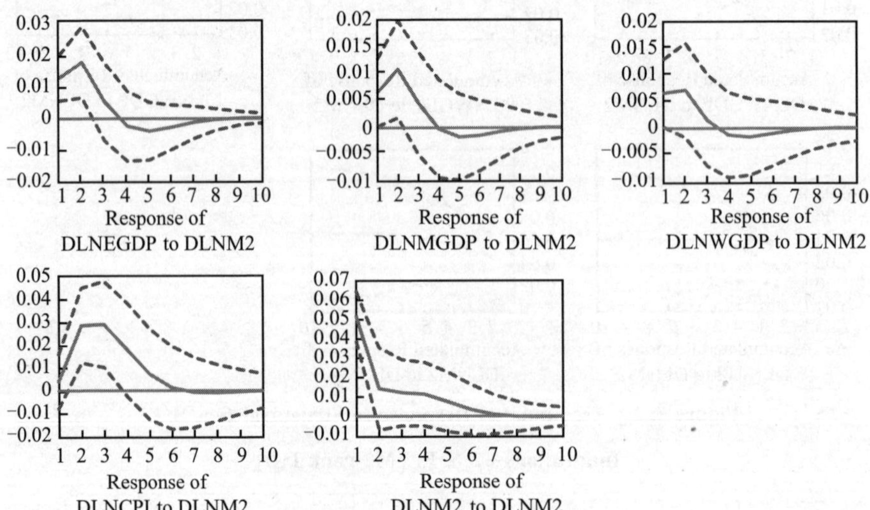

Figure 5. 3 Response to Structural One S. D. Innovations ±2 S. E. (M2 rank first)

Figure 5. 3 displays the impulse responses to structural one-standard-deviation (5. 1580%) unanticipated increase in M2 Change. *EGDP* growth begins to increase at the 1st year and reaches a significant maximum 1. 7955% increase at the 2nd year. Then the response is insignificant and becomes negative after the 4th year and then dies out to zero gradually. The growth of *MGDP* has its maximum increase of 1. 0990% at the 2nd year and the maximum increase (0. 7182%) of *WGDP* growth is at the 2nd year. While the response of MGDP is significant within 2 years, the response of WGDP is not significant during the whole period. The response of the price level reaches its peak (2. 9162%) at the 3rd year, then decreases gradually to zero.

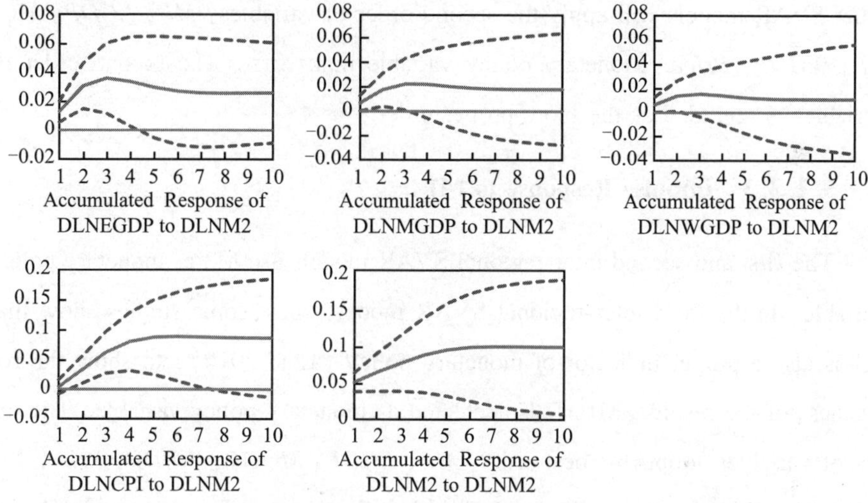

Figure 5. 4 Accumulated Response to Structural One S. D. Innovations ±2 S. E. (M2 rank first)

Figure 5. 4 shows accumulated response to structural one S. D. (5. 1580%) unanticipated increase in M2 Change. The maximum cumulative increase of *EGDP* growth is 3. 6293% at the 3rd year. After 6 years, the cumulative response remains stable (2. 6072%, at the 10th year). The cumulated maximum increase of *MGDP* growth is 2. 2309% at the 3rd year. Then the response decreases gradually and remain stable (1. 8056%) at the 10th year. The maximum cumulative increase of *WGDP* growth is 1. 5365% at the 3rd year and the response remains stable at 1. 0991% at the 10th year. The responses of M2 and CPI increase gradually and remain stable after 6 years.

Comparing the impulse responses of the first and second inter-regional

SVAR models, the results of the second one are much better. Allowing monetary policy to influence output and price instantaneously, the responses of all variables are much bigger. The cumulative response of *MGDP* growth in the first model becomes stable after 6 years and remains at 0. 5756% in the 10th year, after allowing monetary policy to influence output and price instantaneously, the cumulative response of *MGDP* growth remains stable at 1. 8056% in the 10th year. Therefore, the second order of variables is better than the first order. So later on other SVAR models will apply the second order of variables: *MP*, *EGDP*, *MGDP*, *WGDP*, *Price*. Monetary policy variable ranks first. The second order of variables is regarded as the more proper order.

5. 2. 3. 3 Impulse Response to M1

The first and second inter-regional SVAR models use M2 as monetary policy variable. In the third inter-regional SVAR model, since some studies show that M1 is also a proper indicator of monetary policy (Liu, 2010), to show the robustness of the results, M1 is also selected as monetary policy variable. The order of variables adopts the best order: *MP*, *EGDP*, *MGDP*, *WGDP*, *Price*. M1 ranks first. The lag length is one. The identification matrices are matrix *A* and matrix *B*. This model is also stable and the third inter-regional SVAR generated impulse response graphs are plotted in Figure 5. 5 and Figure 5. 6.

Figure 5. 5 displays the impulse responses to structural one-standard-deviation (7. 0196%) unanticipated increase in M1 Change. Three regions' changes of GDP growth have the same trend. They firstly increase and reach a peak within 2 years. Then the responses become negative after the 3rd year and converge to zero gradually in the long-run. The *EGDP* growth reaches a peak (1. 3085%) at the 2nd year. The growth of *MGDP* displays its maximum increase of 1. 0049% at the 2nd year and the maximum increase of the *WGDP* growth (0. 7098%) is at the 2nd year. The response of the price reaches its peak (3. 0541%) at the 2nd year, and decreases gradually and finally converges to zero.

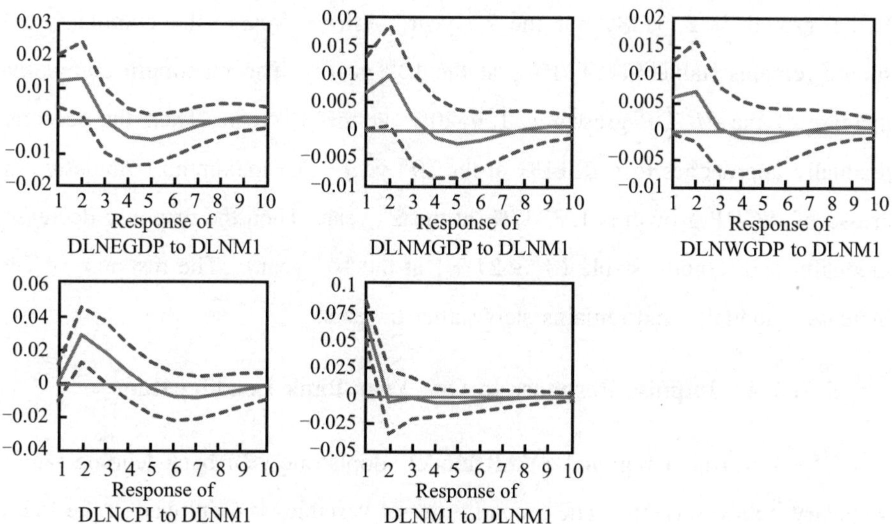

Figure 5.5 Response to Structural One S. D. Innovations ±2 S. E. (M1)

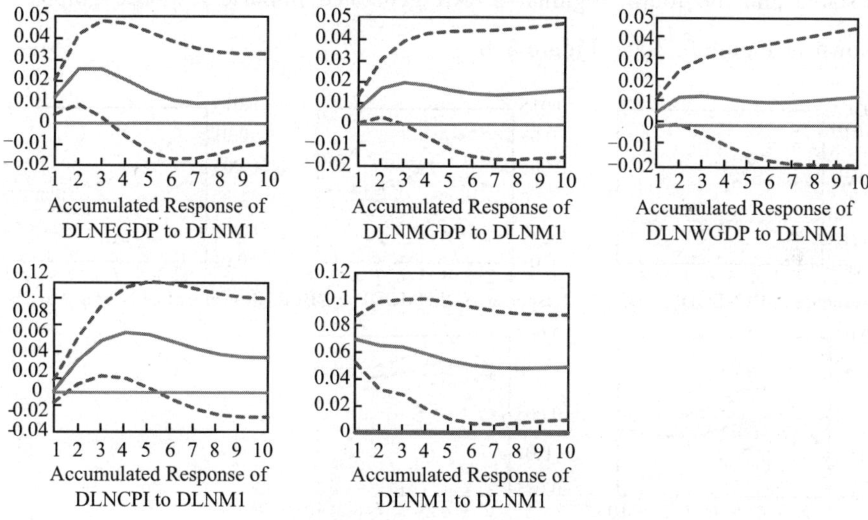

Figure 5.6 Accumulated Response to Structural One S. D. Innovations ±2 S. E. (M1)

Figure 5.6 shows accumulated response to the innovation (7.0196%) of M1. In the whole period, the cumulative responses of three regions' GDP growth remain positive. Cumulated responses of three regions reach a peak within 3 years and goes to stable after 6 years. The maximum cumulated increase of the

EGDP growth is 2.5443% at the 2nd year. After 6 years, the cumulative response remains stable (1.2143%, at the 10th year). The maximum cumulative increase of the *MGDP* growth is 1.9520% at the 3rd year. Then the response gradually approaches to 1.6114% at the 10th year. The maximum cumulative increase of *WGDP* growth is 1.3737% at the 3rd year. Then the response decreases gradually and remains stable (1.3624%, at the 10th year). The response of CPI increases gradually and remains stable after 6 years.

5.2.3.4 Impulse Response to One Year Bank Lending Rate

The fourth inter-regional SVAR model adopts one year bank lending rate as monetary policy variable. The second order of variables is employed in the fourth model. Bank lending rate (BLR) ranks first. The lag length is one. This model is stable and the fourth regional SVAR generated impulse response graphs are shown in Figure 5.7 and Figure 5.8.

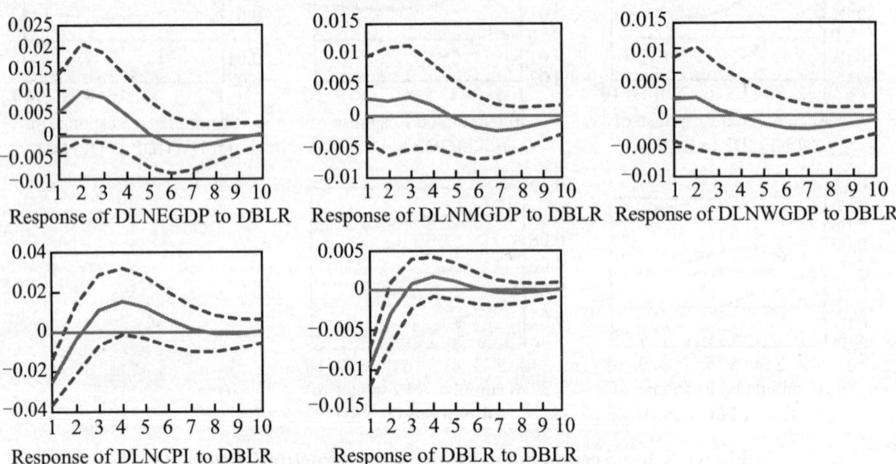

Figure 5.7 Response to Structural One S. D. Innovations ±2 S. E. (BLR)

Figure 5.7 displays the impulse response to structural one-standard-deviation (0.9533%, about 95 basis points) unanticipated decrease in the BLR Change. Three regions' changes of GDP growth firstly increase (the response of *MGDP* display a little reduce at the 2nd year) and reach a peak within 3 years. Then the responses decrease gradually and become negative after the 4th year (*WGDP*) or the 5th year (*EGDP* and *MGDP*). Finally they approach to zero gradually. The *EGDP* growth increases maximum 1. 0015% at the 2nd year. The growth of *MGDP* has its maximum increase (0. 2991%) at the 3rd year and the maximum increase (0. 2897%) of *WGDP* growth is at the 2nd year. In the whole period, the responses of three regions' GDP growth are not significant. In the 1st year, the change of price decreases, indicating that the price feels the shock of interest rate with a lag. Then it increases gradually and reaches its peak (1. 5577%) at the 4th year, then decrease gradually to zero.

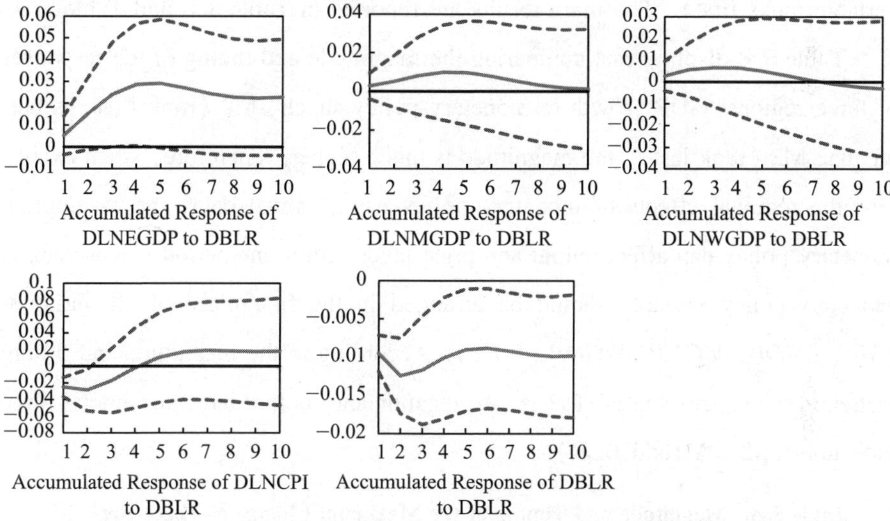

Figure 5. 8 Accumulated Response to Structural One S. D. Innovations ±2 S. E. (BLR)

Figure 5. 8 shows accumulated response to the innovation (0. 9533%, about 95 basis points, decrease) of BLR. The maximum cumulative increase of *EGDP* growth is 2. 9019% at the 5th year. After 6 years, the cumulative response remains stable (2. 2692%, at the 10th year). The maximum cumulative increase of *MGDP* growth is 0. 9882% at the 4th year. Then the response decreases gradually and converges to 0. 1250% at the 10th year. Maximum cumulative increase of *WGDP* growth is 0. 6557% at the 3rd year. Later the response decreases gradually and remains stable (−0. 3027% , at the 10th year). The response of CPI change is negative within 4 years (price puzzle) and then increases gradually and remains stable (positive) after 6 years.

5. 2. 3. 5 Summary

In summary, four inter-regional SVAR models with spillover effect display three regions' responses to monetary policy variable (M2, M1 and BLR). The order of variables is also changed to test the robustness of the results. After comparison, the results show that the second order is more proper (monetary policy variable ranks first). The main results are reported in Table 5. 8 and Table 5. 9.

Table 5. 8 displays that comparing the magnitude and timing of the responses of three regions' GDP growth to monetary policy shock, M2 (rank first) is better than M2 (rank last), the magnitude is much bigger. Therefore, when examining the regional effects of monetary policy using annual data, the assumption monetary policy can affect output and price level within one period is reasonable. Monetary policy variable should be arranged in the first place of all variables (*MP*, *EGDP*, *MGDP*, *WGDP*, *Price*). According to the magnitude and timing of three regions' responses, M2 is a better monetary policy indicator among three indicators (M2, M1 and BLR).

Table 5. 8 Magnitude and Timing of the Maximum Change of Three Regions' GDP Growth to Monetary Policy Innovation

Item	Monetary Policy	EGDP Growth		MGDP Growth		WGDP Growth	
	Innovation (%)	Mag. (%)	Timing	Mag. (%)	Timing	Mag. (%)	Timing
M2 (rank last)	3. 88	0. 91	2	0. 51	2	0. 39	2
M2 (rank first)	5. 16	1. 80	2	1. 10	2	0. 72	1
M1 (rank first)	7. 02	1. 31	1	1. 00	2	0. 71	2
RATE (rank first)	−0. 95	1. 00	2	0. 30	3	0. 29	2

Table 5. 9 Magnitude and Timing of the Cumulative Change of Three Regions' GDP Growth to Monetary Policy Innovation

Item	Monetary Policy	EGDP Growth		MGDP Growth		WGDP Growth	
	Innovation (%)	Mag. (%)	Timing	Mag. (%)	Timing	Mag. (%)	Timing
M2 (rank last)	3. 88	1. 31	3	0. 82	4	0. 49	3
		0. 83	10	0. 58	10	0. 23	10

continuous

Item	Monetary Policy Innovation (%)	EGDP Growth Mag. (%)	EGDP Growth Timing	MGDP Growth Mag. (%)	MGDP Growth Timing	WGDP Growth Mag. (%)	WGDP Growth Timing
M2 (rank first)	5.16	3.63	3	2.23	3	1.54	3
		2.61	10	1.81	10	1.10	10
Ml (rank first)	7.02	2.54	3	1.95	3	1.37	3
		1.21	10	1.61	10	1.36	10
RATE (rank first)	-0.95	2.91	5	0.99	4	0.66	3
		2.27	10	0.12	10	-0.30	10

Table 5.9 shows the maximum cumulative response and long-run cumulated response (10 years) of three regions. According to the maximum cumulative response (when comparing the magnitude, the monetary policy innovation is adjusted to the same size), as a monetary policy indicator, M2 behaves much better than Ml and BLR. Based on the long-run response level, M2 is also a better indicator of monetary policy stance. Therefore, M2 is considered the best measure of monetary policy. When examining the regional effects of monetary policy, M2 (rank first) is adopted as the benchmark monetary policy variable, Ml and BLR are also used as complementary analysis.

According to Table 5.8 and Table 5.9 (M2 ranks first, the benchmark analysis), when there is an unanticipated increase (5.16%) in M2 change, *EGDP* growth shows the biggest magnitude of increase (1.80%), almost 1.6 times of the response of *MGDP* growth, 2.5 times of the response of WGDP growth. The results are similar as the cumulative maximum change of three regions' GDP growth to M2 shock (3.63%, 2.23% and 1.54%). As for the long-run cumulative response level, the cumulative response of *EGDP* growth is positive (2.61%), the one of *MGDP* growth is about 1.81% and that of *WGDP* growth is 1.10%. The results indicate that common monetary policy greatly prompts the economic growth in the East, while at the same time the Middle and the West get less support from monetary policy. The gap among three regions keeps widening.

5.2.3.6 The Spillover Effect

The main advantage of the former inter-regional SVAR analysis is that it considers the spillover effects among three regions. It is argued that when examining the regional effects of monetary policy, the influence of spillover effect should be emphasized and the shortcoming of previous studies is that they do not consider this effect. As the previous studies without accounting for the spillover effect use different control variables, different periods and different region divisions, furthermore, most of the previous literature does not provide the exact size of monetary policy shock. Therefore, direct comparison of the results is impossible and unmeaning. In this section, inter-regional SVAR models for each region without spillover effect are developed to make a contrast and highlight the importance of the spillover effect.

The inter-regional SVAR models for each region without spillover effect use regional variables. Three SVAR models are estimated for three regions. Eastern SVAR model contains *EM*2, *EGDP* and *ECPI* (price level measured by CPI in the East). Middle SVAR model consists of *MM*2, *MGDP* and *MCPI* (price level measured by CPI in the Middle). Western SVAR model involves *WM*2, *WGDP* and *WCPI* (price level measured by CPI in the West). In the SVAR model for each region, *WDGDP* is also included as an exogenous variable. As the regional data of M2 is not available, total CNY deposits of financial institutions in each region are employed to represent regional M2. The estimation procedures are the same as the regional SVAR model. The lag lengths of three models are both one and the models are stable. The impulse response and cumulative impulse response of each region are reported in Figure 5. 9.

To see the importance of spillover effects clearly, the results of SVAR models for each region with spillover effect and without spillover effect are displayed and compared in Table 5. 10. According to Table 5. 10, when accounting for the spillover effects, in the short-run, three regions respond much bigger. The maximum impulse response and cumulative response of *EGDP* growth increase more than 70%. The one in the Middle increase more than 50%. That in the West also increases about 4% – 15%. This means the spillover effect is very important

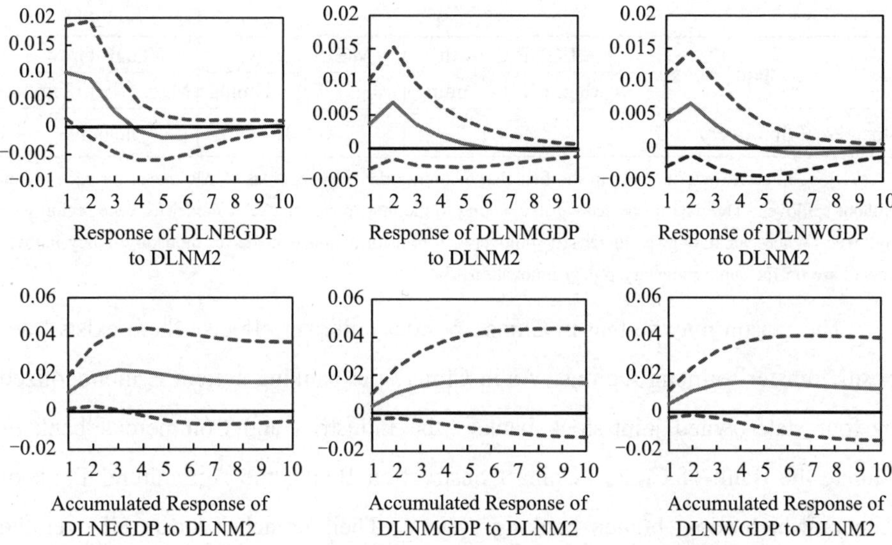

Figure 5. 9 Response and Accumulated Response to Structural One S. D. Innovations ± 2 S. E. (M2)

in the short-run. According to Figure 5. 9, in the long-run, three regions' responses are both positive without accounting for the spillover effects. When considering the spillover effects, the long-run response of *EGDP* growth increases more than 70%, the increase of long-run responses in the Middle is about 32%. However, that in the West is negative.

Table 5. 10 Summary of Responses to M2

Item	EGDP Growth		MGDP Growth		WGDP Growth	
	Mag. (%)	Timing	Mag. (%)	Timing	Mag. (%)	Timing
Monetary policy innovation	5. 52		6. 00		5. 46	
	5. 16		5. 16		5. 16	
Maximum impulse response	1. 01	1	0. 69	2	0. 67	2
	1. 80	2	1. 10	2	0. 72	1
Increase (Spillover)	90. 65		85. 37		13. 71	
Maximum cumulative impulse response	2. 16	3	1. 60	4	1. 56	4
	3. 63	3	2. 23	3	1. 54	3
Increase (Spillover)	79. 78		62. 06		4. 46	
Long run level	1. 57	10	1. 59	10	1. 22	10
	2. 61	10	1. 81	10	1. 10	10

continuous

Item	EGDP Growth		MGDP Growth		WGDP Growth	
	Mag. (%)	Timing	Mag. (%)	Timing	Mag. (%)	Timing
Increase (Spillover)	77.84		32.37		negative	

Notes: In each row, the data in the first line belong to the inter-regional SVAR model for each region without spillover. The data in the second line belong to the inter-regional SVAR model for each region with spillover. When calculating the increase (spillover), a transformation is made for monetary policy innovation (base on the same monetary policy innovation, 5%).

The reason may be that in China, besides spillover effects, there exists "deposits transfer" among regions. As in China, the banking system is monopolized by four state-owned joint-stock banks (the Industrial and Commercial bank of China, the Bank of China, China Construction Bank, the Agricultural Bank of China) which adopt branch banking system. Their branches locate all over the country. In the past fourty years, there is a general phenomenon their branches collect a lot of deposits in the less developed provinces from the West. However, these deposits are not fully used to support the development of these less developed provinces in the West. As the coastal provinces (the East) develop much faster, some of the deposits are transferred to support the development of these coastal provinces by the branches of these four banks. The Research Group of Wuhan Branch of PBC (2002) indicates that the credit supply of financial institutions fails to satisfy the needs of real economy in less developed regions where huge outflow of deposits cause the deposits cannot be translated into investment effectively.

In the inter-regional SVAR model, M2 is used as monetary policy variable. In the short-run, the spillover effect works as the deposits have no time to transfer. Therefore, in the short-run, the spillover effects are very significant. But in the long-run, the deposits have plenty time to transfer from the less developed West to the more developed East. Then in the long-run, when considering the spillover effects, to some extent, the negative influence of the deposits transfer weakens the positive impacts of spillover effects in the West. Thus the long-run cumulative response of *WGDP* growth is rather small. But if it is assumed that all the deposits focus on supporting the development of its own region (the models for each region), the long-run cumulative responses of *WGDP* growth become bigger. Due to the geography and location factor, the West always fails to have enough money to develop its economy in the past. In the long-run, some deposits transfer from the less undeveloped provinces in the West to the more developed provinces in the East. This phenomenon makes the problem of short of money in the West even worse. Meanwhile, the East gets more funds to support its economic growth. The gap among regions keeps widening. This finding also indicates that the previous studies which examine the regional effects of monetary policy region by region without accounting for the spillover effects may to some extent overestimate the response of the West, but underestimate the effects of monetary policy in the East in the long-run.

This explanation also can be proved by Figure 5. 6. M1 mainly contains cash and demand deposit. It is highly liquid and not likely to transfer across regions. Therefore, the long-run level of cumulative response of the East is smaller, the long-run level of cumulative responses of *WGDP* growth is bigger in Figure 5. 6.

Someone may criticize that in the inter-regional SVAR model for each region without spillover effect, total CNY deposits of financial institutions in each region are used as a proxy of regional M2. This proxy itself may account for the spillover effects to some extent. To show the robustness of the results, one year bank lending rate (BLR) is employed as monetary policy variable in three inter-regional SVAR models for each region. The reason is that in the regional model and models for each region, monetary policy indicator is both BLR, not like M2, after all, M2 used in the regional and total CNY deposits of financial institutions in each region employed in the models for each region are not totally the same. The results are shown in Figure 5. 10 and Table 5. 11. The spillover effect is also very important and the findings are rather robust.

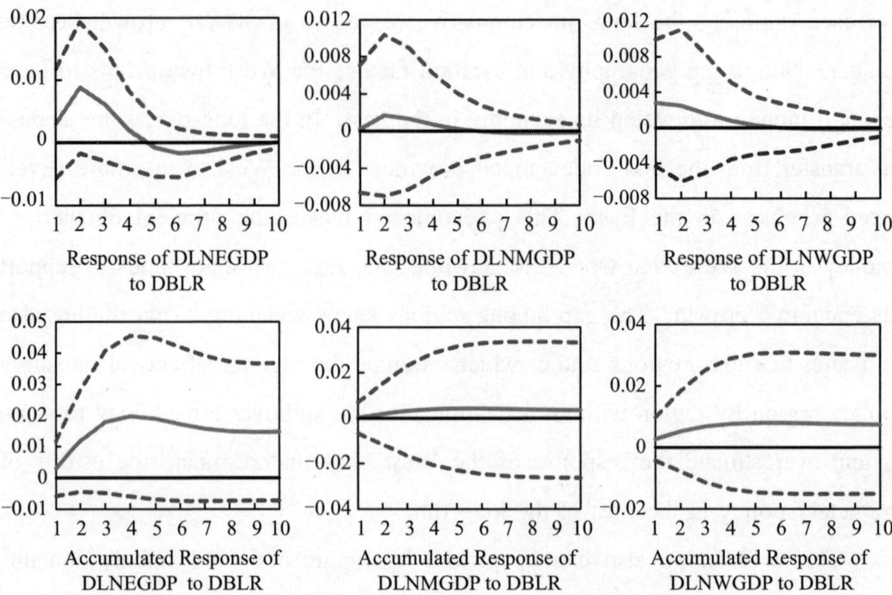

Figure 5.10 Response and Accumulated Response to Structural One S. D. Innovations ±2 S. E. (BLR)

Table 5.11 Summary of Responses to BLR

Item	East GDP Growth		Middle GDP Growth		West GDP Growth	
	Mag. (%)	Timing	Mag. (%)	Timing	Mag. (%)	Timing
Monetary policy innovation	−0.95		−1.00		−1.00	
	−0.95		−0.95		−0.95	
Maximum impulse response	0.88	2	0.17	2	0.28	1
	1.00	2	0.30	3	0.29	2
Increase (Spillover)	14		85		8	
Maximum cumulative impulse response	1.98	4	—	—	—	—
	2.90	5	0.99	4	0.66	3
Increase (Spillover)	47		—		—	
Long run level	1.48	10	0.35	10	1.56	10
	2.27	10	0.13	10	−0.43	10
Increase (Spillover)	52.17		negative		negative	

Notes: In each row, the data in the first line belong to the SVAR model for each region. The data in the second line belong to the regional SVAR model. When calculating the increase (spillover), we make a transformation and base on the same monetary policy innovation (−1%).

5. 2. 3. 7 Summary

This section examines three regions' responses to different monetary policy variables (M2, M1 and BLR). The results show that M2 is a better monetary policy indicator as M2 provides more satisfactory and robust results. This finding is consistent with the results of Song and Zhong (2006) and Kong et al. (2007). This finding is also in accord with the reality, the PBC always regards M2 as intermediate target (Xie, 2004). The two orders of the variables are also checked and the second order (monetary policy variable ranks first) is much better, meaning that when using annual data, the assumption that monetary policy can affect the real economy with one year is more reasonable (Di Giacinto, 2003). The results confirm that three regions respond differently to monetary policy, the East shows the biggest response, the next one is the Middle. The response of the West is smallest among them. These findings confirm that in China, common monetary policy has different impacts on regional economies. The regional effects of monetary policy widen the gap among three regions.

Liu (2010) argues that M1 behaviors better than M2 as a monetary policy indicator, since that the impulse response yields the wrong sign. In this study, the responses of three regions to the innovation of M2 are considered reasonable and consistent with the reality. The results show that both in the short-run and long-run, the spillover effect is very important. But in the long-run, in the west, the negative influence of deposits transfer to some extent weakens the positive impact of the spillover effects.

It is also found that the previous studies which examine the regional effects of monetary policy without accounting for spillover effects may to some extent underestimate the influences of monetary policy on each region in the short-run. They are likely to overestimate the influences of monetary policy in the West, but underestimate the effects of monetary policy in the East in the long-run.

5. 2. 4 Impulse Responses of the Inter-Regional Model for Each Province with Spillover Effect

5. 2. 4. 1 The Results of the Provincial Models

As China is a huge country with many provinces, just dividing China into three regions and considering the responses of only three regions to monetary policy may be too general. To get more detail, the inter-regional models for each province with spillover effect (for simplicity, the provincial SVAR models) are also estimated to examine each province's response to monetary policy. As there are 31 provinces in Mainland China, 31 provincial SVAR models are developed. The lag length of all provincial benchmark models is one. The identification matrices are six order matrix *A* and matrix *B*. All inverse roots lie inside the unit circle, indicating that estimated provincial SVAR models are stable. The models are just identified through structural factorization with matrix *A* and matrix *B*. The results are summarized in Table 5. 12 and Figure 5. 11 – Figure 5. 13①.

Table 5. 12 Impulse Responses of Each Province (Inter-Regional SVAR Model for Each Province with Spillover)

Province	LRIR10	LRIR6	MCIR	Timing	MIR	Timing
Fujian (E)	0. 037383	0. 041907	0. 046712	3	0. 027542	2
Zhejiang (E)	0. 040301	0. 040243	0. 050439	3	0. 027004	2
Jiangsu (E)	0. 033135	0. 034161	0. 045778	3	0. 021869	2
Hainan (E)	-0. 002983	-0. 009101	0. 031264	2	0. 020517	1
Guangdong (E)	0. 034575	0. 034598	0. 040327	3	0. 020083	2
Tianjin (E)	0. 040926	0. 040108	0. 040944	4	0. 019488	1
Shandong (E)	0. 031076	0. 030242	0. 038602	3	0. 018489	2
Henan (M)	0. 035308	0. 032868	0. 034126	4	0. 018374	2
Shanghai (E)	0. 034565	0. 029158	0. 033885	4	0. 018333	2

① In Table 5. 12, we uniformly adjust the monetary policy shock to 5% in order to make a comparison. While in the Figures, we do not adjust the impulse and plot the original impulse response graph.

continuous

Province	LRIR10	LRIR6	MCIR	Timing	MIR	Timing
Hubei (M)	0. 028756	0. 028806	0. 030669	4	0. 016633	2
Chongqing (W)	0. 011428	0. 017485	0. 025281	3	0. 015115	1
Tibet (W)	0. 037550	0. 040469	0. 045100	4	0. 014589	1
Liaoning (E)	0. 013269	0. 013071	0. 028154	3	0. 014574	1
Anhui (M)	0. 026403	0. 027978	0. 035356	4	0. 013195	2
Beijing (E)	0. 003513	0. 005446	0. 017825	3	0. 012877	1
Hebei (E)	0. 025437	0. 022170	0. 022972	3	0. 012843	2
Guangxi (W)	0. 020500	0. 019219	0. 021980	3	0. 011854	2
Jiangxi (M)	0. 013795	0. 012338	0. 019669	3	0. 010331	2
Jilin (M)	0. 010736	0. 011020	0. 019870	2	0. 010232	2
Yunnan (W)	0. 020733	0. 022079	0. 018875	4	0. 010144	2
Shanxi (M)	-0. 008025	-0. 002411	0. 012124	3	0. 010118	1
Sichuan (W)	0. 020758	0. 019581	0. 018109	2	0. 009366	1
Gansu (W)	0. 011110	0. 013165	0. 017540	4	0. 008522	1
Hunan (M)	0. 008607	0. 009274	0. 012720	3	0. 008244	2
Guizhou (W)	-0. 004386	-0. 003887	0. 007994	1	0. 007994	1
Ningxia (W)	-0. 003713	-0. 001094	0. 007919	3	0. 006961	2
Qinghai (W)	0. 008893	0. 005412	0. 011580	3	0. 004613	2
Heilongjiang (M)	0. 015453	0. 013372	0. 011323	4	0. 003938	2
Shaanxi (W)	-0. 010714	-0. 008925	0. 003219	2	0. 002716	2
Xinjiang (W)	0. 001309	-0. 007202	0. 001700	2	0. 001202	1
Inner Mongolia (W)	-0. 030246	-0. 024012	-0. 013452	4	-0. 004095	1

Notes: LRIR10 is long-run (10 years) cumulative impulse response. LRIR6 represents long-run (6 years) cumulative impulse response. MCIR is maximum cumulative impulse response. MIR is maximum impulse response. The unit of timing is year. (E), (M), (W) mean this province belongs to the East, the Middle or the West.

Table 5. 12 displays the impulse responses to structural one standard deviation (5%) unanticipated increase in M2 Change. In Table 5. 12, the data are sorted according to maximum impulse response. We can see that facing a positive monetary shock, all provinces have their maximum impulse responses within two years. Fujian province shows the biggest maximum impulse response (0. 027542), which means if the growth rate of M2 unexpectedly increases 5%, the maximum increase of GDP growth in Fujian province is 2. 75% at the second year, the long-run (6 years) cumulated increase is 4. 19%. Inner Mongolia goes to the bottom with both the negative maximum impulse response and long run

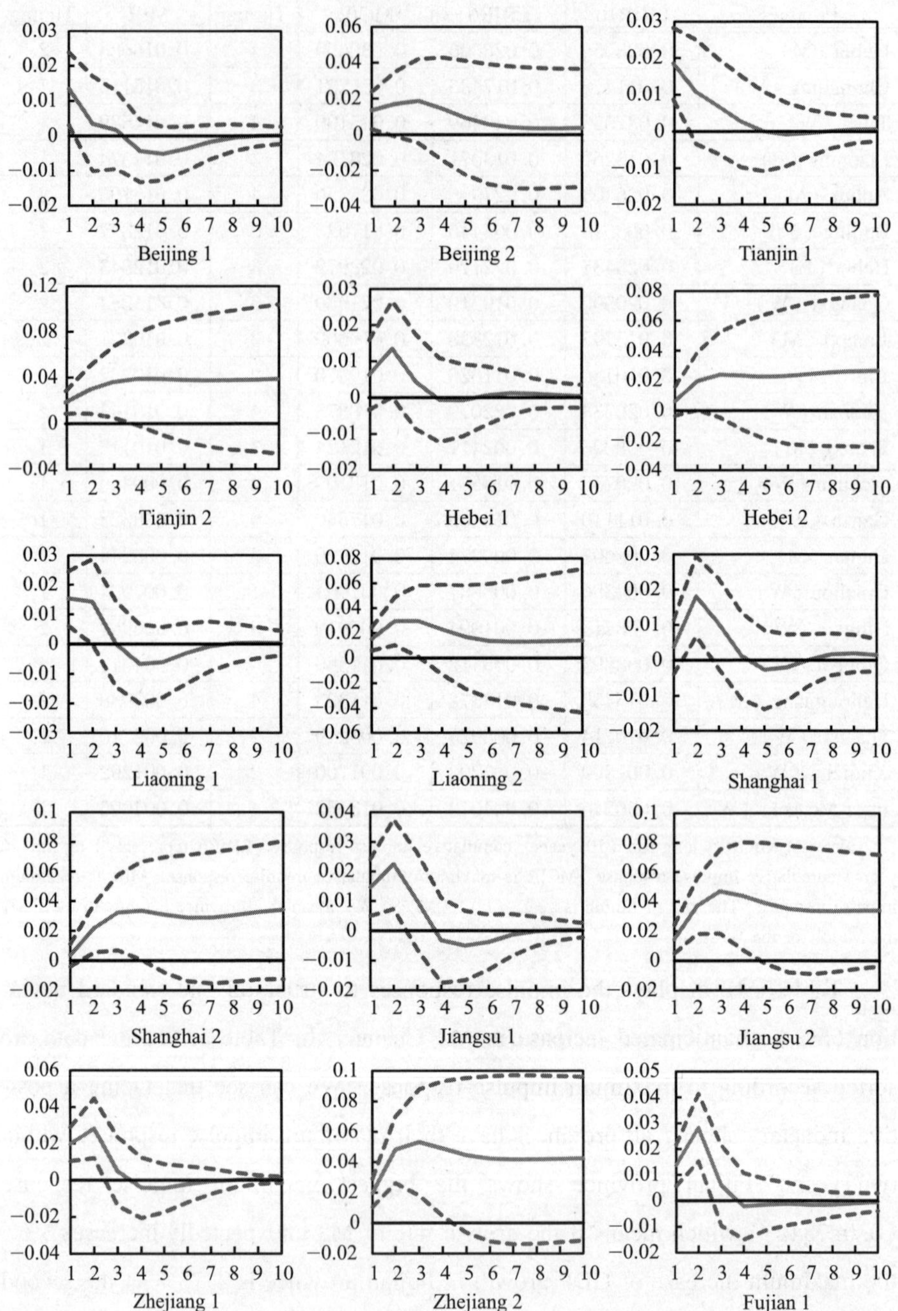
Beijing 1
Beijing 2
Tianjin 1
Tianjin 2
Hebei 1
Hebei 2
Liaoning 1
Liaoning 2
Shanghai 1
Shanghai 2
Jiangsu 1
Jiangsu 2
Zhejiang 1
Zhejiang 2
Fujian 1
1 2 3 4 5 6 7 8 9 10

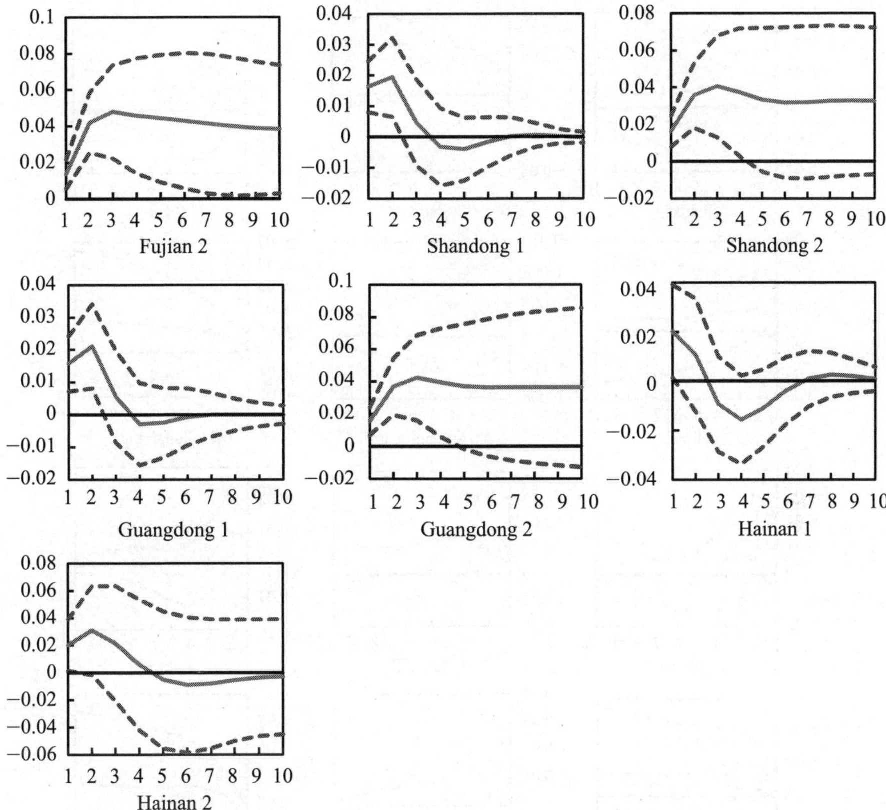

Figure 5. 11 Response and Accumulated Response to Structural One S. D. Innovations ±2 S. E. (M2, the East, provincial SVAR model)

Notes: "Province +1" refers to impulse response of this province to M2. "province +2" means accumulated response of this province to M2.

cumulated response. In top ten maximum impulse responses, eight provinces are located in the East, Henan and Hubei provinces come from the Middle. Liaoning, Beijing and Hebei in the East fail to list in the top ten. In the last ten lists, two provinces belong to the Middle, eight provinces come from the West. Obviously, different provinces respond very differently to the same monetary policy shock. In summary, the provinces in the East show the biggest responses, the next ones are the provinces in the Middle, the provinces in the West rank last. This indicates common monetary policy greatly promotes the economic growth of the East, the Middle is the next one, while at the same time just gives some or

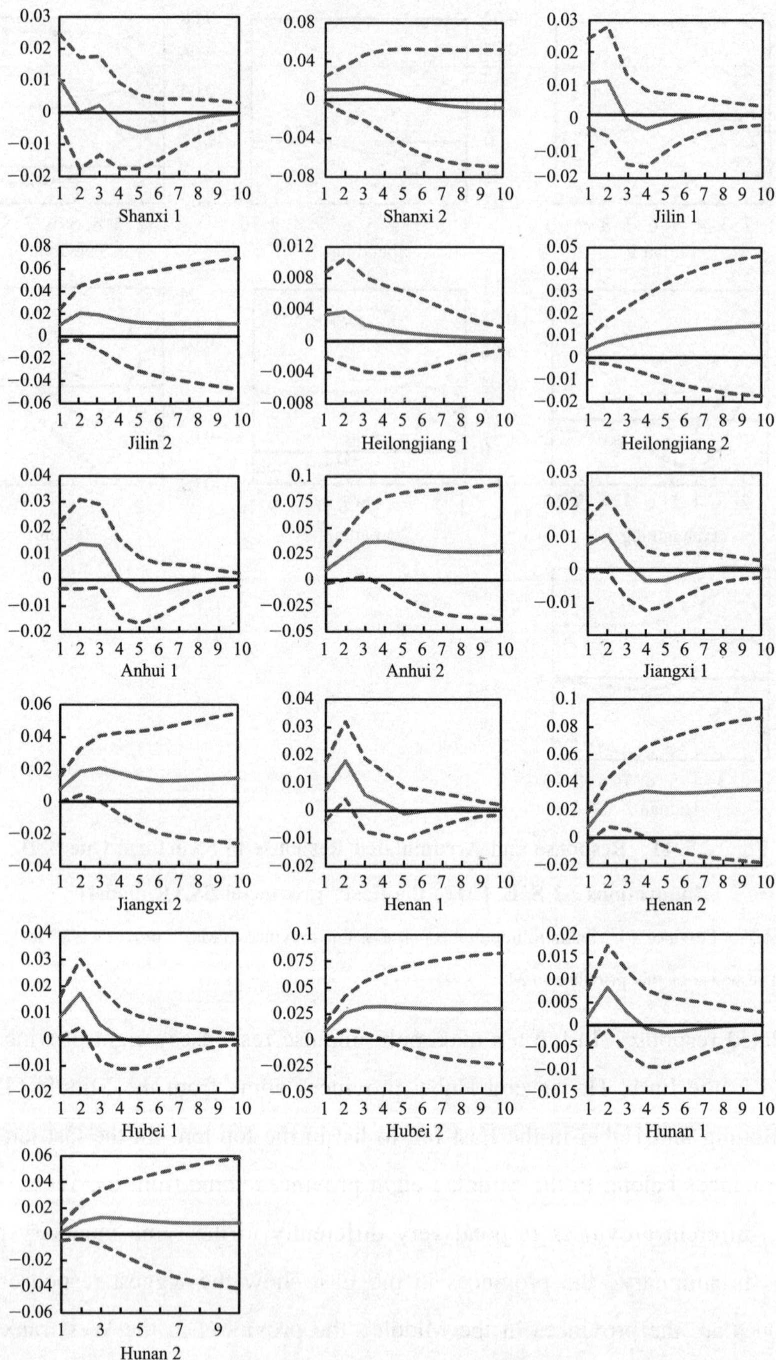

Figure 5. 12 Response and Accumulated Response to Structural One S. D. Innovations ±2 S. E. (M2, the Middle, provincial SVAR model)

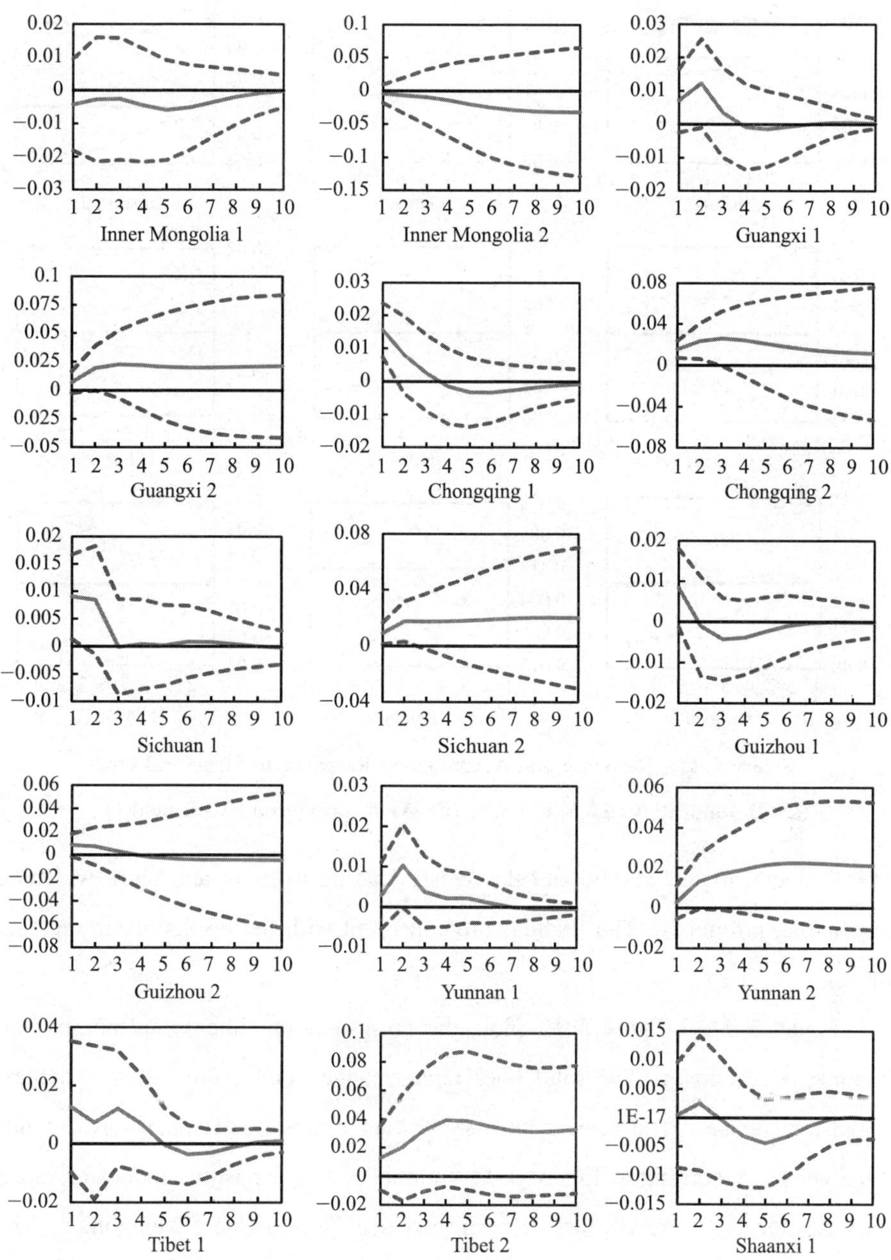
Inner Mongolia 1
Inner Mongolia 2
Guangxi 1
Guangxi 2
Chongqing 1
Chongqing 2
Sichuan 1
Sichuan 2
Guizhou 1
Guizhou 2
Yunnan 1
Yunnan 2
Tibet 1
Tibet 2
Shaanxi 1

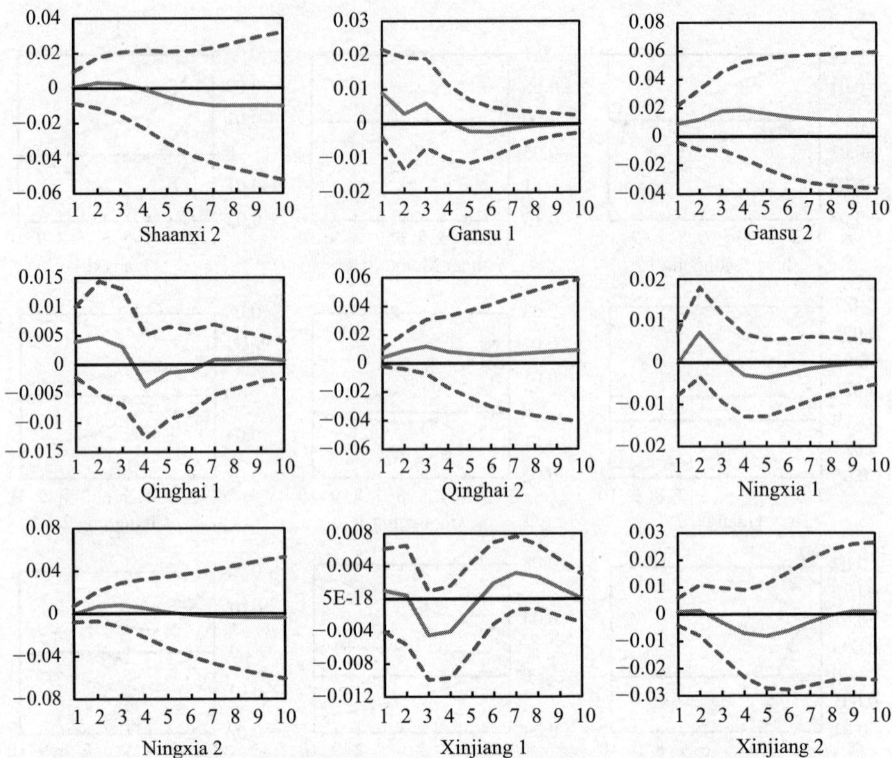

Figure 5.13 Response and Accumulated Response to Structural One S. D. Innovations ±2 S. E. (M2, the West, provincial SVAR model)

little supports to the Middle and the West, leading to more and more widening gap among provinces. The findings are consistent with the results of the regional model.

Figure 5.11 – Figure 5.13 plots the corresponding impulse responses and cumulative responses. The solid lines represent the point estimates of variables' impulse responses. The dashed lines show plus/minus two standard error bands (analytic). According to Figure 5.11 – Figure 5.13, a positive monetary shock increases the GDP growth rate of each province (except Inner Mongolia). The largest impacts reach in the 1st year or the 2nd year after the shock. Then the influences decrease and die out after 4 years in most of the eastern provinces. In a majority of provinces in the Middle or the West, the influences also become small after the peak and 3 or 4 years later, the impacts become negative and die out over time. For cumulative response, most of the provinces display their maximum cumulative responses within 3 or 4 years, long run cumulated responses in a majority of provinces go to stable after 6 years. While the impulse responses and cumulated responses of the eastern provinces are statistically significant within 2 or 3 years, that of most of the middle and western provinces are insignificant in the whole period.

Due to the small sample problem, the performance of analytic confidence interval may be poor in the statistical reliability of estimated impulse response (Kilian, 1998). So the analytic confidence interval may not properly reflect the estimation variability in small sample (Benkwitz et al., 2001; Kilian, 1998). Based on asymptotic distribution theory, for stationary finite order VAR process, the impulse responses are known to taper off to zero after some periods. This is reflected in the confidence bands becoming smaller. Accumulated responses approach to a constant after some periods in general and the confidence bands remain stable (Lütkepohl, 1990). Hence, it is held that the estimated impulse responses and cumulated responses are informative about the actual underlying relations.

5.2.4.2 The Results of the Inter-Regional SVAR Models for Each Province without Spillover Effect

Analogous to the analysis of the inter-regional model for each region, to show the importance of spillover effects, the models for each province without considering the spillover effects are also developed in order to compare the results. To avoid the estimates depend on data availability and the amount of research effort allocated to a specific province, model uniformity is required and this study estimates the inter-regional SVAR model for each province without spillover effect (for simplicity, the SVAR model for each province). The SVAR model for each province is like this: it has three endogenous variables: P_jGDP,

P_jMP and P_jPrice ($j=1, 2, \cdots, 31$), P_jMP is the monetary policy variable, as the regional data of M2 is not available, total Chinese Yuan (CNY) deposits of financial institutions in each province is used to represent M2. P_jGDP is the real GDP of each province. P_jPrice is the price level measured by the consumer price index in each province (1978 = 100). *WDGDP* is also included as an exogenous variable. The estimation period is also 1978 – 2011.

There are 31 inter-regional SVAR models for each province without spillover effect. Among these models, based on the lag length selection criteria mentioned above, the lag length of eight provincial models (Shanxi, Jiangxi, Henan, Hubei, Hunan, Chongqing, Tibet and Gansu) is two. The lag length of the other 23 models is one. All inverse roots lie inside the unit circle and the estimated SVAR model for each province is stable. The models are just identified. The estimation procedure is the same as the benchmark provincial SVAR models. The results are summarized in Table 5. 13 and Figure 5. 14 – Figure 5. 17.

Table 5. 13 displays the impulse responses to structural one-standard-deviation (5%) unanticipated increase in M2 change of the model for each province. The data are sorted according to maximum impulse response. One implicit hypothesis of the model for each province is that it supposes that all the deposits in the province are focused on supporting local economic growth, no deposits transfer among provinces. According to Table 5. 13, although different provinces respond also differently to monetary policy shock, the magnitudes of responses in each province are very different comparing with the results of the benchmark model. In top ten lists, only four provinces belong to the East, four provinces come from the West, the other two are in the Middle. In the last ten lists, three provinces belong to the East, three provinces are in the Middle and the other four are from the West. It is found that if all the deposits in the province are focused on supporting the local economic growth, the East do not have any advantages in economic growth.

Table 5. 13 Impulse Responses of Each Province (Inter-Regional SVAR Model for Each Province without Spillover)

Province	LRIR10	LRIR6	MCIR	Timing	MIR	Timing
Zhejiang (E)	0. 049317	0. 048054	0. 053620	4	0. 025136	2
Qinghai (W)	0. 035092	0. 038803	0. 039141	4	0. 021988	2
Tibet (W)	0. 026437	0. 021564	0. 021403	3	0. 015221	1
Fujian (E)	0. 024095	0. 024093	0. 025984	2	0. 013983	1
Ningxia (W)	0. 024272	0. 024149	—	—	0. 012177	2
Hubei (M)	0. 022993	0. 020840	—	—	0. 012032	2
Guangxi (W)	0. 024212	0. 025475	0. 026343	4	0. 011262	2
Shanxi (M)	0. 015080	0. 014756	0. 015476	3	0. 010619	1
Shandong (E)	0. 012431	0. 012972	0. 015429	3	0. 010427	1
Tianjin (E)	0. 034034	0. 032626	—	—	0. 010312	2
Jiangsu (E)	0. 011624	0. 011781	0. 013735	3	0. 010115	2
Jiangxi (M)	0. 009885	0. 009774	0. 015728	2	0. 010061	2
Chongqing (W)	0. 028687	0. 025592	—	—	0. 009734	1
Yunnan (W)	0. 018283	0. 017467	—	—	0. 009246	1
Jilin (M)	0. 013816	0. 013986	0. 015276	3	0. 007772	1
Inner Mongolia (W)	0. 003385	0. 008684	0. 014528	3	0. 007704	1
Hainan (E)	0. 006316	0. 006482	0. 009800	2	0. 007410	1
Hebei (E)	0. 014654	0. 014206	—	—	0. 007117	2
Anhui (M)	0. 014504	0. 014513	—	—	0. 007052	2
Beijing (E)	0. 009315	0. 009812	—	—	0. 006946	2
Shaanxi (W)	0. 009340	0. 010100	0. 010995	4	0. 006761	2
Liaoning (E)	-0. 017389	-0. 014960	0. 006635	1	0. 006635	1
Gansu (W)	0. 005797	0. 005758	—	—	0. 006267	2
Heilongjiang (M)	0. 007397	0. 007452	0. 007329	3	0. 005551	1
Xinjiang (W)	0. 002739	0. 003446	0. 007084	3	0. 005349	2
Guangdong (E)	0. 006653	0. 006426	0. 008647	3	0. 004832	2
Shanghai (E)	0. 011104	0. 010873	—	—	0. 004614	2
Guizhou (W)	0. 006007	0. 006467	0. 008090	3	0. 004029	1
Sichuan (W)	0. 005307	0. 005944	0. 006369	4	0. 003447	2
Henan (M)	0. 002960	0. 002713	0. 003679	3	0. 002182	3
Hunan (M)	-0. 006835	-0. 005978	0. 000308	1	0. 000308	1

Notes: LRIR10 is long-run (10 years) cumulative impulse response. LRIR6 represents long-run (6 years) cumulative impulse response. MCIR is maximum cumulative impulse response. MIR is maximum impulse response. The unit of timing is year. (E), (M), (W) mean this province belongs to the East, the Middle or the West.

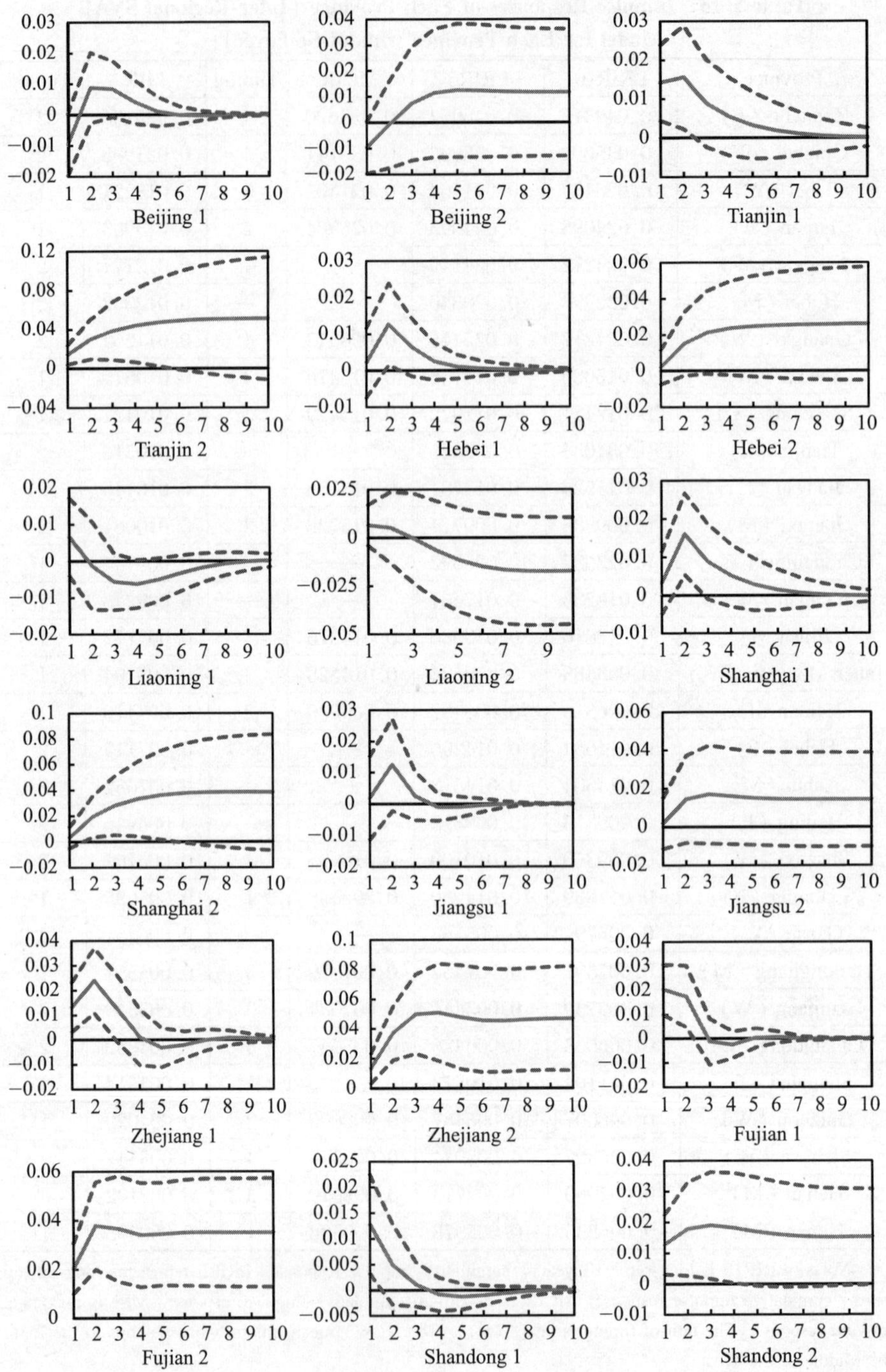
Beijing 1
Beijing 2
Tianjin 1
Tianjin 2
Hebei 1
Hebei 2
Liaoning 1
Liaoning 2
Shanghai 1
Shanghai 2
Jiangsu 1
Jiangsu 2
Zhejiang 1
Zhejiang 2
Fujian 1
Fujian 2
Shandong 1
Shandong 2

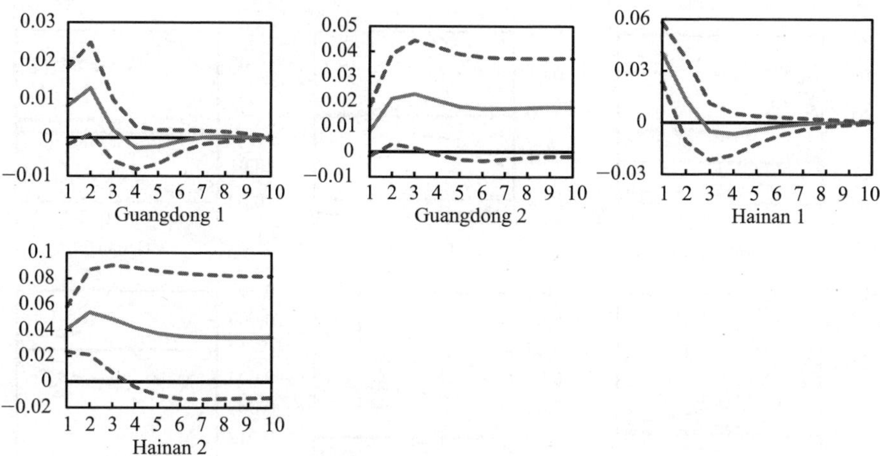

Figure 5.14 Response and Accumulated Response to Structural One S. D. Innovations ±2 S. E. (M2, the East, SVAR model for each province)

Notes: "Province +1" refers to impulse response of this province to M2. "province +2" means accumulated response of this province to M2.

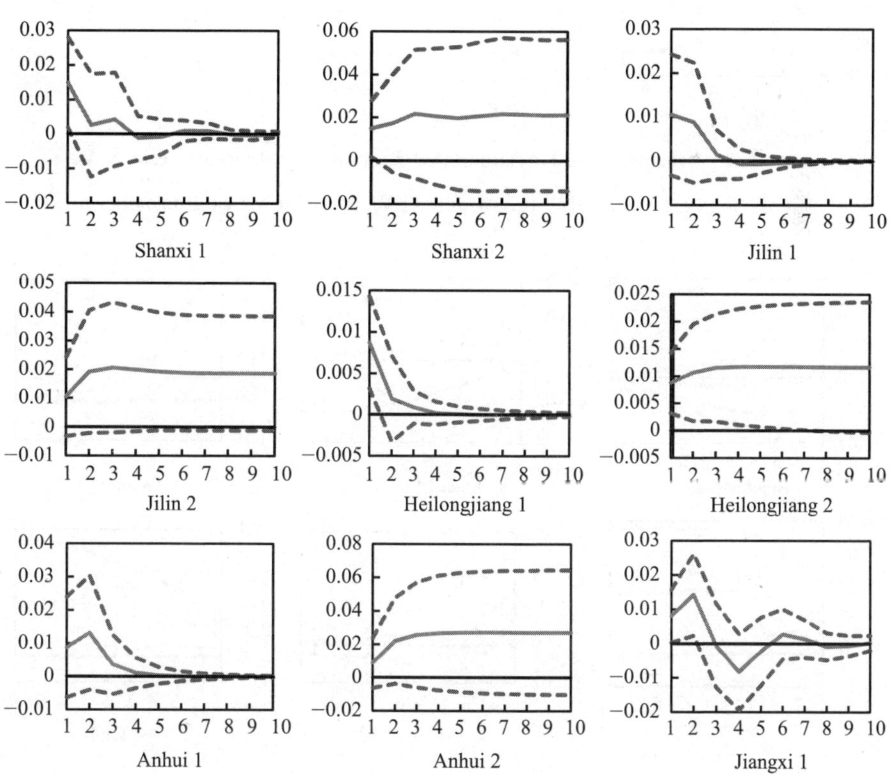

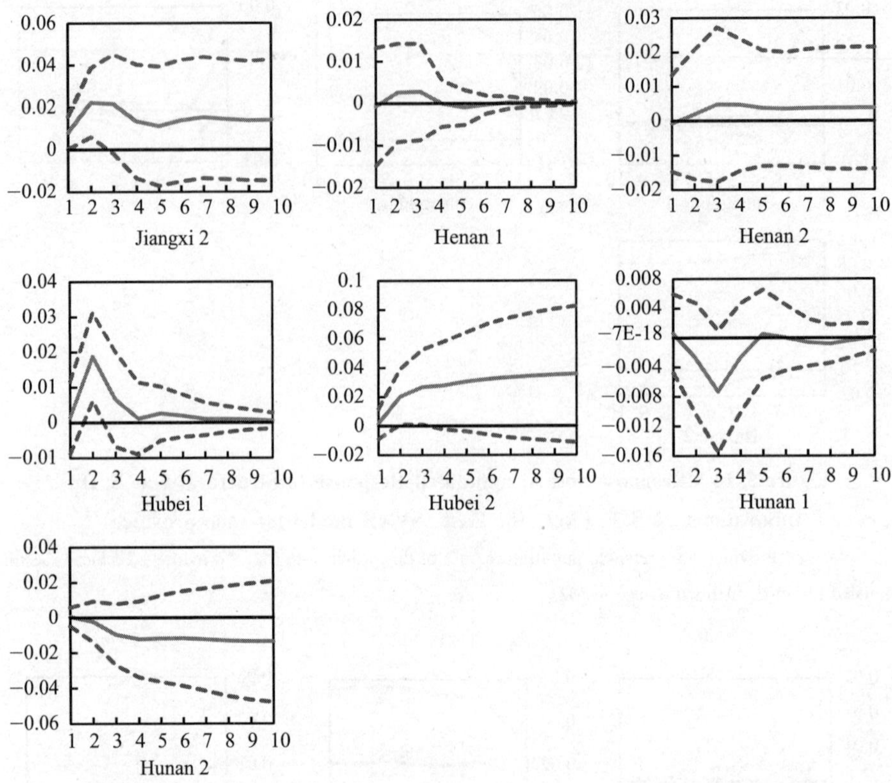

Figure 5.15 Response and Accumulated Response to Structural One S. D. Innovations ± 2 S. E. (M2, the Middle, SVAR model for each province)

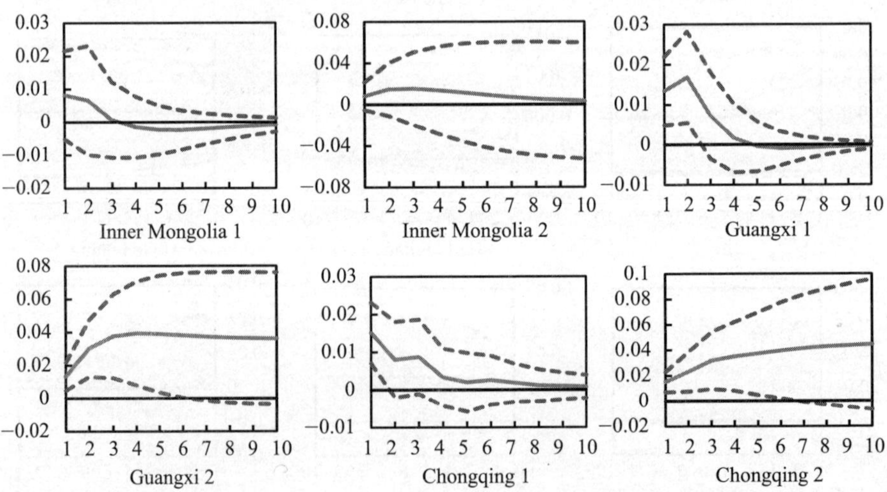

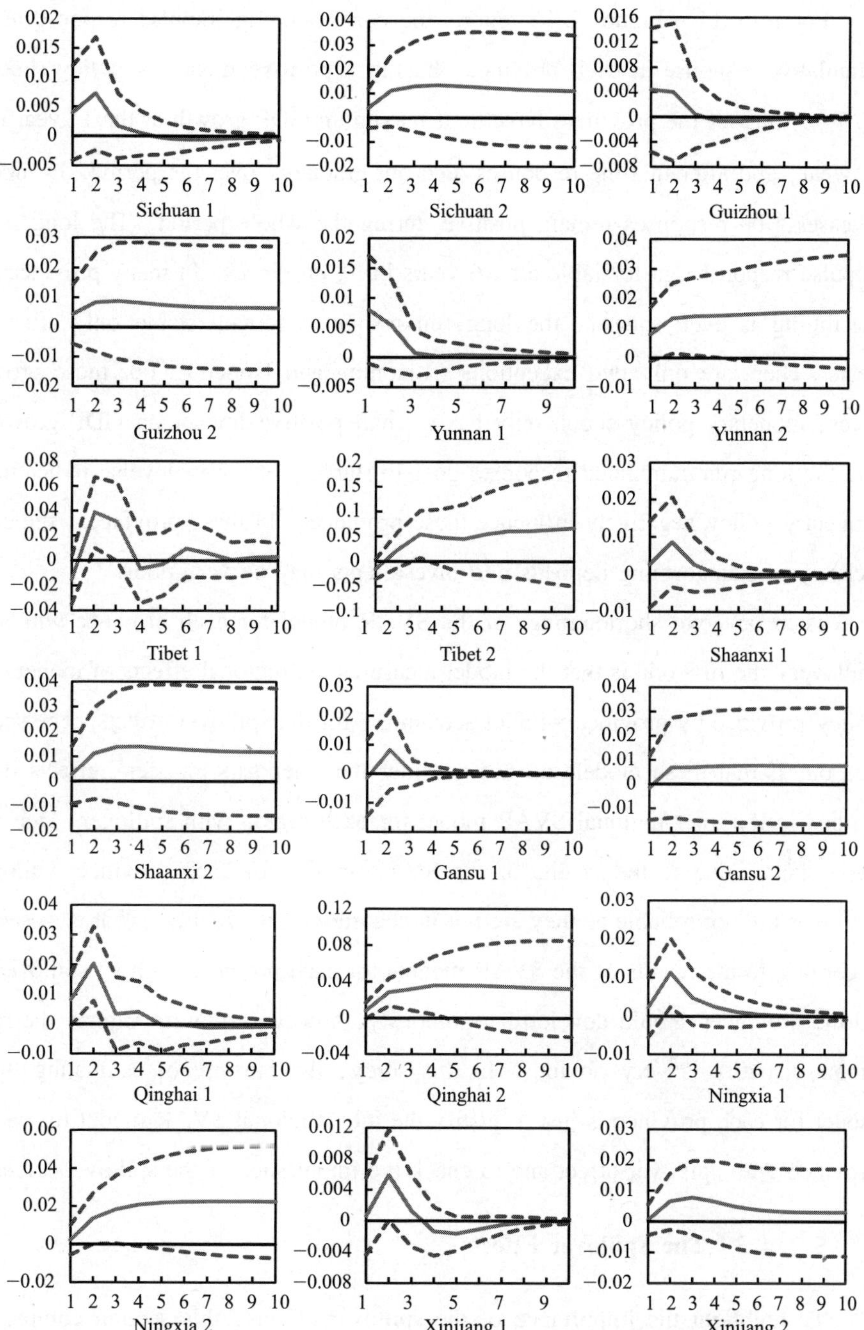

Figure 5. 16 Response and Accumulated Response to Structural One S. D. Innovations ±2 S. E. (M2, the West, SVAR model for each province)

Figure 5. 14 – Figure 5. 16 reports the corresponding impulse response and cumulative response in each province. Facing a positive monetary policy shock (5%), most of the provinces have their maximum GDP growth at the 1st year or 2nd year, and after that the responses died out gradually over the period. In most of cases, the responses remain positive during the whole period. The long run impulse responses go to stable after 6 years in 31 provinces. In many provinces, the timing is even shorter, the long run responses remain stable only after 4 years. There are only two exceptions (Liaoning and Hunan). For these provinces, monetary policy shock only has a small positive impact on GDP growth and the long-run cumulated responses goes to stable at negative levels, indicating monetary policy negatively influence these provinces. In these provinces, the efficiency of transforming deposits into investments may be very poor.

There are two shortcomings of the SVAR model for each province without spillover: the first one is that the model measures the regional effects of monetary policy province by province without accounting for the spillover effects. The second one is that these models do not consider the "deposits transfer" effects described in the inter-regional SVAR model for each region with spillover. Due to these shortcomings, the results of the SVAR model for each province without spillover are not reliable as they are not in accord with the reality. That is to say, according to the results of the SVAR models for each province without spillover, all the provinces should develop harmoniously, however, now in China, the regional disparity is very obvious. In this study, the purpose of estimating this model for each province is just to justify the inter-regional SVAR model for each province with spillover effect and to check the importance of the spillover effect.

5. 2. 4. 3 The Spillover Effects

To highlight the importance of the spillover effects, this section compares the results of the inter-regional SVAR model for each province with spillover effect and without spillover effect. Table 5. 14 plots the comparison and the spillover effects. As some of the models for each province without spillover effect do not have maximum cumulative impulse responses, this section just compares the results of maximum impulse response and the long-run (6 years and 10 years) cumulated impulse responses.

According to Table 5. 14, maximum impulse response shows the maximum increase of real GDP growth of each province to the monetary policy innovation (5%) in the short-run (1 - 2 years). In the short-run, when considering the spillover effects, most of the provinces have much bigger impulse responses. The increases of the magnitudes are more than 50% for many provinces, showing the importance of the spillover effects. 8 out of 31 provinces display less magnitude of impulse response when considering the spillover effects. Among these provinces, 2 belongs to the Middle, others are from the West. These 8 provinces may benefit very little or even negatively from the spillover effects.

Long-run cumulative response shows the total cumulated increase of real GDP growth of each province to monetary policy innovation (5%) in the long-run (6 years or 10 years). Table 5. 14 shows that in the East, long-run cumulated responses increase when considering the spillover effects in 7 provinces (except 4 provinces: Beijing, Liaoning, Hainan and Zhejiang). In the Middle, 6 provinces (except Shanxi and Jilin) have larger magnitudes of long-run cumulative responses. While in the West, the number is only 4, the magnitudes of 8 provinces are much smaller when considering the spillover effects. The reason may be explained as follows: there are two effects among provinces: the spillover effects and the deposits transfer effects, in the short-run, the deposits have no time to transfer, the spillover effects dominate, thus most of provinces show much bigger magnitude of maximum impulse responses. However, in the long-run, deposits can transfer among provinces by the branches of big four banks. To some extent the negative deposits transfer effects may weaken the positive spillover effects, moreover, a number of deposits flow from the less developed western provinces to the more developed coastal provinces in the East. Therefore, in the

Table 5. 14 Comparison of the Results and the Spillover Effects

Spillover	East	LRIR10	LRIR6	MIR	West	LRIR10	LRIR6	MIR
Comparison	Beijing	-0. 0058	-0. 004367	0. 005931	Inner Mongolia	-0. 03363	-0. 032696	-0. 0118
Change(%)		-62. 28	-44. 50	85. 38		-993. 52	-376. 50	-153. 16
Comparison	Tianjin	0. 006892	0. 007482	0. 009176	Guangxi	-0. 00371	-0. 006257	0. 000592
Change(%)		20. 25	22. 93	88. 99		-15. 33	-24. 56	5. 26
Comparison	Hebei	0. 010784	0. 007964	0. 005726	Chongqing	-0. 01726	-0. 008106	0. 005381
Change(%)		73. 59	56. 06	80. 45		-60. 16	-31. 68	55. 28
Comparison	Liaoning	0. 030658	0. 028031	0. 007939	Sichuan	0. 015451	0. 013637	0. 005918
Change(%)		-176. 30	-187. 37	119. 66		291. 11	229. 42	171. 68
Comparison	Shanghai	0. 023461	0. 018285	0. 013719	Guizhou	-0. 01039	-0. 010354	0. 003965
Change(%)		211. 29	168. 16	297. 34		-173. 01	-160. 10	98. 40
Comparison	Jiangsu	0. 021511	0. 022380	0. 011754	Yunnan	0. 00245	0. 004612	0. 000898
Change(%)		185. 05	189. 96	116. 20		13. 40	26. 40	9. 71
Comparison	Zhejiang	-0. 00902	-0. 007810	0. 001867	Tibet	0. 011113	0. 018906	-0. 00063
Change(%)		-18. 28	-16. 25	7. 43		42. 04	87. 67	-4. 15
Comparison	Fujian	0. 013288	0. 017815	0. 013558	Shaanxi	-0. 02005	-0. 019025	-0. 00405
Change(%)		55. 15	73. 94	96. 96		-214. 72	-188. 37	-59. 83
Comparison	Shandong	0. 018645	0. 017270	0. 008062	Gansu	0. 005313	0. 0074063	0. 002255
Change(%)		149. 98	133. 13	77. 31		91. 64	128. 62	35. 98
Comparison	Guangdong	0. 027922	0. 028172	0. 015252	Qinghai	-0. 0262	-0. 033391	-0. 01737
Change(%)		419. 68	438. 41	315. 66		-74. 66	-86. 05	-79. 02
Comparison	Hainan	-0. 0093	-0. 015583	0. 013107	Ningxia	-0. 02799	-0. 025242	-0. 00522
Change(%)		-147. 23	-240. 41	176. 88		-115. 30	-104. 53	-42. 84
Comparison	—	—	—	—	Xinjiang	-0. 00143	-0. 010648	-0. 00415
Change(%)		—	—	—		-52. 22	-308. 98	-77. 53

continuous

Spillover	Middle	LRIR10	LRIR6	MIR	Middle	LRIR10	LRIR6	MIR
Comparison	Shanxi	−0. 02311	−0. 017167	−0. 0005	Jiangxi	0. 003909	0. 002564	0. 000271
Change(%)		−153. 22	−116. 34	−4. 72		39. 54	26. 23	3
Comparison	Jilin	−0. 00308	−0. 002965	0. 00246	Henan	0. 032348	0. 030155	0. 016192
Change(%)		−22	−21	32		1092. 99	1111. 57	742
Comparison	Heilongjiang	0. 008057	0. 005920	−0. 00161	Hubei	0. 005764	0. 007966	0. 004601
Change(%)		108. 93	79. 43	−29. 05		25. 07	38. 22	38. 24
Comparison	Anhui	0. 011898	0. 013465	0. 006142	Hunan	0. 015442	0. 015251	0. 007936
Change(%)		82	93	87		225. 92	255. 14	2578. 75

Notes: LRIR10 is long-run (10 years) cumulative impulse response. LRIR6 represents long-run (6 years) cumulative impulse response. MIR is maximum impulse response. Comparison = Impulse Response of the provincial SVAR model with spillover—Impulse Response of the SVAR model for each province without spillover, Change = Comparison/Impulse Response of the SVAR model for each province without spillover. We use "Change" to measure the spillover effects.

long-run, most of the provinces in the East display larger magnitudes of cumulated impulse responses, while most of the provinces in the West have much smaller or even negative long-run cumulative impulse responses when considering the spillover effects. The Research Group of Wuhan Branch of PBC (2002) also proves this view. The findings further confirm the findings of the regional SVAR model, indicating that the results are robust.

Liu (2010) regards M1 as monetary policy variable and examines the provinces' responses to monetary policy shock. Based on his results, Liu develops a mark sheet of provinces' responses to monetary policy shock. Though using different control variables and methods, this section makes a rough comparison of this mark sheet and the findings of this study (See table 5.15).

Table 5.15 Comparison of the Results of Liu (2010) and this Study

Province	Score	Ranking	Province	Score	Ranking	Province	Score	Ranking
Guangdong	13	5	Hubei	50	10	Yunnan	79	20
Zhejiang	16	2	Hunan	54	24	Shaanxi	81	29
Beijing	19	15	Henan	61	8	Gansu	82	23
Liaoning	21	13	Fujian	64	1	Guangxi	82	17
Jilin	23	19	Anhui	72	14	Jiangxi	85	18
Shanxi	25	21	Shanghai	72	9	Ningxia	91	26
Hainan	27	4	Tianjin	72	6	Qinghai	95	27
Inner Mongolia	37	31	Sichuan	75	22	Shangdong	95	7
Heilongjiang	47	28	Guizhou	77	25	Xinjiang	99	30
Hebei	48	16	Jiangsu	78	3			

Notes: The "Score" is the result of Liu (2010). Lower score stands for stronger response. The "Ranking" is the findings of provincial SVAR model with spillover in this study (sorted based on maximum impulse response).

In Table 5.15, the data are sorted according to the score. Liu (2010) uses M1 as monetary policy variable, as M1 is consisted of cash and demand deposit. Using M1 as monetary policy indicator means neglecting the deposits transfer effect. Thus in the results of Liu (2010), the eastern provinces do not have much advantages to gain more growth when facing an expansionary monetary policy, all provinces tend to develop harmoniously. Liu (2010) argues that M1 behaviors better than M2 as a monetary policy indicator, since that the impulse response yields the "wrong" sign. In fact, he fails to take account the spillover effects and deposits transfer effects. In this study, M2 is used as monetary policy variable. The findings indicate that when considering the spillover effect and deposits transfer effect, the eastern provinces respond more to monetary policy shock. Monetary policy tends to enlarge the regional disparity. The results in this study are more consistent with the reality.

Kong et al. (2007) also examine the regional effects of monetary policy. They use M2 to measure monetary policy. The main shortcoming of Kong et al. (2007) is it estimates VAR model province by province neglecting the spillover effects. This study also provides their results to make a rough comparison (see Table 5. 16).

Table 5. 16 Comparison of the Results of Kong et al. (2007) and this Study

Province	LRIR1	LRIR2	Province	LRIR1	LRIR2	Province	LRIR1	LRIR2
Zhejiang	0. 3959	0. 0402	Liaoning	0. 2742	0. 0131	Ningxia	0. 2204	-0. 0011
Fujian	0. 3859	0. 0419	Jilin	0. 2716	0. 0110	Hainan	0. 2195	-0. 0091
Jiangsu	0. 3764	0. 0342	Tianjin	0. 2670	0. 0401	Shanxi	0. 2108	-0. 0024
Shanghai	0. 3331	0. 0292	Heilongjiang	0. 2668	0. 0134	Beijing	0. 2069	0. 0054
Henan	0. 3173	0. 0329	Hebei	0. 2615	0. 0222	Yunnan	0. 1971	0. 0221
Anhui	0. 3135	0. 0280	Sichuan	0. 2611	0. 0196	Qinghai	0. 1928	0. 0054
Hunan	0. 3054	0. 0093	Shandong	0. 2547	0. 0302	Shaanxi	0. 1781	-0. 0089
Guangxi	0. 3049	0. 0192	Guangdong	0. 2377	0. 0346	Gansu	0. 1730	0. 0132
Hubei	0. 2918	0. 0288	Xinjiang	0. 2346	-0. 0072	Guizhou	0. 1616	-0. 0039
Jiangxi	0. 2879	0. 0123	Inner Mongolia	0. 2310	-0. 0240			

Notes: LRIR refers to long-run cumulative impulse response (6 years). LRIR1 is the result of Kong et al. (2007). LRIR2 is the results of provincial SVAR model with spillover in this study. The data are sorted by LRIR1.

In the provincial SVAR model with spillover in this study, the size of monetary policy shock is 5%. However, Kong et al. (2007) do not clearly point out the exact size of monetary policy shock. Therefore, a direct comparison is meaningless. But when taking a rough look, it is found that as Kong et al. (2007) do not consider the influence of spillover effect and deposits transfer effects, the underlying assumption of their study is that they assume all the deposits focus on the local economic development. As a result, generally speaking, according to Table 5. 16, in the long-run, the magnitudes of provinces' responses to monetary policy shock in Kong et al. (2007) are much bigger than the results in this study. This is consistent with the finding in this study: in the long-run, the previous studies may to some extent overestimate the influences of monetary policy in the West.

5. 3 The Factors Affecting Regional Effects of Monetary Policy in China

This section explores the factors explaining the regional effects of monetary policy in China. The long-run (6 years) cumulative impulse response① is used as the dependent variable to represent the magnitude of regional effects of monetary policy. To show the robustness of the results, the long-run (10 years) cumulated responses and maximum cumulated responses are also chosen as alternative dependent variables. As the impulse responses represent average behavior during the sample period, averaging data for independent variables is appropriate. The data availability limited averaging to the period from 2000 to 2011. This section will run cross sectional (31) multiple linear regressions to check the relationship of independent and dependent variables. Table 5. 17 displays the descriptive statistics and a correlation matrix of all variables. LR6 is positively related to the SE, and negatively related to the SB and the SOE. The SI and the LB are weakly related to LR6. The correlations among independent variables are not very large, eliminating the problem of multicollinearity.

Table 5. 17 Descriptive Statistics and Correlations of Variables

Item	Mean	SD	LR6	LR10	MC	SI	SB	LB	SE	SOE
LR6	0. 0164	0. 0173	1. 00							
LR10	0. 0163	0. 0176		1. 00						
MC	0. 0238	0. 0152			1. 00					

① At this level (6 years), the cumulated impulse responses of most of provinces go to stable.

continuous

Item	Mean	SD	LR6	LR10	MC	SI	SB	LB	SE	SOE
SI	0. 4672	0. 4896	0. 17	0. 14	0. 01	1. 00				
SB	0. 4789	0. 4668	−0. 29	−0. 32	−0. 43	0. 54	1. 00			
LB	0. 2233	0. 2423	0. 05	0. 06	0. 09	−0. 51	−0. 40	1. 00		
SE	0. 8643	0. 8685	0. 56	0. 55	0. 55	−0. 08	−0. 24	0. 16	1. 00	
SOE	0. 2367	0. 2553	−0. 49	−0. 46	−0. 47	−0. 54	−0. 23	0. 63	−0. 28	1. 00

Notes: SD represents standard deviation. LR6 refers to long-run cumulative impulse response (6 years). LR10 stands for long-run cumulative impulse response (10 years). MC is maximum cumulated response. SI is the secondary industry. SB is small bank. LB is large bank. SE is small sized enterprise. SOE refers to state-owned and state-holding enterprise.

The results of regressions are presented in Table 5. 18 – Table 5. 20. In all equations, the percent of secondary industry is included to represent the interest rate channel. In equation 1, the proportion of small banks and the percent of small enterprises are employed to represent the traditional bank lending channel. In equation 2, this study uses the proportion of large banks and the percent of state-owned and state-holding enterprises to measure the bank lending channel with Chinese characteristics (soft budget constraint: large banks—SOEs). In equation 3, both the traditional bank lending channel and the bank lending channel with Chinese characteristics are included. In equation 4, equation 5 and equation 6, a dummy variable is added to control for the influences of the provinces in the developed eastern coastal region.

Table 5. 18 Estimated Equations Explaining Cross-Province Variation in Impulse Responses (Dependent Variable: Long-Run 6-year Cumulative Impulse Response)

Variable	Equation 1	Equation 2	Equation 3	Equation 4	Equation 5	Equation 6
Intercept	−2. 2319 *** (0. 0688)	−0. 0141 (0. 0285)	−0. 1243 (0. 0738)	−0. 2185 *** (0. 0716)	−0. 0197 (0. 0309)	−0. 1178 (0. 0754)
Percent Secondary Industry	0. 0938 ** (0. 0372)	0. 0013 (0. 0385)	0. 0525 (0. 0390)	0. 0873 ** (0. 0385)	0. 0088 (0. 0418)	0. 0489 (0. 0399)
Percent Small Bank	−0. 1017 ** (0. 0440)		−0. 0872 ** (0. 0400)	−0. 0881 * (0. 0478)		−0. 0998 ** (0. 0452)
Percent Large Bank		0. 1212 *** (0. 0373)	0. 0749 * (0. 0374)		0. 1181 *** (0. 0383)	0. 0755 * (0. 0379)
Percent Small Sized Enterprise	0. 2628 *** (0. 0763)		0. 1380 * (0. 0801)	0. 2456 *** (0. 0801)		0. 1400 * (0. 0812)
Percent State-Owned Enterprise		−0. 1190 *** (0. 0261)	−0. 0825 *** (0. 0279)		−0. 1088 *** (0. 0333)	−0. 0934 *** (0. 0330)

continuous

Variable	Equation 1	Equation 2	Equation 3	Equation 4	Equation 5	Equation 6
Dummy East Region				0. 0044 (0. 0058)	0. 0033 (0. 0065)	-0. 0041 (0. 0065)
Model Criteria						
Adjusted R^2	0. 4047	0. 4063	0. 5250	0. 3952	0. 3894	0. 5132
S. E. of Regression	0. 0133	0. 0133	0. 0119	0. 0134	0. 0135	0. 0120
F-statistic	7. 7986	7. 8441	7. 6307	5. 9002	5. 9837	6. 2711
Prob. (F-statistic)	0. 0007	0. 0006	0. 0002	0. 0016	0. 0018	0. 0005
Durbin-Watson Stat	2. 1066	1. 9998	1. 9253	2. 1136	2. 0016	1. 8994

Notes: Standard errors in the parentheses. *, **, and *** indicates that a null hypothesis of zero is rejected at the 10%, 5%, and 1% levels, respectively.

Each regression is significant at the 1% level, explaining between 38% and 51% of the cross-provincial variation in long-run cumulated response. Adjusted R^2s are a little low as the dependent variable impulse responses are measured error term. White heteroskedasticity test shows that there are no heteroskedasticity among independent variables. Two-tailed test is used to test the hypotheses.

In Table 5. 18, the dependent variable is the long-run (6 years) cumulated response. The coefficients of the percent of secondary industry are rather unstable. The coefficient is positive and significant in equation 1 and equation 4. In equation 2, equation 3 equation 5 and equation 6, the coefficient is positive but insignificant. Therefore, there are no apparent evidences of existence of interest rate channel at the regional level. The results are consistent with the findings of Jiang and Chen (2009). Actually, in China, most of interest rates are regulated by the PBC, although interest rate liberalization is in process, it is far to the end. Hence, the interest rate channel is rather weak at the regional level in China.

The coefficients of the proportion of small sized enterprises in equation 1, equation 3, equation 4 and equation 6 are positive and significant, and that of the proportion of state-owned and state-holding enterprises in equation 2, equation 3, equation 5 and equation 6 are negative and significant, indicating that a province with large proportion of small sized enterprises and small proportion of state-owned and state-holding enterprises will be more sensitive to monetary policy shocks. This is consistent with the idea of bank lending channel.

The coefficients of the percent of small banks in equation 1, equation 3, equation 4 and equation 6 are negative and significant, while that of the percent of large banks in equation 2, equation 3, equation 5 and equation 6 are positive and significant, indicating that a province with a larger proportion of small banks and smaller percent of large banks will respond less to monetary policy shock. These findings are inconsistent with the hypothesis proposed by bank lending channel. But the finding is the same as Carlino and DeFina (1998). Carlino and DeFina (1998) explain that one possible reason is that the banks' assets size may be a poor indicator of its ability to adjust their balance sheets to monetary policy shocks. For example, Peek and Rosengren (1995) suggest that bank capital should be a better measure—better capitalized banks may have more and cheaper other sources of funds. Kashyap and Stein (1995) consider the types of loans being made by small banks might be proper indicator.

This study offers another possible explanation. As in China, the four large banks are state-owned commercial banks which have been listed only since 2006. Their top leaders are appointed by Chinese government. So the actions of four large banks are consistent with the monetary policy actions implemented by the PBC. Besides interest rates and reserve requirements, the PBC still relies on non-market tools such as "loan quotas" and "window guidance" to banks. In recent years, the main objective of the PBC's "loan quotas" and "window guidance" policy is four large banks. Sun et al. (2010) find that four large banks react quickly to a contractionary monetary policy, as these banks often follow the signals of central bank quickly because of political factors (Sun et al., 2010). Therefore, as the actions of four banks are consistent with the PBC's monetary policy action, the province with a relatively big proportion of large banks would be more sensitive to monetary policy actions. Small banks mainly contain city commercial banks and rural credit cooperative in China. Compared with the four big banks, city commercial banks have more freedom to monetary policy actions and their funds are supported by the local governments. In recent years, Chinese government has implemented many preferential policies so as to support the development of the rural area. Since 2003, when the PBC raised the reserve requirement ratio, the rural credit cooperative still applied a relatively lower preferential reserve requirement ratio. Therefore, there is possible that a province with relatively big proportion of small banks is less sensitive to monetary policy actions. However, this possible reason should be tested in more details in future.

Table 5.19 Estimated Equations Explaining Cross-Province Variation in Impulse Responses (Dependent Variable: Long Run 10-year Cumulative Impulse Response)

Variable	Equation 1	Equation 2	Equation 3	Equation 4	Equation 5	Equation 6
Intercept	-0.2287*** (0.0702)	-0.0123 (0.0301)	-0.1270 (0.0772)	0.2114*** (0.0726)	-0.0226 (0.0325)	-0.1246 (0.0795)
Percent Secondary Industry	0.0932** (0.0380)	-0.0025 (0.0407)	0.0539 (0.0408)	0.0847** (0.0390)	0.0113 (0.0438)	0.0526 (0.0421)
Percent Small Bank	-0.1111** (0.0449)		-0.0976** (0.0419)	-0.0936* (0.0484)		-0.1024** (0.0476)
Percent Large Bank		0.1197*** (0.0394)	0.0699* (0.0391)		0.1142*** (0.0401)	0.0702* (0.0399)
Percent Small Sized Enterprise	0.2618** (0.0778)		0.1444* (0.0839)	0.2396*** (0.0813)		0.1451* (0.0856)
Percent State Owned Enterprise		-0.1167*** (0.0276)	-0.0777** (0.0292)		-0.0979*** (0.0349)	-0.0818*** (0.0348)
Dummy East Region				0.0056 (0.0058)	0.0060 (0.0068)	-0.0015 (0.0068)
Model Criteria						
Adjusted R^2	0.4049	0.3614	0.5001	0.4033	0.3562	0.4804
S. E. of Regression	0.0136	0.0141	0.0124	0.0136	0.0141	0.0127
F-statistic	7.8041	6.6591	7.0027	6.0684	5.1493	5.6222
Prob. (F-statistic)	0.0007	0.0016	0.0003	0.0014	0.0034	0.0009
Durbin-Watson Stat	2.1637	2.0891	2.0203	2.1814	2.0957	2.0105

Notes: Standard errors in the parentheses. *, **, and *** indicates that a null hypothesis of zero is rejected at the 10%, 5%, and 1% levels, respectively.

In Table 5.19 and Table 5.20, the dependent variables are long-run (10 years) cumulated responses and maximum cumulated response, respectively. The results are rather similar with that of Table 5.18, indicating the robustness of the results. For the dummy variable eastern region, we can see that in Table 5.18 and Table 5.19, it is not significant, but in Table 5.20, it is positive and significant. As for the long-run cumulated responses (6 or 10 years), in the East, although most of the provinces respond significantly to monetary policy shock, some provinces (Beijing, Liaoning and Hainan) have smaller responses, leading to the insignificance of the coefficient of dummy variable. But in the short-run responses (maximum cumulative impulse response), the provinces in the East have apparent much bigger responses to monetary policy shock. Therefore, the coefficient of dummy variable in Table 5. 20 is positive and significant, indicating the location factor would affect the province's response to monetary policy.

Table 5. 20 Estimated Equations Explaining Cross-Province Variation in Impulse Responses (Dependent Variable: Maximum Cumulative Impulse Response)

Variable	Equation 1	Equation 2	Equation 3	Equation 4	Equation 5	Equation 6
Intercept	-0. 1651 ** (0. 0609)	0. 0206 (0. 0245)	-0. 0468 (0. 0610)	-0. 1300 ** (0. 0577)	0. 0015 (0. 0247)	-0. 0553 (0. 0615)
Percent Secondary Industry	0. 0594 * (0. 0329)	-0. 0407 (0. 0330)	0. 0104 (0. 0322)	0. 0422 (0. 0310)	-0. 0152 (0. 0332)	0. 0151 (0. 0615)
Percent Small Bank	-0. 1088 *** (0. 0389)		-0. 0967 *** (0. 0330)	-0. 0735 * (0. 0385)		-0. 0803 ** (0. 0369)
Percent Large Bank		0. 1026 *** (0. 0320)	0. 0638 ** (0. 0309)		0. 0923 *** (0. 0305)	0. 0630 * (0. 0309)
Percent Small Sized Enterprise	0. 2146 *** (0. 0675)		0. 0891 *a (0. 0662)	0. 1695 ** (0. 0646)		0. 0865 *a (0. 0663)
Percent State Owned Enterprise		-0. 1136 *** (0. 0224)	-0. 0852 *** (0. 0230)		-0. 0791 *** (0. 0265)	-0. 0711 ** (0. 0270)
Dummy East Region				0. 0114 ** (0. 0047)	0. 0111 ** (0. 0052)	0. 0053 (0. 0053)
Model Criteria						
Adjusted R^2	0. 4022	0. 4376	0. 5836	0. 4960	0. 5035	0. 5837
S. E. of Regression	0. 0116	0. 0114	0. 0098	0. 0108	0. 0107	0. 0098
F-statistic	7. 7282	8. 7796	9. 4082	8. 3801	8. 6071	8. 0113
Prob. (F-statistic)	0. 0007	0. 0003	0. 0000	0. 0002	0. 0001	0. 0001
Durbin-Watson Stat	1. 7546	2. 0346	2. 0896	1. 8450	2. 0938	2. 0854

Notes: Standard errors in the parentheses. *, **, and *** indicates that a null hypothesis of zero is rejected at the 10%, 5% and 1% levels, respectively. a Null hypothesis is tested against alternative hypothesis of a theoretically prescribed positive coefficient (one-tailed test).

In summary, the interest rate channel at the regional level is rather weak. To some extent, the bank lending channel can explain the regional effects of monetary policy in China. A province becomes more sensitive to monetary policy shock as the percent of small sized enterprises increase and the percent of state-owned and state-holding enterprises decrease. This idea is consistent with the proposition of bank lending channel. However, it is also found provinces containing a large concentration of small banks or small percent of large banks will be less sensitive to monetary policy innovations. This finding is conflicted with bank lending channel.

5.4 The Role of DRRR Policy on the Earthquake-Stricken Counties

In this section, panel data is used to test the third model: the role of DRRR policy on the earthquake-stricken counties. In panel data analysis, three models are estimated: pooled regression model, fixed effects model and random effects model. This study uses the pooled ordinary least squares (POLS) to estimate the pooled regression model, uses within estimator to estimate the fixed effects and the generalized least squares (GLS) to estimate random effects model. In addition, the first difference (FD) estimator is also provided for fixed effects model estimation. The results are reported in Table 5.21.

In Table 5.21, model A is estimated for the 39 earthquake badly hurt counties with the DRRR policy, model B is tested for the other 39 counties with normal RRR policy in Sichuan province. At the first glance, it can be seen the coefficients of the interaction part $DRRR \times LOAN$ of model A is bigger than that of model B in all regressions.

Then the Likelihood ratio test and Hausman test are run to see which model is the best one. For model A, when running the Likelihood ratio test, the cross-

Table 5.21 Results of the Models

Item	Dependent Variable (DV): GDP							
	Pooled Regression		Fixed Effects (Within)		Fixed Effects (FD)		Random Effects	
IV	Model A	Model B	Model A	Model B	Model A	Model B	Model A	Model B
Intercept	0.6356 (1.2395)	1.2107 *** (3.2775)	2.7597 *** (4.3027)	4.7895 *** (13.8243)	0.0870 *** (3.1577)	0.0875 *** (4.8278)	1.6893 *** (3.7311)	3.9675 *** (13.7078)
GOV	0.0222 (0.4836)	0.2201 *** (4.0883)	0.0191 (0.6397)	0.0993 *** (2.9413)	0.0245 (1.2616)	0.0152 (0.6846)	0.0442 * (1.6710)	0.0822 *** (2.6529)
LOAN	0.0721 (1.4833)	0.1460 *** (3.2571)	0.1014 * 1.9053	0.0971 *** (3.2937)	0.0816 (0.6312)	0.0378 (0.9161)	0.1065 ** (2.5912)	0.1002 *** (3.6568)
DRRR * LOAN①	0.4365 *** (3.7606)	0.0763 (1.1443)	0.2849 *** (5.2299)	0.2114 *** (11.9360)	0.2074 *** (4.1866)	0.1336 *** (6.3916)	0.3006 *** (5.8805)	0.1890 *** (11.1380)
OI	0.2298 *** (4.6212)	0.1249 *** (2.5728)	0.1309 *** (4.7792)	0.1308 *** (5.5908)	0.1108 *** (3.2884)	0.0655 ** (2.4810)	0.1196 *** (4.7748)	0.1034 *** (4.7247)
CONS	0.6269 *** (20.5969)	0.4893 *** (9.1563)	0.5502 *** (8.5782)	0.3380 *** (6.4859)	0.1669 ** (2.5908)	0.1007 (1.4622)	0.6199 *** (15.9608)	0.4489 *** (10.4446)
Adj. R^2	0.9445	0.9129	0.9932	0.9962	0.2050	0.3646	0.9006	0.9342
Obs.	156	156	156	156	117	117	156	156

Notes: T-statistics in parentheses. *, **, and *** indicates that a null hypothesis of zero is rejected at the 10%, 5%, and 1% levels, respectively. Adj. R^2 is adjusted R^2. Obs. is observations. The variables are in logarithm except DRRR and RRR.

① For Model B, the interaction part is $RRR \times LOAN$.

section F-statistic is 29. 4352, the P-value is 0. 0000, so the null hypothesis that the proper model is pooled regression model is rejected. Then the Hausman test is run to compare the fixed effects and random effects, if the Hausman test rejects the null hypothesis, the fixed effects model (entity fixed effects model) is appropriate, or the random effects model is estimated (Hausman, 1978). The Chi-Sq. Statistic for model A is 19. 3821 and P-value is 0. 0016, thus the null hypothesis is rejected, the final model is fixed effects model (entity fixed effects model). In model B, for Likelihood ratio test, the cross-section F-statistic is 88. 2973, the P-value is 0. 0000, for the Hausman test, the Chi-Sq. Statistic is 28. 0772 and P-value is 0. 0000, the null hypothesis can be rejected and the fixed effects model (entity fixed effects model) is chosen as the best model.

For fixed effects model (within estimator), according to Table 5. 21, in model A (the earthquake-stricken counties), the coefficient of government expenditure is positive and non-significant. The coefficients of other independent variables are both positive and statistically significant. In model B, all the coefficients are positive and significant. The coefficient of the interaction part is the combined effect of the DRRR and loans on the GDP. This coefficient in model A is bigger than that in model B (fixed effects model). Ceteris paribus, considering all these 78 counties are in the same province Sichuan, located in the adjacent places, almost share the same economic development level, thus this study concludes that it is the DRRR policy which mainly causes the difference. In earthquake-stricken counties, the combined effect of the lower DRRR and more loans is about 34. 77% bigger than that in the other 39 counties, indicating that the preferential DRRR in the earthquake-stricken counties is effective and does can help the economy of the less developed disaster counties to gain more growth than the normal RRR in other counties. The results of fixed effects model (FD) are also provided in Table 5. 20. In addition, this study estimates the fixed effects model using the LSDV (the results are available on request), the results are rather stable and confirm the robustness of the findings.

5.5 Summary

In this chapter, this study tests three models corresponding to the three objectives. For the first objective, examining the regions' responses to monetary policy when considering the spillover effects, the results of the first model confirm that different regions and provinces respond to monetary policy differently. Generally speaking, the developed region (the East) and the coastal provinces (such as Zhejiang, Shanghai, Shandong and Guangdong) have a much bigger responses to common monetary policy. The less developed region (the West) and the inland western provinces respond less to monetary policy. Moreover, the regional effects of monetary policy widen the regional disparity and undermine the regional coordinated economic development.

In the first model, the importance of the spillover effects is also checked. The results show that in the short-run, when examining the regional or provincial effects of monetary policy, the spillover effects are very important. In most of cases, it can significantly increase the responses of regions and provinces to monetary policy. In the long-run, the spillover effects are also very important in the East and the Middle. However, in the West, to some extent the negative influence of another effect "deposit transfer" may weaken the positive influence of the spillover effects. As most of the deposits flow to the more developed eastern provinces through four large commercial banks, it is found that, in the long-run, the expansionary monetary policy mostly supports the economic growth of the East, it also support the Middle while at the same time, it give less or even no supports to the West in the long-run. Thus to some extent, monetary policy enlarges the gap of regional economies.

In the second model, the factors affecting the regional effects of monetary policy are examined. The results show that in China, the interest rate channel is rather weak at the regional level. Regions or provinces with a large proportion of small enterprises or small percent of state-owned or state-holding enterprises respond more to monetary policy. At the regional level, to some extent, bank lending channel is more effective than interest rate channel.

The role of the DRRR policy on the earthquake-stricken counties is tested in the third model. The findings show that comparing with the role of the normal RRR on other counties, the preferential DRRR policy does can help the economy of the less developed disaster counties to gain more growth.

Chapter 6

Conclusion

6.1 Introduction

This chapter begins by the recapitulation of this study followed by the main findings of this study. The next section is implication of this study which covers the theoretical and practical implications and in what follow, limitations of the study and some suggestions for future study are put forward. This chapter is closed with the conclusion of this study.

6.2 Recapitulation of the Study

This study tries to examine and propose solutions to reduce the regional effects of monetary policy in China. To achieve this general objective, three sub-objectives are raised. The first one is to evaluate the magnitude and timing of regions' and provinces' output responses to monetary policy when considering spillover effects across regions or provinces. The second one is to examine whether or not provincial different size distributions of small banks can explain the regional effects of monetary policy. The third one is to examine whether the

DRRR policy has some effects on the outputs of earthquake-stricken areas so as to reduce the regional effects of monetary policy.

For the first objective, this study attempts to examine the regional effects of monetary policy in China more precisely and pay special attention to the influence of spillover effects on the regional effects of monetary policy. For the second objective, this study tries to explain the factors affecting the regional effects of monetary policy. Among these factors, this study emphasizes and examines the role of small bank based on the bank lending channel. For the third objective, in fact, this study tries to find some solutions to reduce the regional effects of monetary policy in China from the perspective of monetary policy. Therefore, this study takes the examination of the role of DRRR policy (one instrument of monetary policy in China) on the earthquake-stricken area for a case study, while the real purpose is to check whether this differentiated reserve requirement ratio can reduce the regional effects of monetary policy and make a more balanced regional economic development.

In achieving these objectives, research questions are raised. The general research question this study wants to address is to how to examine and reduce the regional effects of monetary policy in China. In order to explore this issue in more detail, this study also comes up with three sub-research questions which are: how much of the magnitude and timing of regions' and provinces' output responses to monetary policy when considering spillover effects in China? Can provincial different size distributions of small banks explain the regional effects of monetary policy in China? Does the DRRR policy have any effects on the outputs of the earthquake-stricken areas so as to reduce the regional effects of monetary policy?

The first question is actually consisted of two aspects: the regions' responses and the provinces' responses to monetary policy shock in China. In order to resolve this research question, two SVAR models are developed: the inter-regional SVAR model for each region and the inter-regional SVAR model for each province. As the regional model just contains three regions: the East, the Middle and the West, this division may be too general to examine the regional effects of monetary policy. Thereafter, this study develops the provincial SVAR model to examine 31 provinces' responses to monetary policy shock in more detail so as to get a comprehensive understanding of the regional effects of monetary policy in China. In the first research question, the main contribution is that this study examines the regional effects of monetary policy with accounting for the spillover effects which the previous literature in China neglects. Carlino and DeFina (1995) find important and persistent interregional spillovers exist and suggest that when examining the regional effects of macro-policies scholars should incorporate this interregional spillover effects. To highlight the spillover effects, this study also develops the SVAR models for each region and for each province without accounting for spillover effects in order to make a comparison.

For the second question, this study tries to examine the reasons why monetary policy influences different regions differently. This study uses the provincial SVAR model with spillover effect generated impulse responses as dependent variable. Based on monetary transmission mechanism theory, this study mainly checks two monetary transmission channels: interest rate channel and bank lending channel. The percent of the second industry in each province is employed to represent interest rate channel. As for bank lending channel, this study uses the proportion of small bank and the percent of small enterprises in each province to represent the traditional bank lending channel, uses the percent of large commercial banks and the proportion of state-owned and state-holding enterprises in each province to represent the bank lending channel with soft budget constraints. This study runs cross-sectional multiple linear regressions to test the relationship between the dependent and independent variables.

The purpose for the third question is to find a monetary policy instrument which to some extent can reduce the regional effects of monetary policy and promote the coordinated regional economies. As the PBC has implemented the

DRRR policy on certain region (the disaster area), this study uses this implementation as a case study to check the role of the DRRR policy on the earth quake-stricken counties. If the positive role of the DRRR policy on these areas can be confirmed, maybe the application of the DRRR policy can be extended to the more less developed western provinces and rural areas so as to promote the economic growth of these areas.

6.3 Main Findings of the Study

6.3.1 The Existence of Regional Effects of Monetary Policy and Importance of Spillover Effects

First of all, the first objective of this study is to evaluate the magnitude and timing of regions' and provinces' output responses to monetary policy when considering the spillover effects. To achieve this objective, this study develops two benchmark SVAR models with accounting for the spillover effect: the inter-regional SVAR model for each region and for each province. Meanwhile, with the purpose of emphasizing the importance of the spillover effect, two SVAR models for each region and each province with no consideration for spillover effects are also developed in order to make a comparison. Both of the models confirm the existence of regional effects of monetary policy in China and the importance of spillover effect.

For the benchmark inter-regional SVAR model with spillover effect, the results show that in the short-run, when there is an unexpected increase of M2 change, the output growth of the East displays the biggest magnitude of increase, almost 1.6 times the increase of output growth in the Middle and 2.5 times that of the West. In long-run level, the results are rather similar as that in the short-run, indicating that current monetary policy promotes its economic growth of the

East more, while at the same time gives less supports to the Middle and the West. In China, it is clear that common monetary policy has different effects across regions. What is more, these regional effects widen the gap among regions.

When comparing the benchmark inter-regional SVAR model with the spillover effect and without the spillover effect, the results are as expected. The spillover effect is of special importance when examining the regional effects of monetary policy in China. In the short-run, when considering the spillover effects, three regions respond much bigger to monetary policy shocks, indicating that the spillover effects are very important in the short-run. When examining the regional effects of monetary policy, the spillover effects should be taken into account. In the long-run, when considering this effect, the long-run response of the East and the Middle increases more than 30%, while the increase of long-run responses in the West is negative. That implies in the long-run level, besides the spillover effect, other factors may affect the responses of the West to monetary policy shock. The explanations will be provided later.

To measure the regional effects of monetary policy in more detail, this study further estimates the inter-regional SVAR model for each province with the spillover effect and without the spillover effect. The results of the provincial SVAR model are quite consistent with that of the regional model. Provinces show considerable different responses to monetary policy innovation. For example, an unexpected 5% increase of M2 change can increase the GDP growth of Zhejiang province by 2.70% within two years, while at the same time it can only increase the GDP growth of Qinghai province by 0.46%. Generally speaking, the provinces in the East show much bigger responses, the provinces in the Middle and the West display relative smaller responses. For the long-run cumulative responses, most of the eastern provinces display positive responses, meanwhile a big part of provinces in the West show negative long-run cumulative impulse responses. The results are in accord with the finding of the regional model.

The results of provincial SVAR model indicate that in the short-run, when considering the spillover effects, most of the provinces have much bigger maximum impulse responses. The increases of the magnitudes are more than 70% for many provinces, showing the importance of the spillover effects.

As for long-run cumulative impulse response, this study finds that in the East, long-run responses increase when considering the spillover effects in seven provinces (except four provinces: Beijing, Liaoning, Hainan and Zhejiang). In the Middle, Six provinces (except Shanxi and Jilin) have larger magnitudes of long-run cumulative responses. While in the West, the number is only four, the magnitudes of eight provinces are much smaller when considering the spillover effects. The finding is quite similar with that of the regional model, showing the robustness of the results.

In short, both the findings of the regional model and provincial model confirm that in China, regions and provinces respond differently to monetary policy shock. In the short-run, the spillover effect is very important when examining the regional effects of monetary policy. Regions and provinces show much bigger responses to monetary policy shock when considering the spillover effect in the short-run. If scholars examine the regional effects of monetary policy without accounting for the spillover effect, the results may be biased and not reliable.

In the long-run level, when considering the spillover effect, the results indicate that the long-run accumulated responses of the East and its affiliated provinces increase the most, the long-run accumulated responses in the Middle also increase a lot, but the increase of long-run accumulated responses in the West and most of their affiliated provinces are negative. The explanation is as follow. In China, besides spillover effects, there exists "deposits transfer" among regions. This is related to China's banking system. As in China, traditionally, the banking system is almost monopolized by four large commercial banks which adopt branch banking system. Their branches spread all over the country. In the past forty years, the branches of four large banks collect a lot of deposits in the

West. However, these deposits are not fully used to support the development of the West. As the East is more developed with a relatively full-fledged market economy and some better investment opportunities, some of the deposits are transferred to support the development of the East by their branches of the four large banks.

In the benchmark regional and provincial SVAR model, M2 is used as monetary policy variable. In the short-run, the spillover effects work as the deposits have no time to transfer. But in the long-run, the deposits have plenty time to transfer from the less developed western region to the more developed eastern coastal region. The negative influence of deposits transfer to some extent weakens the positive influence of the spillover effects in the West. Thus in the long-run, when considering the spillover effects, the increase of long-run cumulative response in the West is negative. If assuming all the deposits focus on the development of its own region (the SVAR models for each region), the long-run cumulative responses of the outputs in the West would increase more. This is also proved by the provincial SVAR model. This phenomenon also indicates that the previous studies which examine the regional effects of monetary policy region by region without accounting for the spillover effects are likely to overestimate the response of the West, but underestimate the effects of monetary policy in the East in the long-run. While in the short-run, to some extent they may underestimate the regions' responses to monetary policy shock.

The results and explanations are robust as they are confirmed by the regional SVAR models with M1 and one year bank lending rate as monetary policy variables. As M1 is mainly consisted of cash and demand deposit which are highly liquid and not likely to transfer across regions. Hence, the long-run level of cumulative response of the East is smaller, the long-run level of cumulative responses of WGDP growth is bigger. When this study runs the estimation of the regional SVAR model with one year bank lending rate, the impulse responses of three regions are similar to that of the benchmark regional model.

When estimating the inter-regional SVAR model, this study also checks two questions: the first one is which one is the best order of all the endogenous variable, monetary policy variable ranks first or last. The second one is which variable (M2, M1, and one year bank lending rate) can better represent monetary policy stance. For the first one, this study finds that if M2 ranks first, the responses of three regions increase more than 50% comparing with that with M2 ranking last. Thus the best order is the one which monetary policy variable ranks first, meaning that monetary policy can affect the real variables within one year. For the second one, the results show that M2 (rank first) is the better monetary policy variable as three regions apparently respond more to the change of M2.

6.3.2 The Second Objective of this Study

This study runs multiple linear regressions using cross sectional data (31 provinces) to check the factors influencing the regional effects of monetary policy in China. Using the provincial SVAR (with spillover effect) generated impulse responses as dependent variable, the results show that the coefficient of the percent of secondary industry in each province is rather unstable, meaning there are no apparent evidences of existence of interest rate channel at the regional level. This finding is consistent with Jiang and Chen (2009). Thus interest rate channel is rather weak at the regional level in China.

The results display that a province with large proportion of small sized enterprises and small percent of state-owned and state-holding enterprises will be more sensitive to monetary policy shocks. This is consistent with the bank lending channel. Kashap and Stein (1995), Carlino and DeFina (1998) both point out that contractionary monetary policy would pose more of a problem for small firms than large firms who usually have greater access nonbank sources of external finance.

However, the coefficients of the percent of small banks are negative and significant. Moreover, the coefficients of the percent of large banks are positive and significant. That is to say, a province with a bigger proportion of small banks and smaller percent of large banks will respond less to monetary policy shock. These findings are inconsistent with the hypothesis proposed by bank lending channel. Carlino and DeFina (1998) explain that one possible reason is that the banks' assets size may be a poor indicator of its ability to adjust their balance sheets to monetary policy shocks. This study also tries to provide some possible explanations. However, the explanations should be tested in more details in future.

Above all, this study finds that the interest rate channel is rather weak at the regional level. To some extents, bank lending channel plays a certain role at the regional level. However, the role of small banks and large commercial banks is conflict with the proposition of bank lending channel. The location whether this province is located in the East will significantly influence its response to monetary policy shocks.

6. 3. 3 The Third Objective of this Study

This study checks the role of the DRRR policy on the earthquake-stricken counties. Previously it is confirmed that monetary policy indeed has regional effects and the regional effects enlarge regional disparity. Consequently, this study wants to find some solutions to reduce the regional effects of monetary policy and narrow the gap among regions. Accordingly, panel data analysis is employed to examine the effects of the DRRR policy on the earthquake-stricken area during 2008 – 2011. This study makes a comparison between 39 earthquake badly hurt counties with preferential DRRR policy and the other 39 counties with the normal RRR policy in Sichuan province. The results confirm that the preferential DRRR policy really can quicken the recovery process of the earthquake-stricken counties comparing with the normal RRR in other counties. That is to say, if certain less developed region is applied this preferential DRRR policy by the PBC, its economy will grow much faster than before. To some extents, the PBC can use this policy to reduce the regional effects of monetary policy.

6.4 Implications of the Study

6.4.1 Policy Implication

6.4.1.1 Pay Attention to Spillover Effects

In order to formulate proper monetary policy, it is necessary for the PBC to measure the regional effects of monetary policy. The results of this study indicate that the PBC should pay special attention to the influence of spillover effects when examining the regional effects of monetary policy in China. Given the influence of the spillover effects, there are some differences between the national monetary policy transmission channel and the regional monetary transmission channel. For the whole country, monetary policy directly affects the whole economy through monetary transmission channels. But at the regional level, besides this direct influence, monetary policy also can indirectly influence the economy of certain region through the spillover effects. And what is more, the empirical results show that these spillover effects can increase the responses of most provinces and regions by more than 50% , so it is very crucial and cannot be neglected in the short-run for the PBC to formulate monetary policy.

If the PBC neglects the spillover effects when measuring the regional effects of monetary policy, the consequence may be very serious. For instance, based on the direct impacts on regional economies of monetary policy, the PBC implements expansionary monetary policy and reduce reserve requirement ratio by 1% in order to pull the economy out of recession. In facts, if considering both the direct influence (monetary transmission channel) and the indirect influence (spillover effects) of monetary policy on regional economies, as the spillover effects actually amplify the influence, the PBC can achieve its goals by just reducing reserve requirement ratio by 0.5%. Thus the 1% reduction of the RRR is too large, the consequence may be that it can pull the economy out of recession, while at the same time causing high inflation. The loss exceeds the gain. Therefore, when examining the regional effects of monetary policy in China, the PBC had better pay attention to the spillover effects and consider both the direct impacts and the indirect impacts of monetary policy on regional economies.

In the long-run, there exists another effect: deposits transfer effect, which means the four large banks adopting branch banking system transfer the deposits from the less developed middle and western provinces to the more developed eastern coastal provinces. In fact, in the long-run level, the East benefits more while the Middle and the West suffer losses from the deposits transfer effect.

In order to reduce the deposits transfer effects, the PBC should continue to reduce the market share of four large banks, support the development of rural credit cooperatives and city commercial banks which businesses are focused on local economies, improving the competitiveness in the banking industry and reducing the influences of deposits transfer effects gradually.

In reality, the PBC has always taken M2 as intermediate target (Xie, 2004). The results show that when the PBC selects M2 as monetary policy indicator or intermediate target, especially when it wants to monitor the amount of regional or provincial money supply (M2) in order to formulate monetary policy, the PBC should notice this influence of deposits transfer effects. For example, the PBC may care about how many funds are really used to support the economic growth of certain region. The amount of funds can be calculated like this: the amounts of M2 plus the deposits flowed in, and minus the deposits flowed out.

6. 4. 1. 2 Regional Interest Rate Channel and Bank Lending Channel

This study explains the regional effects of monetary policy based on monetary transmission channels. The results show that at the regional level, bank lending channel is effective to some extent. This study checks two types of bank lending channels, the traditional channel: small banks—small enterprises channel and the channel with Chinese characteristic: large banks—state-owned and state-holding enterprises channel. One of an unexpected finding is that provinces with a large proportion of small banks and a relatively small percent of large banks respond less to monetary policy shock. Although this study offers some explanations based on the real condition of China's banking industry, these explanations only provide some possibilities. In fact, it is not consistent with the basic idea of traditional bank lending channel. What should be done should still follow the view of bank lending channel.

In a market economy, the traditional channel should be basic bank lending channel. Therefore, the PBC should give more supports to develop small banks whose loans mainly flow to the S&M sized enterprises so as to let the traditional bank lending channel play a more and more important role. Meanwhile, the PBC should further reduce the market share of four large banks and reform the property rights of state-owned and state-holding enterprises, let their decisions be more decided by market or not the PBC.

At the regional level, this study finds that the interest rate channel is rather weak. Industry and construction in a region do not respond sensitively to the change of interest rate in China. The reason is that as China is a transition economy from planned economy to market economy. Traditionally the PBC regulated all the interest rates, since 1994 the PBC has start the interest rate liberalization process. Although in recent years this reform has got some progress, it is still a long journey and far from the end. The results indicate that the PBC should further liberalize the interest rates, allowing interest rate play a fundamental role in resources allocation.

6. 4. 1. 3 Structural Adjustment with the DRRR Policy

The results of this study show that the preferential DRRR policy (a ratio lower than normal RRR) implemented in the earthquake-stricken counties during certain period can significantly quicken the reconstruction and development of the disaster area. This case gives the PBC an idea to reduce the regional effects and promote coordinated regional economic development from the perspective of monetary policy.

The results of this study show that in the long-run, monetary policy greatly supports the economic growth of the East, while at the same time gives little or no supports to the Middle and the West. To some extent, the DRRR policy can be applied to reduce the different effects of monetary policy and narrow the gap of regional economies. For example, the PBC can apply a lower reserve requirement ratio to the less developed middle and western provinces to promote their economic growths, while implement a higher reserve requirement ratio for the developed eastern provinces.

The results indicate monetary policy can play a role in adjusting and optimizing economic structure through differentiated monetary policy instruments such as the DRRR policy. This type of instrument gives certain flexibility to monetary policy. From this finding, this study observes that the inefficiency of monetary policy can be further improved by offering specific growth-enhancing instruments such as DRRR. However, since changing the RRR is not favorable to long-run prospect of attracting foreign investors, especially to China, other possible instruments can be time to time introduced to the middle and/or the western regions. The PBC can use differential monetary policy instruments to guide credit funds flow to the area which government policy focus on. Besides the DRRR policy, other differentiated instruments, such as preferential interest rate for certain region can also be implemented by the PBC.

6. 4. 1. 4 The Design of Monetary Policy Should Consider Regional Information

China is a huge and multinational country with big regional disparity. The implementation of monetary policy in China is made difficult due to the existence of regional effects of monetary policy. Therefore, it is not enough for the PBC to formulate monetary policy based on the Taylor rule and McCallum rule while just considering economic growth rate and inflation rate of the whole nation. The PBC should take into account the different impacts of common monetary policy across regions. A better design of monetary policy should account for regional data as the existence of different regional effects. Considering national information together with regional information about real economic condition, monetary policy can be set optimally by the PBC in China.

To be successfully conducting monetary policy, the PBC has to weigh the different consequences of monetary policy actions on different regions and reconcile the economic interests of different regions. Given the different effects across regions of monetary policy, it may be better that regions with different economic and financial structures could have their own voices at the central bank in order to account their welfare interests.

6. 4. 1. 5 Certain Autonomous Right for the Branches of the PBC

Because of the existence of regional effects of monetary policy, under the background of common monetary policy, the PBC may assign its regional branches a certain autonomous right, allowing them to make a fine adjustment according to the real economic condition of their own regions. To some extent, this action can help to reduce the regional effects of common monetary policy and promote balanced regional economic development.

Until 1998, the branch network of the PBC was based on Chinese administrative system, with 31 branch offices located at the provincial level. In 1998, the branches of the PBC underwent a major restructuring. The 31 provincial branches of the PBC were replaced by nine regional branches that are in a better position to conduct common monetary policy (see Table 6. 1).

Table 6. 1 The Regional Branches of the PBC

Branch	Tianjin	Shenyang	Shanghai	Nanjing	Jinan
Jurisdiction	Tianjin	Liaoning	Shanghai	Jiangsu	Shandong
	Hebei	Jilin	Zhejiang	Anhui	Henan
	Shanxi	Heilongjiang	Fujian		
	Inner Mongolia				
Branch	Wuhan	Guangzhou	Chengdu	Xi'an	
Jurisdiction	Jiangxi	Guangdong	Sichuan	Shaanxi	Gansu
	Hubei	Guangxi	Guizhou	Qinghai	Ningxia
	Hunan	Hainan	Yunnan	Xinjiang	
			Tibet		

Sources: The People's Bank of China

The regional branches have analyzed regional economic and financial conditions in detail and provided plenty of useful information for the PBC to formulate monetary policy in the past years. However, the main problem bothered the regional branches is that their scopes of job is just to provide information to the PBC. They should be offered job scope covering research on the real regional monetary policy and providing useful suggestions to the PBC. Especially when the China Banking Regulatory Commission (CBRC) separated from the PBC in 2003, the role of regional branches has reduced gradually.

In fact now the regional branches do not have any autonomous right, what they do is just following instructions of the PBC and implementing standard monetary policy. To reduce different impacts of monetary policy, the PBC needs to grant regional branches certain autonomous right to certain extent. For instance, the PBC can give regional branches permission to set certain monetary policy instrument above or less than the standard level according to real economic conditions of their own regions. The regional branches can provide useful suggestions based on regional economic and financial conditions to the PBC and the PBC should take them seriously. If regional branches have such kind of decision-making power, when the PBC changes monetary policy stance, they have the right to make a fine adjustment according to the real economic conditions of their own regions in order to promote regional economic growth at best. This can help to reduce the gap of regional economies and promote harmonious develop of China's regional economy.

6. 4. 1. 6 Coordination of Monetary and Fiscal Policies

As macro-control policies, a well coordination of monetary and fiscal policies is necessary. While fiscal policy can be tailored for a particular region or sector, the consequences of common monetary policy are national by nature. However, the effects of monetary policy will not be uniform as countries are typically composed of diverse regions. Therefore, it is very helpful to understand regional effects of monetary policy, if one region experiences negative influence of monetary policy, it can be compensated by the fiscal policy. For example, the government's grants program. If monetary policy has differential impacts upon provinces, there is a rationale for increasing government grants to those provinces which are adversely affected. Monetary and fiscal policies can make a better coordination to stabilize and promote regional economic development.

6. 4. 2 Theoretical Implication

6. 4. 2. 1 Formulation and Implementation of Monetary Policy

Traditionally, monetary policy is formulated by the central bank following the Taylor rule and McCallum rule based on the national output gap and inflation gap. The results show that for a large country with obvious regional disparity, the formulation and implementation of monetary policy can be divided into two stages: at the first stage, the formulation and implementation of monetary policy should consider the regional effects of monetary policy. In other words, under this circumstance, when the central bank formulates monetary policy, they should not only consider the national economic growth and the inflation level, but also pay attention to the information of regional economies. After careful consideration of national and regional economic information, the implementation of monetary policy formulated by the central bank should help to promote the coordinated regional economic development. At the second stage, when all regions have a balanced economic development, then the central bank can implement a common and unified monetary policy.

Mundell (1961) first put forward the single currency conception and the optimum currency area (OCA) theory. He argues that a currency area should be a region, whose borders need not necessarily coincide with the state borders, it may be beyond the state borders or within the borders. Now single currency is very common in one country or one region (European Union, EU) even they do not satisfy the OCA standards. In these countries or regions, especially the geographically diversified country like China or the eastern enlargement of EU where single currency applies with unbalanced regional economies, they should consider the suggestions of this study such as under common monetary policy, giving more autonomous right to the branches of European central bank in each country and allowing them to make a fine adjustment of common monetary policy according to their own economic condition, or applying differentiated monetary policy instrument on different regions depending on the real economic condition. After satisfying the OCA standards, common monetary policy can be implemented.

6.4.2.2 Consideration of the Spillover Effects

The findings of this study broaden the perspective of monetary policy transmission mechanism, especially at the regional level. As well known, at the national level, monetary policy directly influence the national economy through different monetary transmission channels. However, at the regional level, monetary policy can affect regional economies through two mechanisms: direct influences through monetary transmission channels and indirect influences through the spillover effects among regions. Moreover, the results show these indirect influences are very important and cannot be neglected. Therefore, at the regional level, when examining the regional effects of monetary policy, two mechanisms should be considered: the monetary transmission channel and the spillover effects.

6.4.2.3 Differentiated Monetary Policy Instrument

The findings also provide some new innovations to the implementation of monetary policy. If one country is very big and geographically diversified, the central bank of this county can try to implement differentiated monetary policy instruments for structural adjustment of the economy, such as the DRRR policy, the central bank can apply a lower RRR on the less developed region and at the same time apply a little higher RRR on the more developed region. Nevertheless, the implementation of differentiated monetary policy instruments has an important precondition: a large country with an unbalanced regional economy. If common monetary policy is implemented in such a country, regional effects of monetary policy will generated and these regional effects will enlarge the regional disparity. In addition, the implementation period of differentiated monetary policy instrument is limited. It can be implemented when there exists regional disparity in one country and common monetary policy has differential effects across regions. Once the regional economies become balanced, the differentiated monetary policy instrument no longer applies, instead, common and unified monetary policy will be proper.

6.5 Limitations of the Study

This study also has several limitations. First, as short of quarterly or monthly data of regional GDP, this study can only use the annual data for the regional and the provincial SVAR model. From 1978 to 2011, just 34 years, the data may be not enough. Moreover, as in the past three decades, China has undergone substantial changes in its economic and financial fields. Due to data limitation, this study cannot check structural break by dividing the estimation period.

For cross sectional multiple linear regressions (the second model), because of data limitation, this study just averages the data of the factors explaining the regional effects of monetary policy for twelve years, which may be not enough. As the data how many loans small banks lend to small enterprises and how many loans large banks lend to state-owned and state-holding enterprises are not available, this study uses the proportion of assets of small banks as a proxy for the percent of small banks. The results indicate that they show an adverse direction as the bank lending channel predicted. One possible reason is that the banks' assets size may be a poor indicator of its ability to adjust their balance sheets to monetary policy actions. For the panel model (the third model), in fact, the best data used in the model should be monthly data or seasonal data. But due to data limitation, this study can only get yearly data (only four years) which seems to be a little short.

Second, in the past forty years, monetary policy instruments which the PBC used have changed several times. Now the PBC uses variety of monetary policy instruments to regulate the economy simultaneously. Some studies such as Sun (2013) indicate perhaps one single instrument would not constitute an adequate representation of the monetary policy stance. He, Leung and Chong (2013) also point out that the analysis based on a single monetary tool may not provide a good evaluation of its monetary policy. Xiong (2012) summarizes the information of some monetary policy instruments and develops a new policy stance index. He et al. (2013) suggest a factor that tracks a wide range of market-based policy instruments at the disposal of the PBC to represent a general stance of monetary policy. Unfortunately, their empirical periods are both in recent years (after 1998). As the estimation period is from the economic reform and opening up (1978) until 2011, due to the data problem, this study cannot get such a policy stance index. These shortcomings may be overcome when the information and data problem are solved.

Third, this limitation comes from the SVAR model itself. As well known, there is a particular asymmetry about the effects of monetary policy which we call the "traditional Keynesian asymmetry" (Weise, 1999; Ravn & Sola, 2004; Tan, Habibullan & Mohamed, 2010), which states that positive monetary policy shocks have smaller real effects than negative monetary policy shocks. However, the SVAR model treats tightening and easing of M2 symmetrically, that is to say, an unexpected increase in M2 temporarily increase the GDP growth relative to what it would be otherwise. Therefore, an important limitation of this study is that the results cannot reflect the asymmetric effect of monetary policy in China.

6.6 Suggestions of Future Study

This study expects the future studies develop this research from the following aspects:

First, if the seasonal data or monthly data about the information of the GDP of China and its provinces are available, future study can do a more in-depth and detailed research on the regional effects of monetary policy in China. Since economic reform and opening up, China has undergone comprehensive changes in the field of economy and finance. The future study should check structural break when examining the regional effects of monetary policy in China. Although this study accounts for differences in the effects of monetary policy across regions, differences in the effects of monetary policy over time are not allowed due to the data limitation. This is not proper. In future, when the data problem is solved, the studies should examine whether the regional effects of monetary policy in China has changed over time.

Second, future study should pay more attention to monetary policy transmission channels at the regional level. Most of the previous studies focus on the national monetary transmission channel. Due to the existence of regional disparity, it is necessary to study the regional effects of monetary policy and the regional monetary policy transmission channels. This study just examines the factors affecting the regional effects of monetary policy based on regional monetary transmission channels. Future studies should give a more detailed description and examination of monetary transmission channel at the regional level. In this study, the proportion of assets of small banks is used as a proxy for the percent of small banks. The result is not as the bank lending channel predicted. If future studies can get the data how many loans small banks lend to small enterprises and use this variable as the indicator of bank lending channel, the results may be improved.

Third, this study just does a simple case study to examine the effects of the DRRR policy on the disaster area. In fact, the PBC also applies this policy to other fields, such as the large commercial banks and the S&M sized banks, certain rural areas, and some rural credit cooperatives. If relevant data is available, future studies can further examine the effects of the DRRR policy on these fields. Confirming by various aspects of the effects of the DRRR policy can give us more supports to extend the application of the DRRR policy.

Moreover, if it is confirmed that the DRRR policy can reduce the regional effects of monetary policy, future studies should focus on how to extend its application, in which area, how long this policy should be implemented and how much this preferential DRRR policy lower than the normal RRR.

Finally, lots of previous studies analyze which is the best monetary policy indicator in China. In summary, it seems that a policy stance index can better reflect the monetary policy stance. However, the previous studies construct this policy index mainly after 1998. This period is too short if you want to examine the effects of monetary policy. At present, the estimation period of most of studies is from economic reform and opening up (1978) until now. Future studies should try to construct a policy index which can better measure monetary policy stance from 1978 until now.

6.7 Conclusion

China is a large country with great regional disparity. Monetary policy exerts different impacts across regions. The main objective of this study is to examine and reduce the regional effects of monetary policy in China. This study employs the SVAR model to study the regional and provincial effects of common monetary policy with accounting for spillover effect in China. To reduce the regional effects of monetary policy, this study also explores the factors affecting regional effects of monetary policy. Finally the DRRR policy is tested whether it can reduce the regional effects of monetary policy. The findings show that in China, regions and provinces respond differently to monetary policy shock. The spillover effect exerts a significant influence on the magnitude of regions' and provinces' responses to monetary policy innovations. In China, bank lending channel is more effective than interest rate channel. The DRRR policy does can help the earthquake-stricken counties to gain more economic growth in Sichuan province. Then it is suggested that the PBC can consider expanding to apply this DRRR policy to more less developed provinces (Such as some provinces in the Middle and the West) or some rural areas in order to reduce the regional effects of monetary policy and promote a more coordinated regional economic development.

References

[1] Agenor, P. & Montiel, J. Monetary Policy Analysis in a Small Open Credit Based Economy [J]. *Open Economic Review*, 2008, 9: 423 – 455.

[2] Andersen, L. C., & Jordon, J. L. Monetary and Fiscal Actions: A Test of their Relative Importance in Economic Stabilization [J]. *Federal Reserve Bank of St. Louis*, *Review* 1968: 11 – 23.

[3] Arnold, I. J. M. The Regional Effects of Monetary Policy in Europe [J]. *Journal of Economic Integration*, 2001, 16 (3): 399 – 420.

[4] Arnold, I. J. M. & Vrugt, E. B. Regional Effects of Monetary Policy in the Netherlands [J]. *International Journal of Business and Economics*, 2002, 1 (2): 123 – 134.

[5] Arnold, I. J. M. & Vrugt, E. B. Firm Size, Industry Mix and the Regional Transmission of Monetary Policy in Germany [J]. *German Economic Review*, 2004, 5 (1): 35 – 59.

[6] Baek, S. W. Does China Follow "the East Asian Development Model"? [J] *Journal of Contemporary Asia*, 2005, 35 (4): 485 – 498.

[7] Barrios, S., & Strobl, E. The Dynamics of Regional Inequalities [J]. *Regional Science and Urban Economics*, 2009, 39 (5): 575 – 591.

[8] Beare, J. B. A Monetarist Model of Regional Business Cycles [J]. *Journal of Regional Science*, 1976, 16 (1): 57.

[9] Benkwitz, A., Lütkepohl, H., & Wolters, J. Comparison of Bootstrap Confidence Interval for Impulse Responses of German Montary Systems [J]. *Macroeconomic Dynamics*, 2001, 5 (01): 81 – 100.

[10] Bennett, J., & Dixon, D. H. Monetary Policy and Credit in China: A Theoretical Analysis [J]. *Journal of Macroeconomics*, 2001, 23 (2): 297 – 314.

[11] Bernanke, B. S. How Important is the Credit Channel in the Transmission of Monetary Policy?: A Comment [M]. *Carnegie-Rochester Conference Series on Public Policy*, 1993, 39: 47 – 52.

[12] Bernanke, B. S. & Blinder, A. S. Credit, Money and Aggregate Demand [J]. *American Economic Review*, 1988, 78: 435 – 439.

[13] Bernanke, B. S. & Blinder, A. S. The Federal Funds Rate and the Channels of Monetary Transmission [J]. *American Economic Review*, 1992, 82 (4): 901 – 921.

[14] Bernanke, B. S. & Boivin, J. Monetary Policy in a Data-rich Environment [J]. *Journal of Monetary Economics*, 2003, 50 (3): 525 – 546.

[15] Bernanke, B. S., Boivin, J. & Eliasz, P. Measuring the Effects of Monetary Policy: A Factor-Augmented Vector Autoregressive (FAVAR) Approach [J]. *The Quarterly Journal of Economics*, 2005, 120 (1): 387 – 422.

[16] Bernanke, B. S. & Gertler, M. Inside the Black Box: The Credit Channel of Monetary Policy Transmission [J]. *Journal of Economic Perspectives*, 1995, 9 (4): 27 – 48.

[17] Bernanke, B. S., Gertler, M. & Waston, M. Systematic Monetary Policy and the Effects of Oil Price Shocks [J]. *Brookings Papers on Economic Activity*, 1997 (1): 91 – 142.

[18] Bernanke, B. S. & Mihov, I. Measuring Monetary Policy [J]. *The Quarterly Journal of Economics*, 1998, 113 (3): 869 – 902.

[19] Bewley, R., Orden, D., Yang, M., & Fisher, L. A. Comparison of Box-Tiao and Johansen Canonical Estimators of Cointegrating Vectors in VEC (1) Models [J]. *Journal of Econometrics*, 1994, 64 (1 – 2): 3 – 27.

[20] Black, F. Bank Funds Management in an Efficient Market [J]. *Journal of Financial Economics*, 1975, 2 (4): 323 – 339.

[21] Boivin, J. & Giannoni, M. P. Has Monetary Policy Become more Effective [J]? *Review of Economics and Statistics*, 2006, 88 (3): 445 – 462.

[22] Borio, C. & Disyatat, P. Unconventional Monetary Policies: An Appraisa [J]. *The Manchester School*, 2010, 78: 53 – 89.

[23] Braun, P. A. & Mittnik, S. Misspecifications in Vector Autoregressions and their Effects on Impulse Responses and Variance Decompositions [J]. *Journal of Econometrics*, 1993, 59: 319 – 341.

[24] Brun, J. F., Combes, J. L. & Renard, M. F. Are there Spillover Effects between Coastal and Noncoastal Regions in China? [J] *China Economic Review*, 2002, 13 (2 – 3): 161 – 169.

[25] Burdekin, R. C. K. & Siklos, P. L. What has Driven Chinese Monetary Policy since 1990? Investigating the People's Bank's Policy Rule [J]. *Journal of International Money and Finance*, 2008, 27 (5): 847 – 859.

[26] Cameron, A. C. & Trivedi, P. K. *Microeconometrics: Methods and Applications* [M]: New York: Cambridge university press, 2005.

[27] Campbell, J. Y. & Perron, P. Pitfalls and Opportunities: What Macroeconomists should Know about Unit Roots [J]. *In I. National Bureau of Economic Research* (Ed.), *NBER Macroeconomics Annual*, 1991 (6): 141 – 220.

[28] Cargill, T. F. & Mayer, T. The Effect of Changes in Reserve Requirements during the 1930s: The Evidence from Nonmember Banks [J]. *Journal of Economic History*, 2006, 66 (2): 417.

[29] Carlino, G. & Defina, R. Regional Income Dynanmics [J]. *Journal of Urban Economics*, 1995, 37: 88 – 106.

[30] Carlino, G. & DeFina, R. The Differential Regional Effects of Monetary Molicy [J]. *Review of Economics & Statistics*, 1998, 80 (4): 572 – 587.

[31] Carlino, G. & DeFina, R. The Differential Regional Effects of Monetary Policy: Evidence from the U. S. States [J]. *Journal of Regional Science*, 1999, 39 (2): 339 – 358.

[32] Cecchetti, S. G. Distinguishing Theories of the Monetary Transmission Mechanism [J]. *Federal Reserve Bank of St. Louis Economic Review*, *Federal Reserve Banks of San Francisco*, 1995, 77: 83 – 97.

[33] Chase Econometric Associates, I. Rural Impacts of Monetary Policy [J]. *Agricultural Economics Research*, 1981, 33: 1 – 11.

[34] Chen, A. & Groenewold, N. Reducing Regional Disparities in China: An Evaluation of Alternative Policies [J]. *Journal of Comparative Economics*, 2010, 38 (2): 189 – 198.

[35] Chen, A. & Groenewold, N. Does Investment Allocation Affect the Inter-Regional Output Gap in China? A Time-series Investigation [J]. *China Economic Review*, 2012, 26: 197 – 206.

[36] Christiano, L. & Eichenbaum, M. Identification and the Liquidity Effect of a Monetary Policy Shock. In Z. H. A. Cukierman, and L. Leiderman (Ed.), *Political Economy, Growth, and Business Cycles* [M]. Cambridge MA: MIT Press.

[37] Christiano, L. J. Modeling the Liquidity Effect of a Money Shock [J]. *Quarterly Review* (win), 1991: 3 – 34.

[38] Christiano, L. J., Eichenbaum, M. & Evans, C. L. Monetary Policy Shocks: What have we Learned and to What End? [C] *National Bureau of Economic Research Working Paper Series*, 1998, *No.* 6400.

[39] Cortes, B. S. & Kong, D. Regional Effects of Chinese Monetary Policy [J]. *The International Journal of Economic Policy Studies*, 2007, 2, 15 – 28.

[40] Cosimano, T. F. & McDonald, B. What's Different among Banks? [J] *Journal of Monetary Economics*, 1998, 41 (1): 57 – 70.

[41] Dai, G. China's Monetary Policy: Retrospect and Prospect [J]. *China & World Economy*, 2001, 3.

[42] Davidson, R. & MacKinnon, J. G. *Estimation and Inference in Econometrics* [M]. Oxford: Oxford University Press, 1993.

[43] De Grauwe, P. Monetary Policies in the Presence of Asymmetrie [J]. *Journal of Common Market Studies*, 2000, 38 (4): 593 –612.

[44] De Lucio, J. J. & Izquierdo, M. Local Responses to a Global Monetary Policy—the Regional Structure of Financial System [J]. *Fundación de Estudios de Economía Aplicada*, *FEDEA-D. T*, 1999, 14: 1 –24.

[45] Di Giacinto, V. Differential Regional Effects of Monetary Policy: A Geographical SVAR Approach [J]. *International Regional Science Review*, 2003, 26 (3): 313 –341.

[46] Dickey, D. A. & Fuller, W. A. Likeliood Ratio Statistics for Autoregressive Time Series with a Unit Root [J]. *Econometria*, 1981, 49: 1057 –1072.

[47] Dickinson, D. & Liu, J. The Real Effects of Monetary Policy in China: An Empirical Analysis [J]. *China Economic Review*, 2007, 18 (1): 87 –111.

[48] Dornbusch, R. , Favero, C. & Giavazz, F. Immediate Challenges for the ECB [J]. *Economic Policy*, 1998, 4: 17 –63.

[49] Du, Y. *Monetary Policy and Bank Loan Supply in China* [D]. Bachelor of Arts Williams College, 2010.

[50] Eichenbaum, M. Comments on 'Interpreting the Time Series Facts: The Effects of Monetary Policy' by Christopher Sims [J]. *European Economic Review*, 1992, 36: 1001 –1011.

[51] Elbourne, A. & de Haan, J. Financial Structure and Monetary Policy Transmission in Transition Countries [J]. *Journal of Comparative Economics*, 2006, 34 (1): 1 –23.

[52] Fabozzi, F. J. & Thurston, T. B. State Taxes and Reserve Requirements as Major Determinants of Yield Spreads among Money Market Instruments [J]. *Journal of Financial and Quantitative Analysis*, 1986, 21 (4): 427 –436.

[53] Fan, L. , Yu, Y. & Zhang, C. An Empirical Evaluation of China's Monetary Policies [J]. *Journal of Macroeconomics*, 2011, 33 (2): 358 –371.

[54] Fan, S. , Kanbur, R. & Zhang, X. China's Regional Disparities: Experience and Policy [J]. *Review of Development Finance*, 2011, 1 (1): 47 –56.

[55] Faust, J. & Leeper, E. M. When do Long-Run Identifying Restrictions Give Reliable Results? [J] *Journal of Business & Economic Statistics*, 1997, 15 (3): 345 –353.

[56] Fielding, D. & Shields, K. Regional Asymmetries in the Impact of Monetary Policy Shocks on Prices: Evidence from US Cities [J]. *Oxford Bulletin of Economics and Statistics*, 2011, 73 (1): 79 –103.

[57] Fishkind, H. H. The Regional Impact of Monetary Policy: An Economic Simulation Study of Indiana 1958 –1973 [J]. *Journal of Regional Science*, 1977, 17 (1): 77.

[58] Fleisher, B. M. & Chen, J. The Coast-Noncoast Income Gap, Productivity, and Region-

al Economic Policy in China [J]. *Journal of Comparative Economics*, 1997, 25 (2): 220 – 236.

[59] Friedman, M., & Schwartz, A. J. *A Monetary History of the United States*, 1867 – 1960 [M]. Princeton: Princeton University Press, 1963.

[60] Fu, X. Limited Linkages from Growth Engines and Regional Disparities in China [J]. *Journal of Comparative Economics*, 2004, 32 (1): 148 – 164.

[61] Ganley, J., & Salmon, C. The Industrial Impact of Monetary Policy Shocks; Some Stylised Facts [R]. *Bank of England Working Paper*, 1997, *No.* 68.

[62] Garrison, C. B., & Chang, H. S. The Effect of Monetary and Fiscal Policies on Regional Business Cycles [J]. *International Regional Science Review*, 1979, 4 (2): 167 – 180.

[63] Geiger, M. *Instruments of Monetary Policy in China and their Effectiveness*: 1994 – 2006 [C]. Paper presented at the United Nations Conference on Trade and Development, 2008.

[64] Georgopoulos, G. Measuring Regional Effects of Monetary Policy in Canada [J]. *Applied Economics*, 2009, 41 (16): 2093 – 2113.

[65] Gerlach, S. Interest Rate Setting by the ECB: Words and Deeds [C]. *Discussion paper of centre for economic policy research*, 2004, *No.* 4775.

[66] Gerlach, S., & Svensson, L. E. O. Money and Inflation in the Euro-Area: A Case for Monetary Indicators? [C] *Center for Economic Policy Research Discussion Paper, series*, 2002, *No* 3392.

[67] Gertler, M. Financial Structure and Aggregate Economic Activity: An Overview [J]. *Journal of Money, Credit & Banking*, 1988, 95: 559 – 588.

[68] Gertler, M., & Gilchrist, S. The Role of Credit Market Imperfections in Monetary Transmission Mechanism: Arguments and Evidence [J]. *Scandinavian Journal of Economics*, 1993: 43 – 64.

[69] Goodfriend, M., & Prasad, E. A Framework for Independent Monetary Policy in China [J]. *CESifo Economic Studies*, 2007, 53 (1): 2 – 41.

[70] Gray, S. Central Bank Balances and Reserve Requirements [C]. *International Monetary Fund*, 2011, 11.

[71] Green, S. Making Monetary Policy Work in China: A Report from the Money Market Front Line [J]. *Stanford Center for International Development.*, 2005, 245.

[72] Grilli, V., & Roubini, N. Liquidity, Capital Controls, and Exchange Rates [J]. *Journal of International Money and Finance*, 1993, 12 (2): 139 – 153.

[73] Groenewold, N., Lee, G., Lee, & Chen, A. Regional Output Spillovers in China: Estimates from a VAR Model [J]. *Papers in Regional Science*, 2007, 86 (1): 101 – 122.

[74] Gros, D. & Hefeker, C. One Size must Fit all: National Divergences in a Monetary Union [J]. *German Economy Review*, 2002, 3 (3): 1-16.

[75] Guimarães, R. R. d. S. & Monteiro, S. M. M. Monetary Policy and Regional Output in Brazil [J]. *Revista Brasileira de Economia*, 2014, 68: 73-101.

[76] Gujarati, D. N. *Basic Econometric* (4th ed.): The Mc Graw Hill Cooperation [M]. New Pelhi: Tata McGraw-Hill Education, 2004.

[77] Gunji, H. & Yuan, Y. Bank Profitability and the Bank Lending Channel: Evidence from China [J]. *Journal of Asian Economics*, 2010, 21 (2): 129-141.

[78] Habibullah, M. S. Divisia Money and Income in Indonesia: Some Results from Error-Correction Models, 1981: 1-1994: 4 [J]. *Applied Economics Letters*, 1998, 5 (6): 387-391.

[79] Habibullah, M. S., Dayang-Affizzah, A. & Puah, C. -H. Regional Income Disparities in Malaysia: A Stochastic Convergence Analysis [J]. *Geografia: Malaysian Journal of Society and Space*, 2012, 8 (5): 100-111.

[80] Habibullah, M. S. & Eng, Y. -K. Does Financial Development Cause Economic Growth? A Panel Data Dynamic Analysis for the Asian Developing Countries [J]. *Journal of the Asia Pacific Economy*, 2006, 11 (4): 377-393.

[81] Hanson, S. J. & Christoph, W. Empirical Evidence of a Credit Channel Using Regional Data [R]. *Unpublished manuscript*, 1996.

[82] Harrigan, F. J. & McGregor, P. G. Interregional Arbitrage and the Supply of Loanable Funds: A Model of Intermediate Financial Capital Mobility [J]. *Journal of Regional Science*, 1987, 27 (3): 357-367.

[83] Hausman, J. A. Specification Tests in Econometrics [J]. *Econometrica: Journal of the Econometric Society*, 1978, 46 (6): 1251-1271.

[84] Hayo, B. & Uhlenbrock, B. *Sectoral Effects of Monetary Policy in Germany* [M]. Kluwer Academic Publishers, 1999.

[85] He, D. & Pauwels, L. What Prompts the People's Bank of China to Change its Monetary Policy Stance? Evidence from a Discrete Choice Model [J]. *China & World Economy*, 2008, 16 (6): 1-21.

[86] He, D. & Wang, H. Dual-Track Interest Rates and The Conduct of Monetary Policy in China [J]. *SSRN Electronic Journal*, 2011, 23 (4): 928-947.

[87] He, L. *An Empirical Analysis on the Asymmetric Regional Effects of Chinese Monetary Policy——Based on the VAR models of Jiangsu and Henan province* [C]. Paper presented at the 1st International Conference on Information Science and Engineering (ICISE), 2009.

[88] He, L. Empirical Research of Asymmetry Regional Effects of Monetary Policy in China [J]. *Financial Theories and Practice (in Chinese)*, 2010, 5: 57-60.

[89] He, Q. Leung, P. -H. , & Chong, T. T. -L. Factor-augmented VAR Analysis of the Monetary Policy in China [J]. *China Economic Review*, 2013, 25: 88 – 104.

[90] Hein, S. E. & Jonathan, D. S. Reserve Requirements: A Modern Perspective [J]. *Economic Review-Federal Reserve Bank of Atlanta*, 2002, 87 (4): 41 – 52.

[91] Heinemann, F. & Huefner, F. P. Is the View from the Eurotower Purely European? National Divergence and ECB Interest Rate Policy [J]. *Scottish Journal of Political Economy*, 2004, 51 (4): 544 – 558.

[92] Hsiao, C. *Analysis of panel data* (2nd ed. Vol. 34) [M]. Cambridge university press, 2003.

[93] Hsing, Y. & Hsieh, W. -J. Impacts of Monetary, Fiscal and Exchange Rate Policies on Output in China: A VAR Approach [J]. *Economics of Planning*, 2004, 37 (2): 125 – 139.

[94] Ibrahim, M. H. Sectoral Effects of Monetary Policy: Evidence from Malaysia [J]. *Asian Economic Journal*, 2005, 19 (1): 83 – 102.

[95] Jarociński, M. Responses to Monetary Policy Shocks in the East and the West of Europe: A Comparison [J]. *Journal of Applied Econometrics*, 2010, 25 (5): 833 – 868.

[96] Jiang, Y. & Chen, Z. Empirical Analysis of Regional Effects of Monetary Policy Employing SVAR in China [J]. *Journal of Financial Research (in Chinese)*, 2009, 346 (4): 180 – 195.

[97] Jiang, Y. , Liu, Y. & Zhao, Z. Empirical Analysis of Effectiveness of Monetary Channel and Credit Channel [J]. *Journal of Financial Research (in Chinese)*, 2005, 299 (5): 70 – 79.

[98] Jiao, J. , Sun, T. & Liu, X. Analysis of Regional Differences of the Effectiveness of Monetary Policy in China [J]. *Journal of Financial Research (in Chinese)*, 2006, 309 (3): 1 – 15.

[99] Johansen, S. Estimation and Hypothesis Testing of Cointegration Vectors in Gaussian Vector Autoregressive Models [J]. *Econometrica*, 1991, 59 (6): 1551 – 1580.

[100] Johansen, S. & Juselius, K. Maximum Likelihood Estimation and Inference on Cointegration-with Application to the Demand for Money [J]. *Oxford Bulletin of Economics and Statistics*, 1990, 52 (2): 169 – 210.

[101] Johansson, A. C. Is U. S. Money Causing China's Output? [J] *China Economic Review*, 2009, 20 (4): 732 – 741.

[102] Jones, D. C. , Li, C. & Owen, A. L. Growth and Regional Inequality in China During the Reform Era [J]. *China Economic Review*, 2003, 14 (2): 186 – 200.

[103] Kashyap, A. K. , & Stein, J. C. The Impact of Monetary Policy on Bank Balance Sheets [C]. *Carnegie-Rochester Conference Series on Public Policy*, 1995, 42:

151 – 195.

[104] Kashyap, A. K. & Stein, J. C. The Role of Banks in Monetary Policy: A Survey with Implications for the European Monetary Union [J]. *Economic Perspectives, Federal Reserve Bank of Chicago*, 1997, 21 (5): 2 – 18.

[105] Kashyap, A. K. & Stein, J. C. What do a Million Observations on Banks Say about the Transmission of Monetary Policy? [J] *American Economic Review*, 2000, 90 (3): 407 – 428.

[106] Kashyap, A. K. Stein, J. C., & Wilcox, D. W. Monetary Policy and Credit Conditions: Evidence From the Composition of External Finance [J]. *American Economic Review*, 1993, 83 (1): 78 – 98.

[107] Keating, J. W. Structural Approaches to Vector Autoregressions [J]. *Fderal Reserve Bank of St. Louis Review*, 1992, 74: 37 – 57.

[108] Kieler, M., & Saarenheimo, T. Differences in Monetary Policy Transmission? A Case not Closed [J]. *European Commission, Directorate-General for Economic and Financial Affairs*, 1998.

[109] Kilian, L. Small-Sample Confidence Intervals for Impulse Response Functions [J]. *The Review of Economics and Statistics*, 1998, 80 (2): 218 – 230.

[110] Kishan, R. P. & Opiela, T. P. Bank Size, Bank Capital, and the Bank Lending Channel [J]. *Journal of Money, Credit and Banking*, 2000: 121 – 141.

[111] Koivu, T. Has the Chinese Economy Become more Sensitive to Interest Rates? Studying Credit Demand in China [J]. *China Economic Review*, 2009, 20 (3): 455 – 470.

[112] Kong, D. On China's Monetary Policy Framework [R]. *The Keizai Gaku, Annual Report of the Economic Society, Tohoku University, Sendai, Japan.*, 2003, 65 (2).

[113] Kong, D., Cortes, B. S. & Qin, D. Empirical Ananlysis of Provincial Effectiveness of Monetary Policy in China [J]. *Journal of Financial Research (in Chinese)*, 2007, 330 (12): 17 – 26.

[114] Kornai, J. The Soft Budget Constraint [J]. *Kyklos*, 1986, 39 (1): 3 – 30.

[115] Kwiatkowski, D., Phillips, P. C. B., Schmidt, P., & Shin, Y. Testing the Null Hypothesis of Stationarity against the Alternative of a Unit Root: How Sure are we that Economic Time Series have a Unit Root? [J] *Journal of Econometrics*, 1992, 54: 159 – 178.

[116] Lütkepohl, H. *Introduction to Multiple Time Series Analysis* (2nd ed.) [M]. Berlin: Springer-Verlag, 1993.

[117] Lütkepohl, H. *New Introduction to Multiple Time Series Analysis* [M]. Springer-Verlag Berlin Heidelberg, 2005.

[118] Lütkepohl, H. *Structural Vector Autoregressive Analysis for Cointegrated Variables*

[M]. Springer Berlin Heidelberg, 2006.

[119] Lütkepohl, H. & Krätzig, M. *Applied time series econometrics* [M]. Cambridge University Press, 2004.

[120] Lau, C. K. M. New Evidence about Regional Income Divergence in China [J]. *China Economic Review*, 2010, 21 (2): 293 – 309.

[121] Leeper, E. & Gordon, D. B. In Search of the Liquidity Effect [J]. *Journal of Monetary Economics*, 1992, 29: 341 – 369.

[122] Lessmann, C. Foreign Direct Investment and Regional Inequality: A Panel Data Analysis [J]. *China Economic Review*, 2013, 24: 129 – 149.

[123] Liu, P. & Xie, T. The Monetary Policy Transmission in China: "Credit Channel" and its Limitations [R]. *Working Papers of the Business Institute Berlin at the Berlin School of Economics (FHW-Berlin)* 2006, 22: 1 – 28.

[124] Liu, Y. *The Effects of Monetary Policy Shocks in China* 1997 *to* 2005 [D]. Ph. D thesis, University of Aix-Marseille Ⅱ, 2010.

[125] Lu, M. & Wang, E. Forging Ahead and Falling Behind: Changing Regional Inequalities in Post-Reform China [J]. *Growth and Change*, 2002, 33 (1): 42 – 71.

[126] Lutkepohl, H. Asymptotic Distributions of Impulse Response Functions and Forecast Error Variance Decompositions of Vector Autoregressive Models [J]. *Review of Economics & Statistics*, 1990, 72 (1): 116 – 125.

[127] Ma, G. Yan, X. & Liu, X. China's Evolving Reserve Requirements [J]. *Journal of Chinese Economic and Business Studies*, 2013, 11 (2): 117 – 137.

[128] Mathur, V. K. & Stein, S. Regional Impact of Monetary and Fsical Policy: An Investigation into the Reduced Form Approach [J]. *Journal of Regional Science*, 1980, 20 (3): 343 – 351.

[129] McCallum, B. T. Robustness Properties of a Rule for Monetary Policy [C]. *Carnegie Rochester Conference Series on Public Policy*, 1988, 29: 173 – 203.

[130] Meade, E. & Sheets, N. Regional Influences on U. S. Monetary Policy: Some Implications for Europe [R]. *Centre for Economic Performance, London School of Economics and Political Science, London, UK.*, *CEPDP*, 2002: 523.

[131] Mehrotra, A. N. Exchange and Interest Rate Channels during a Deflationary Era—Evidence from Japan, Hong Kong and China [J]. *Journal of Comparative Economics*, 2007, 35 (1): 188 – 210.

[132] Menon, J. Exchange rate pass-through [J]. *Journal of Economic Surveys*, 1995, 9 (2): 197 – 231.

[133] Mishkin, F. Symposium on the Monetary Transmission Mechanis [J]. *Journal of Economic Perspectives*, 1995, 9 (4): 3 – 10.

[134] Montoro, C. & Moreno, R. The Use of Reserve Requirements as a Policy Instrument in

Latin America [J]. *BIS Quarterly Review*, 2011, 5: 53 –65.

[135] Moore, C. L. & Hill, J. M. Interregional Arbitage and the Supply of Loanable Funds [J]. *Journal of Regional Science*, 1982, 22 (4): 499 –512.

[136] Morrison, W. M. China's Economic Conditions [R]. *Library of Congress Washington Dc Congressional Research Service*, 2009.

[137] Mundell, R. A. A Theory of Optimum Currency Areas [J]. *The American Economic Review*, 1961, 51 (4): 657 –665.

[138] Nachane, D. M. , Ray, P. & Ghosh, S. Does Monetary Policy have Differential State-Level Effects? An Empirical Evaluation [J]. *Economic and Political Weekly*, 2002, 37 (47): 4723 –4728.

[139] Naka, A. & Tufte, D. Examining Impulse Response Functions in Cointegrated Systems [J]. *Applied Economics*, 1997, 29 (12): 1593 –1603.

[140] Osborne, D. K. & Zaher, T. S. Reserve Requirements, Bank Share Prices, and the Uniqueness of Bank Loans [J]. *Journal of Banking & Finance*, 1992, 16 (4): 799 –812.

[141] Owyang, M. T. & Wall, H. J. Regional VARs and the Channels of Monetary Policy [J]. *Applied Economics Letters*, 2009, 16 (12): 1191 –1194.

[142] Park, A. & Sehrt, K. Tests of Financial Intermediation and Banking Reform in China [J]. *Journal of Comparative Economics*, 2001, 29: 608 –644.

[143] Pedroni, P. & Yao, J. Y. Regional Income Divergence in China [J]. *Journal of Asian Economics*, 2006, 17 (2): 294 –315.

[144] Peek, J. & Rosengren, E. S. Bank Lending and the Transmission of Monetary Policy [C]. *Conference series-Federal Reserve Bank of Boston*, 1995, 39: 47 –79.

[145] Peersman, G. & Smets, F. The Industry Effects of Monetary Policy in the Euro Area [J]. *The Economic Journal*, 2005, 115 (503): 319 –342.

[146] Phillips, P. C. B. & Perron, P. Testing for a Unit Root in Time Series Regression [J]. *Biometrika*, 1988, 75: 335 –346.

[147] Qin, D. , Quising, P. , He, X. & Liu, S. Modeling Monetary Transmission and Policy in China [J]. *Journal of Policy Modeling*, 2005, 27 (2): 157 –175.

[148] Ravn, M. O. & Sola, M. Asymmetric Effects of Monetary Policy in the United States [J]. *Review-Federal Reserve Bank of Saint Louis*, 2004, 86, 41 –58.

[149] Reichenstein, W. The Impact of Money on Short-Term Interest Rates [J]. *Economic Inquiry*, 1987, 25 (1): 67 –82.

[150] Ridhwan, M. M. , de Groot, H. L. F. , Rietveld, P. & Nijkamp, P. The Regional Impact of Monetary Policy in Indonesia [J]. *Growth and Change*, 2014, 45 (2): 240 –262.

[151] Ridhwan, M. M. , Nijkamp, P. Rietveld, P. & de Groot, H. L. F. Regional Develop-

ment and Monetary Policy: A Review of the Role of Monetary Unions, Capital Mobility and Locational Effects [R]. *VU University Amsterdam, Faculty of Economics, Business Administration and Econometrics, Serie Research Memoranda*, 2008, 7: 1 -27.

[152] Roberts, R. B. & Fishkind, H. The Role of Montary Force in Regional Economic Activity: An Econometric Simulation Analysis [J]. *Journal of Regional Science*, 1979, 19 (1): 15 -29.

[153] Rodríguez-Fuentes, C. & Dow, S. EMU and the Regional Impact of Monetary Policy [J]. *Regional Studies*, 2003, 37 (9): 969 -980.

[154] Rodríguez-Fuentes, C. J. Credit Availability and Regional Development [J]. *Papers in Regional Science*, 1998, 77 (1): 63 -75.

[155] Rodríguez-Fuentes, C. J. *Regional monetary policy* [M]. Routledge, 2006.

[156] Romer, C. D. & Romer, D. H. Does Monetary Policy Matter? A New Test in the Spirit of Friedman and Schwartz [C]. In O. J. B. a. S. Fischer (Ed.), *NBER Macroeconomics Annual*, MIT Press, 1989, 4: 121 -184.

[157] Said, S. E. & Dickey, D. A. Testing for Unit Roots in ARMA (P, Q) Models with Unknown P and Q [J]. *Biometrika*, 1984, 71, 599 -607.

[158] Samolyk, K. A. The Role of Banks in Influencing Regional Flows of Funds [R]. *Working Paper, Federal Reserve Bank of Cleveland*, 1989: 8914.

[159] Samolyk, K. A. A Regional Perspective on the Credit View [J]. *Federal Reserve Bank of Cleveland, Economic Review*, 1991, 27: 27 -38.

[160] Samolyk, K. A. Bank Performance and Regional Economic Growth: Evidence of A Regional Credit Channel [R]. *Federal Reserve Bank of Cleveland, Working Paper*, 1992: 9204.

[161] Samolyk, K. A. Banking Conditions and Regional Economic Performance Evidence of a Regional Credit Channel [J]. *Journal of Monetary Economics*, 1994, 34 (2): 259 -278.

[162] Schunk, D. L. The Differential Impacts of Monetary Policy: Are the Differences Diminishing? [J]. *Papers in Regional Science*, 2005, 84 (1): 127 -136.

[163] Scott, I. O., Jr. The Regional Impact of Monetary Policy [J]. *The Quarterly Journal of Economics*, 1955, 69 (2): 269 -284.

[164] Sims, C. A. Macroeconomics and Reality [J]. *Econometrica*, 1980, 48: 1 -48.

[165] Sims, C. A. Interpreting the Macroeconomic Time Series Facts: The Effects of Monetary Policy [J]. *European Economic Review*, 1992, 36 (5): 975 -1000.

[166] Sims, C. A. & Zha, T. Error Bands for Impulse Responses [J]. *Econometrica*, 1999, 67 (5): 1113 -1155.

[167] Sims, C. A. & Zha, T. A. Does Monetary Policy Generate Recessions [R]. *Yale*

University, *Working Paper*, 1995.

[168] Song, W. & Zhong, Z. The Existence and Origin of Regional Effects of Monetary Policy in China: An Analysis Based on the Theory of Optimum Currency Areas [J]. *Economic Research Journal (in Chinese)*, 2006, 3: 46-58.

[169] Stewart, J. D. & Hein, S. E. An Investigation of the Effect of the 1990 Reserve Requirement Change on Financial Asset Prices [J]. *Journal of Financial Research*, 2002, 25 (3): 367-382.

[170] Stock, J. H. & Watson, M. W. Variable Trends in Economic Time Series [J]. *Journal of Economics Perspectives*, 1998, 2: 147-174.

[171] Strongin, S. The Identification of Monetary Policy Disturbances: Explaining the Liquidity Puzzle [J]. *Journal of Monetary Economics*, 1995, 35: 463-498.

[172] Sun, H. Foreign Direct Investment and Regional Export Performance in China [J]. *Journal of Regional Science*, 2001, 41 (2): 317-336.

[173] Sun, H. Autonomy and Effectiveness of Chinese Monetary Policy under the De Facto Fixed Exchange Rate System [J]. *China & World Economy*, 2009, 17 (3): 23-38.

[174] Sun, L., Ford, J. L. & Dickinson, D. G. Bank Loans and the Effects of Monetary Policy in China: VAR/VECM Approach [J]. *China Economic Review*, 2010, 21 (1): 65-97.

[175] Sun, R. Does Monetary Policy Matter in China? A Narrative Approach [J]. *China Economic Review*, 2013, 26: 56-74.

[176] Tan, S. H., Habibullah, M. S. & Mohamed, A. Asymmetric Effects of Monetary Policy in ASEAN-4 Economies [J]. *International Research Journal of Finance and Economics*, 2010, 44 (3): 1-38.

[177] Taylor, J. B. Discretion versus Policy Rules in Practice [C]. *Carnegie-Rochester Conference Series on Public Policy*, 1993, 39 (1): 195-214.

[178] Taylor, J. B. The Monetary Transmission Mechanism: An Empirical Framework [J]. *The Journal of Economic Perspectives*, 1995, 9 (4): 11-26.

[179] The Research Group of Wuhan branch of PBC, M. P. Constraint of Inner Regulations And Macro Policies: A Case Study on the Blocks of Monetary transmission Channel in Undeveloped regions in China [J]. *Journal of Financial Research (in Chinese)*, 2002, 269 (11): 20-27.

[180] Tong, J. Analysis of the Effectiveness of Monetary Policy in China [J]. *Journal of Northeast Financial and Economic University*, 2011, 5.

[181] Van den Heuvel, S. J. Does Bank Capital Matter for Monetary Transmission? [J]

Economic Policy Review, 2002, 8 (1), 259 – 265.

[182] Walsh, C. E. What Caused the 1990 – 1991 Recession? [J] *Economic Review, Federal Reserve Banks of San Francisco*, 1993, 2, 33 – 48.

[183] Walter Isard. The Value of the Regional Approach in Economic Analysis [C]. In C. i. R. i. I. a. Wealth (Ed.), *Regional Income*: NBER, 1957: 69 – 86.

[184] Wang, S. & Handa, J. Monetary Policy Rules under a Fixed Exchange Rate Regime: Empirical Evidence from China [J]. *Applied Financial Economics*, 2007, 17 (12): 941 – 950.

[185] Weber, E. J. Monetary Policy in a Heterogeneous Monetary Union: the Australian Experience [J]. *Applied Economics*, 2006, 38 (21): 2487 – 2495.

[186] Wei, K., Yao, S. & Liu, A. Foreign Direct Investment and Regional Inequality in China [J]. *Review of Development Economics*, 2009, 13 (4): 778 – 791.

[187] Weise, C. L. The Asymmetric Effects of Monetary Policy: A Nonlinear Vector Autoregression Approach [J]. *Journal of Money, Credit and Banking*, 1999, 31 (1): 85 – 108.

[188] Wooldridge, J. *Introductory Econometrics: A Modern Approach* (5th ed.) [M]. Cengage Learning, 2012.

[189] Xie, P. China's Monetary Policy: 1998 – 2002 [R]. *Stanford Center for International Development Working Paper*, 2004, *No.* 217.

[190] Xie, P. & Luo, X. Taylor Rule and its Empirical Test in China's Monetary Policy [J]. *Economic Research Journal (in Chinese)*, 2002, 3: 3 – 12.

[191] Xiong, W. Measuring the Monetary Policy Stance of the People's Bank of China: An Ordered Probit Analysis [J]. *China Economic Review*, 2012, 23 (3): 512 – 533.

[192] Yao, S. & Zhang, Z. Regional Growth in China Under Economic Reforms [J]. *The Journal of Development Studies*, 2001, 38 (2), 167 – 186.

[193] Yi, G. The Framework of China's Monetary Policy [C]. *Presented at the PBC-IMF International Seminar on Monetary Policy Operations, Suzhou, China*, 2001, 5.

[194] Ying, L. G. Measuring the Spillover Effects: some Chinese Evidence [J]. *Papers in Regional Science*, 2000, 79 (1), 75 – 89.

[195] Zhang, J., Wang, L. & Wang, S. Financial Development and Economic Growth: Recent Evidence from China [J]. *Journal of Comparative Economics*, 2012, 40 (3): 393 – 412.

[196] Zhang, Q. & Zou, H. F. Regional Inequality in Contemporary China [J]. *Annals of Economics and Finance*, 2012, 13 (1), 113 – 137.

[197] Zhang, X. & Zhang, K. H. How Does Globalisation Affect Regional Inequality within

A Developing Country? Evidence from China [J]. *The Journal of Development Studies*, 2003, 39 (4): 47 -67.

[198] Zhou, Y. & Jiang, Z. Monetary Channel, Credit Channel and the Effectiveness of Monetary Policy in China [J]. *Journal of Financial Research* (*in Chinese*), 2002, 267 (9): 34 -43.